KANSAS C.U.S.D.#3
3 6221 00018 0166

MW00416350

Ghosts of Old Europe

GHOSTS of Old Europe

Hans Holzer

Dorset Press • New York

This collection published by Dorset Press,
a division of Marboro Books Corp.,
by arrangement with Hans Holzer.
1992 Dorset Press
ISBN 0-88029-718-2

Printed in the United States of America

M 9 8 7 6 5 4 3 2

Contents

Introduction vii

England

The Tower of London 3

Her Name was Trouble:
The Secret Adventure of Nell Gwyn 6

Encountering the Ghostly Monks 43

Bloody Mary's Ghost 57

Midland Ghosts 66

Longleat's Ghosts 76

The Ghost on Television 93

The Ghosts at Blanchland 113

The Real Camelot 124

Scotland

The Ghosts Around Edinburgh 153

Spectral Mary, Queen of Scots 177

The Ghostly Monk of Monkton 179

Scottish Country Ghosts 188
Border Country Ghosts 192

Ireland

The Ghost on the Kerry Coast 197
Haunted Kilkea Castle, Kildare 209
The Ghosts at Skryne Castle 212
The Haunted Rectory 223
Ghost Hunting in County Mayo 245
The Lovers of Carlingford 258

France

The Musketeer of Avignon 263
The Ghost at La Tour Malakoff, Paris 265
The Eight Young Ladies of the Château de la Caze 271

Germany

Haunted Wolfsegg Fortress, Bavaria 275
The Haunted Ruin at Schwärzenberg, Bavaria 279

Austria

Ghosts Around Vienna 285
The Secret of Mayerling 305
The Black Knight of Pflindsberg 336

Switzerland

A Haunted Former Hospital in Zurich 341

Estonia

The Concerned Castle Ghost 347

Introduction

Many Americans believe that British castles, especially dungeons, have ghosts. This is not necessarily so, although many castles do in fact have that sort of attraction.

Actually, ghosts occur wherever a great tragedy has left an unfortunate person hung up between the spirit worlds and this world, unable to proceed due to the inability to free themselves from emotional turmoil.

The true cases reported in this book are the results of my own personal investigations and travel, not hearsay or other people's research. I am convinced that these hauntings did occur and, in many cases, they are still unresolved.

Therefore, a visit by you, dear reader, might yield interesting results. Perhaps you are psychic enough to feel the presence of a ghost, or possibly only a replay of a scene from the past—not actually a person but something remaining in the atmosphere because of the intensity of the original event.

Either way, be neither afraid nor puzzled. You

are dealing with human events, not demons, devils, or monsters who belong in the realm of phantasy.

As for visiting these haunted places, don't expect ghosts to appear on demand as if they are on the payroll of the local tourist office. But if you are psychically gifted—and nearly everybody is in varying degrees—chances are you may have a true experience, ranging from a psychic impression of past events to a full-blown apparition or a visitation from the resident wraith.

If that happens, enjoy it and don't panic. Send good thoughts to the entity you see or feel present, and go on remembering, as my good friend, the great late medium Eileen Garrett once put it, "It's such a short distance from here to there."

May all the ghosts you encounter be friendly.

Hans Holzer, Ph.D.

New York, 1992

England

The Tower of London

PROBABLY THE most celebrated of British royal ghosts is the shade of unlucky Queen Anne Boleyn, the second wife of Henry VIII, who ended her days on the scaffold. Accused of infidelity, which was a form of treason in the sixteenth century, she had her head cut off despite protestations of her innocence. In retrospect, historians have well established that she was speaking the truth. But at the time of her trial, it was a political matter to have her removed from the scene, and even her uncle, who sat in judgment of her as the trial judge, had no inclination to save her neck.

Anne Boleyn's ghost has been reported in a number of places connected with her in her lifetime. There is, first of all, her apparition at Hampton Court, attested to by a number of witnesses over the years, and even at Windsor Castle, where she is reported to have walked along the eastern parapet. At the so-called Salt Tower within the confines of the Tower of London, a guard observed her ghost walking along headless, and he promptly fainted. The case is on record, and the man insisted over and over again that he had not been drinking.

Perhaps he would have received a good deal of sympathy from a certain Lieutenant Glynn, a member of the Royal Guard, who has stated, also for the record, "I have seen the great Queen Elizabeth and recognized her, with her olive skin color, her fire-red hair, and her ugly dark teeth. There is no doubt about it in my mind." Although Elizabeth died a natural death at a ripe old age, it is in the nature of ghosts that both the victims and the perpetrators of crimes sometimes become restless once they have left the physical body. In the case of good Queen Bess, there was plenty to be remorseful over. Although most observers assume Queen Elizabeth "walks" because of what she did to Mary Queen of Scots, I disagree. Mary had plotted against Elizabeth, and her execution was legal in terms of the times and conditions under which the events took place. If Queen Elizabeth I has anything to keep her restless, it would have to be found among the many lesser figures who owed their demise to her anger or cold cunning, including several ex-lovers.

Exactly as described in the popular English ballad, Anne Boleyn had been observed with "her 'ead tucked under," not only at the Tower of London, but also at Hever Castle, in Kent, where she was courted by King Henry VIII.

As recently as February 1957, a Welsh Guardsman on duty at the Tower reported seeing a ghost on the upper battlements of the Salt Tower on the anniversary of the execution of Lady Jane Grey, who died four hundred years ago after a reign of only nine days. In the Church of St. Peter ad Vincula, within the Tower compound, there have been reports of presences in the pews, like "a second shadow." Only a trance medium could ascertain the truthfulness of these reports. Perhaps I can smuggle one in next time I'm in London. The Queen need never know.

Her Name was Trouble: The Secret Adventure of Nell Gwyn

PICTURE THIS, if you will: All England is rejoicing, the long and bloody Civil War is finally over. Thousands of dead cavaliers and matching thousands of roundheads will never see the light of day again, smoking ruins of burned-down houses and churches and estates have finally cooled off, and England is back in the family of nations. The Puritan folly has had its final run: King Charles II has been installed on his father's throne, and Whitehall Palace rings once again with pleasant talk and music.

The year is 1660. One would never suspect that a scant eleven years before, the King's father had been executed by the parliamentary government of Oliver Cromwell. The son does not wish to continue his revenge. Enough is enough. But the Restoration does not mean a return to the old ways, either. The evils of a corrupt court must not be repeated lest another Cromwell arise. Charles II is a young man with great determination and skilled in the art of diplomacy. He likes his kingship, and he thinks that with moderation and patience the House of Stuart would be secure on the English throne for centuries to come. Although the Puritans are no longer running the country, they are far from gone. The King does not wish to offend their moral sense. He will have his fun, of course, but why flaunt it in their faces?

With the Restoration came not only a sigh of relief from the upper classes, that all was well once again and one could *play*, but the pendulum soon started to swing the other way: Moral decay, excesses, and cynicism became the earmarks of the Restoration spirit. Charles II wanted no part of this, however. Let the aristocracy expose themselves; he would always play the part of the monarch of the people, doing what he wanted quietly, out of sight.

One of the nicest sights in the young King's life was an actress of sorts by the name of Nell Gwyn. She and her mother had come to London from the country, managed to meet the King, and found favor in his eyes. She was a pale-skinned redhead with flash and lots of personality, and evidently she had the kind of attractions the King fancied. Kings always have mistresses, and even the Puritans would not have expected otherwise. But Charles II was also worried about his own friends and courtiers: He wanted the girl for himself, he knew he was far from attractive, and though he was the King, to a woman of Nell's spirit, that might not have been enough.

The thing to do was simply not to sneak her in and out of the Whitehall rear doors for a day or two, and possibly run into the Queen and a barrage of icy stares. A little privacy would go a long way, and that was precisely what Charles had in mind. Nell was not his only mistress by any means—but she was the only one he *loved*. When he gazed into the girl's sky-blue eyes or ran his hands through her very British red hair, it electrified him and he felt at peace. Peace was something precious to him as the years of his reign rolled by. The religious problem had not really been settled; even the Stuarts were split down the middle among Protestants and Catholics. The Spaniards were troublesome, and Louis XIV in league with the "godless" Turks was not exactly a good neighbor. Yes, Charlie needed a little hideaway for his girl and for himself, a place in the country where the pressures of Whitehall would not intrude.

His eyes fell upon a partially dilapidated old manor house near St. Albans, about an hour and a half from London by today's fast road, in the vicinity of an old Roman fortress dominating the rolling lands of Herfordshire. Nearby was the site of the Roman strong city of Verulamium, and the place had been a fortified manor house without interruption from Saxon times onward. It had once belonged to the Earl of Warwick, the famed "King maker," and in 1471, during an earlier civil war period, the Wars of the Roses, the house had been in the very center of the Battle of Barnet. To this day the owners find rusty fifteenth-century swords and dead soldiers' remains in the moat or on the grounds.

By the middle of the sixteenth century, however, the manor house, known as Salisbury Hall, had gradually fallen into a state of disrepair, partially due to old age and partially as a consequence of the civil war, which was fought no less savagely than the one two centuries later which brought Charles II to the throne.

A certain country squire named John Cutte had then acquired the property, and he liked it so much he decided to restore the manor house. He concentrated his rebuilding efforts on the center hall, lavishing on the building all that sixteenth-century money could buy. The wings later fell into ruins, and have now completely disappeared. Only an old battlement, the moat surrounding the property, or an occasional corridor abruptly ending at a wall where there had once been another wing to the house remind one of its early period.

One day Charles and Nell were driving by the place, and both fell in love with it instantly. Discreetly Charles inquired whether it might be for sale, and it so happened it was, not merely because he was the King, but because of financial considerations: The recent political affairs had caused the owners great losses, and they were glad to sell the house. Once again it was almost in ruins, but Charles restored it in the style of his own period. This was a costly operation, of course, and it presented a problem, even for a king. He could not very well ask Parliament for the money to build his mistress a country house. His personal coffers were still depleted from the recent war. There was only one way to do it, and Charles II did not hesitate: He borrowed the money from discreet sources, and soon after installed his lady love at Salisbury Hall.

As time went on, the King's position grew stronger, and England's financial power returned. Also, there was no longer any need for the extreme caution that had characterized the first few years after the Restoration. The King did not wish to bury Nell Gwyn at a distance in the country, especially as he did not fancy riding out there in the cold months of the year. He therefore arranged for her to have a private apartment in a house built above the Royal

Saddlery near the Deanery, in the London suburb called Soho.

In the second half of the seventeenth century, Soho was pretty far uptown from Whitehall, and the young things flitting to and fro through its woods were still four-legged. Today, of course, Soho is the sin-studded nightclub section of London's West End. The old house, built in 1632, still stands, but it has changed over many times since. Next door to it was the Royalty Theatre, where Nell Gwyn had once been among the hopeful young actresses—but not for long. It seems odd to find a theater next door to the stables, but Soho was a hunting suburb and it seemed then logical to have all the different sporting events and facilities close together. Besides, Nell did not mind; she liked peeking in at the Royalty Theatre when she was not otherwise engaged. Unfortunately, the theater is no more; it was destroyed by a Nazi bomb in World War II. But the Saddlery did not get a scratch and that is all to the good, for today it houses a most interesting emporium. The nightclub known as the Gargoyle occupies part of the four-story building, the balance being what is now called the Nell Gwyn Theatre, and various offices and dressing rooms. In the 1920s, Noel Coward was one of the founding members of this club, and Henri Matisse designed one of the rooms. It was highly respectable and private then, and many of the leading artists of the 1920s and 1930s made it their hangout for late-night parties. As Soho became more and more a nightclub area, the Gargoyle could not remain aloof: Today it is London's best-known striptease club. The girls are probably prettier than most of the competition, the owner, Jimmy Jacobs, is a man of breeding and culture, and the proceedings at the Gargoyle are never vulgar. It isn't the place to take your maiden aunt, but you *can* take your wife. The last time I visited Jimmy Jacobs' world, I was somewhat startled by the completely nude bartenders, female, popping up behind the bar of the upstairs club; it seemed a bit incongruous to think that these girls dress to go to work, then take their clothes off for their work, and get dressed to go home. But I think Nell Gwyn would have been quite understanding. A girl's got to make a living, after all. The décor inside is flashy and very much in the style of the 1920s, for Jimmy Jacobs has not touched any of it.

In this "town house" Nell Gwyn lived for many years. But she actually died of a stroke in another house in the Mall which the King had given her in the days when they were close. According to *Burnet's Own Time,* Vol. I, p. 369, she continued in favor with the King for many years, even after she was no longer his mistress, and it is true that the King had words of concern for her on his deathbed: "Let not poor Nelly starve," he asked of his brother and successor on the English throne, James II.

That of course might have been an expression of remorse as much as a sign of caring. When her royal protector was gone, Nell was most certainly in great debt, and among other things was forced to sell her personal silver. The *Dictionary of National Biographies* is our source of reference for these events that filled her last remaining years. She survived Charles II by only two years, leaving this vale of tears on the thirteenth of November 1687, at the age of thirty-seven, considered middle age in those days, especially for a woman!

But there were periods during which Nell was at odds with her King, periods in which he refused to look after her. Nell, of course, was not a shy wallflower: On one occasion she stuck her head out of her window, when some sightseers were staring at her house, and intoned, "I'm a Protestant whore!" Although her profession had been listed as actress, she herself never made any bones about what she thought she was.

During those lean years she badgered the Court for money, and the sentimental King sent it to her now and then. Their relationship had its ups and downs, and there were periods when Nell was in financial trouble and the King would not help her. Whatever help he gave her was perhaps because of their offspring. The first-born child later became the Duke of St. Albans, taking the title from Charles's romantic memory still attaching to his and Nell's early days (and nights) at Salisbury Hall near St. Albans. The descendants of this child still thrive, and the present duke is the thirteenth to hold the title. Gradually the King's interest started to wander, but not his possessiveness of her. While he allowed himself the luxury of casting an appreciative eye in other directions, he took a dim view of anyone else doing likewise toward his Nell.

There are popular stories that Nell died broke and lonely, but the fact seems to be that while she had years when she was indeed poor and unhappy, at the very end she had a measure of comfort due perhaps to the personal belongings she had managed to save and which she was later able to sell off. The house in the Mall was still hers, and it was there that she passed on. In a final gesture, Nell left the house to the Church and was buried properly in the crypt at St. Martin's in the Fields.

We know very little about her later years except

the bare facts of her existence and continued relationship with the King. But this knowledge is only a skeleton without the flesh and blood of human emotions. The story fascinated me always from the purely historical point of view, but it was not until 1964 that I became interested in it as a case of psychic phenomena.

The English actress Sabrina, with whom I shared an interest in such matters, called my attention to an incident that had occurred a short time before my arrival in London.

One of the girls in the show got locked in by mistake. It was late at night, and she was the only one left in the building. Or so she thought. While she was still trying to find a way to get out, she became aware of the sounds of footsteps and noises. Human voices, speaking in excited tones, added to her terror, for she could not see anyone. Not being a trained psychic researcher, she reacted as many ordinary people would have reacted: She became terrified with fear, and yelled for help. Nobody could hear her, for the walls of the building are sturdy. Moreover, she was locked in on the top floor, and the noises of the Soho streets below drowned out her cries for help. Those who did hear her took her for a drunk, since Soho is full of such people at that time of the night. At any rate, she became more and more panicky, and attempted to jump out the window. At that point the fire department finally arrived and got her out.

Jimmy Jacobs was so impressed with her story that he asked the editor of the *Psychic News* to arrange for an investigation, which yielded two clues: that the Royal Stables were once located in the building, and that Jimmy Jacobs himself was very psychic. The first fact he was able to confirm objectively, and the second came as no surprise to him either. Ever since he had taken over the club, he had been aware of a psychic presence.

"When I bought this place in 1956, I hadn't bargained for a ghost as well, you know," Jimmy Jacobs explained to me, especially as the subject of ESP had always fascinated him and running a burlesque show with psychic overtones wasn't what he had in mind. But he could not discount the strange experiences his employees kept having in the old building, even though he had given explicit instructions to his staff never to tell any new dancer anything about the psychic connotations of the building. If they were to learn of them, they would do so by their own experiences, not from gossip or hearsay, he decided.

One night in 1962, Jimmy was standing in the reception room on the top floor. It was three o'clock in the morning, after the club had shut down and he was, in fact, the only person in the building. He was about to call it a night when he heard the elevator come up to his floor. His first thought was that someone, either an employee or perhaps a customer, had forgotten something and was coming back to get it. The hum of the elevator stopped, the elevator came to a halt, and Jimmy looked up toward it, curious to see who it was. But the doors did not open. Nobody came out of the elevator. His curiosity even more aroused, Jimmy stepped forward and opened the outer iron gates, then the inner wooden gates of the small elevator, which could accommodate only three people at one time. It was empty.

Jimmy swallowed hard. He was well aware of the operating mechanism of this elevator. To make it come up, someone had to be *inside* it to press the button, or someone had to be where *he* was, to call it up. He had not called it up. Nobody was inside it. How did the elevator manage to come up?

For days after the event he experimented with it to try and find *another* way. But there just wasn't any other way, and the mechanism was in perfect working order.

Jimmy stared at the elevator in disbelief. Then, all of a sudden, he became aware of a shadowy, gray figure, about five yards away from him across the room. The figure was dressed in a period costume with a high waist; it wore a large hat and had its face turned away from him—as if it did not wish to be recognized. Jimmy later took this to be a sign that the girl was "an imposter" posing as Nell Gwyn, and did not wish to be recognized as such. That he was wrong in his conclusion I was to learn later.

For the moment Jimmy stared at the shadowy girl, who did not seem to walk the way ordinary humans do, but instead was gliding toward him slightly above floor level. As she came nearer to where he was rooted, he was able to distinguish the details of her hat, which was made of a flowered material. At the same time, his nostrils filled with the strong aroma of gardenias. For days afterward he could not shake the strong smell of this perfume from his memory.

The figure glided past him and then disappeared into the elevator shaft! Since Jimmy was only a yard away from the figure at this point, it was clear that she was not a human being simply taking the elevator down. The elevator did not budge, but the figure was gone nevertheless.

The next morning, when Jimmy returned to his club, he began to put all reports of a psychic nature into a semblance of order, so that perhaps someone —if not he—could make head or tail of it. Clearly, *someone* not of flesh and blood was there because of some unfinished business. But who, and why?

The interesting part seemed to be that most of the disturbances of a psychic nature occurred between 1962 and 1964, or exactly three hundred years after the heyday of Nell Gwyn. It almost looked as if an anniversary of some sort were being marked!

An exotic dancer named Cherry Phoenix, a simple country girl, had come to London to make her fame and fortune, but had wound up at the Gargoyle making a decent enough salary for not-so-indecent exposure, twice nightly. The men (and a few women, too) who came to see her do it were from the same country towns and villages she had originally come from, so she should have felt right at home. That she didn't was partially due to the presence of something other than flesh-and-blood customers.

For the first months of her stay she was too busy learning the routines of her numbers and familiarizing herself with the intricate cues and electrical equipment that added depth to her otherwise very simple performance to allow anything unusual to intrude on her mind. But as she became more relaxed and learned her job better, she was increasingly aware that she was often not alone in her dressing room upstairs. One night she had come in fifteen minutes early, and the stairwell leading up to the roof was still totally dark. But she knew her way around, so she walked up the winding old stairs, using her hands to make sure she would not stumble. Her dressing room was a smallish room located at the top of the stairs and close to a heavy, bolted door leading out to the flat rooftop of the building. There were other dressing rooms below hers, in back of the stage, of course, but she had drawn this particular location and had never minded it before. It was a bit lonesome up there on the top floor, and if anything should happen to her, no one was likely to hear her cries, but she was a self-sufficient young woman and not given to hysterics.

That evening, as she reached the top of the stairs, she heard a peculiar flicking sound. Entering her dressing room in the darkness, she made her way to the familiar dressing table on the right side of the room. Now the noise was even more pronounced. It sounded to her as if someone were turning the pages of a book, a sound for which there was no rational source. Moreover, she suddenly became aware of a clammy, cold feeling around her. Since it was a warm evening, this too surprised her. "I went goosey all over," the girl commented to me in her provincial accent.

In the dark, she could not be sure if there weren't someone else in the dressing room. So she called out the names of the other two girls, Barbara and Isabelle, who shared the room with her. There was no answer. Cherry Phoenix must have stood on that spot for about fifteen minutes without daring to move. Finally, she heard the noise of someone else coming up the stairs. The steps came nearer, but it was one of her dressing room mates. With that, the spell was broken and the noise stopped. Casually, the other girl turned the lights on. Then Cherry told the other girl about her unsettling experience. She got very little sympathy from the other girl, for she had heard the strange noise herself on many occasions. For the first time Cherry found out that the ghost of "Nell" was responsible for all these shenanigans, and was told not to worry about it.

This was of little comfort to the frightened girl,

the more so as other uncanny happenings added to her worries. The door to the roof was always secured by a heavy iron bolt. It would be impossible to open it from the outside, and the girls were safe in this respect even in Soho. But it could be pulled back by someone on the inside of the door, provided the person attempting this had great physical strength. The bolt was rarely pulled as this was an emergency exit only, and it was stiff and difficult to move. Nevertheless, on a number of occasions, when the girls knew there was no one else upstairs, they had found the bolt drawn back and the door to the roof wide open. In fact, it soon became apparent that the rooftop and that door were focal points of the mysterious haunting.

The last time Cherry found the rooftop door wide open was in 1964, and even after she left the show in 1965, it continued to "open itself" frequently, to the consternation of newcomers to the dressing room.

One night, when Cherry was getting ready to leave—about the same time as Jimmy Jacobs' encounter with the gray lady—she heard a rattling sound, as if someone wanted to get out of a cage! There was such an air of oppression and violence about the area then that she could not get out of the dressing room and down the stairs fast enough.

When I visited the haunted stairwell in September of 1966, I clearly heard those terrifying sounds myself. They sounded far away, as if they were coming to my ears through a hollow tunnel, but I could make out the sound of metal on metal . . . such as a sword hitting another sword in combat. Was that perhaps the rattling sound Cherry Phoenix had heard earlier? At the time I heard these metallic sounds I was quite alone on the stairs, having left two friends in the theater with Jimmy Jacobs. When they joined me outside on the stairs a few moments later, the sounds had stopped, but the whole area was indeed icy.

Cherry Phoenix never saw the gray lady the way her boss had seen her. But another girl named Tracy York had been in the Gargoyle kitchen on the floor below the top floor, when she saw to her horror the outline of a woman's figure in a pale lilac dress. She ran out of the kitchen screaming, into the arms of choreographer Terry Brent, who calmed her down. In halting words, Tracy York reported her experience, and added that she had wanted to talk about the strange voice she kept hearing—a voice calling her name! The voice belonged to a woman, and Miss York thought that one of her colleagues had called her. At the time she was usually in the top-floor dressing room, and she assumed the voice was calling her from the next lower floor. When she rushed down, she found there was no one there, either. Terry Brent remembered the incident with the gray lady very well. "Tracy said there was a kind of mistiness about the figure, and that she wore a period costume. She just appeared and stood there."

Brent was not a believer in the supernatural when he first came to work at the Gargoyle. Even the mounting testimony of many girls—noises, apparitions, metallic rattlings, cold spots—could not sway him. He preferred to ascribe all this to the traditional rumors being told and embroidered more and more by each successive tenant of the top-floor dressing room. But one night he came in to work entering through the theater. It was still early, but he had some preliminary work to do that evening. Suddenly he heard the laughter of a woman above his head, coming from the direction of that top-floor dressing room. He naturally assumed that one of the girls had come in early, too. He went upstairs and found Isabelle Appleton all by herself in the dressing room. The laughter had not been hers, nor had the voice sounded like hers at all. The girl was pale with fear. She, too, had heard the violent laughter of an unseen woman!

When I had investigated the Gargoyle and also Salisbury Hall for the first time, I had wondered whether the restless shade of Nell Gwyn might be present in either of the houses. According to my theory she could not very well be in both of them, unless she were a "free spirit" and not a troubled, earthbound ghost. Had there been any evidence of Nell Gwyn's presence at Salisbury Hall, once her country retreat?

Some years ago, Sir Winston Churchill's stepfather, Cornwallis-West, had an experience at Salisbury Hall. A guards officer not the least bit interested in psychic phenomena, Mr. Cornwallis-West was sitting in the main hall downstairs when he became aware of a figure of a beautiful girl with blue eyes and red hair coming down the stairs toward him. Fascinated by her unusual beauty, he noticed that she wore a pale cream dress with blue chiffon, and he heard clearly the rustling of silk. At the same time he became conscious of the heavy scent of perfume, a most unusual scent for which there was no logical explanation, such as flowers or the presence of a lady. The figure reached the heavy oaken door near the fireplace and just disappeared *through* it. Cornwallis-West was aware of her ethereal nature by now, and realized it was a ghost. His first thought, however, was that perhaps something dreadful had happened to his old nanny, for the girl reminded him of her. Immediately he telephoned his sister and inquired if the woman was all right. He was assured that she was. Only then did it strike him that he had seen an apparition of Nell Gwyn, for the nanny had always been considered a veritable double of the celebrated courtesan. He quickly reinforced his suspicions by inspecting several contemporary portraits of Nell Gwyn, and found that he had indeed seen the onetime owner of Salisbury Hall!

Others living at the Hall in prior years had also met the beautiful Nell. There was the lady with several daughters who occupied Salisbury Hall around 1890. On one of several occasions she was met by a beautiful young girl, perhaps in her late teens, with a blue shawl over her shoulders and dressed in a quaint, old-fashioned costume of an earlier age. The lady assumed it was one of her daughters masquerading to amuse herself, and she followed the elusive girl up the stairs. It was nighttime, and the house was quiet. When the girl with the blue shawl reached the top landing of the stairs, she vanished into thin air!

On checking out all her family, she found them safely asleep in their respective rooms. Nobody owned an outfit similar to the one she had seen the vanished girl wear.

But the phenomena did not restrict themselves to the wraith of beautiful Nell. Christopher, the young son of Mr. and Mrs. Walter Goldsmith, the present owners of the Hall, reports an experience he will never forget. One night when he occupied his brother Robin's room upstairs, just for that one night, he had a terrifying dream, or perhaps a kind of vision: Two men were fighting with swords—two men locked in mortal combat, and somehow connected with this house.

Christopher was not the only one who had experienced such a fight in that room. Some years before a girl also reported disturbed sleep whenever she used that particular room, which was then a guest room. Two men would "burst out" of the wall and engage in close combat.

There is an earlier specter authenticated for the Hall, dating back to the Cromwellian period. It is the unhappy ghost of a cavalier who was trapped in the Hall by roundheads outside, and, having important documents and knowledge, decided to commit suicide rather than brave capture and torture. The two fighting men might well have reference to that story, but then again they might be part of Nell's—as I was to find out much later.

The mystery of Nell Gwyn remained: I knew she had died almost forgotten, yet for many years she had been the King's favorite. Even if she had become less attractive with her advancing years, the King would not have withdrawn his favors unless there were another reason. Had something happened to break up that deep-seated love between Charles II and Nell? History is vague about her later years. She had not been murdered nor had she committed suicide, so we cannot ascribe her "continuous presence" in what were once her homes to a tragic death through violence. *What other secret was Nell Gwyn hiding from the world?*

In September of 1966, I finally managed to take up the leads again and visit the house at 69 Deane Street. This time I had brought with me a psychic by the name of Ronald Hearn, who had been recommended to me by the officers of the College of Psychic Science, of which I am a member. I had never met Mr. Hearn, nor he me, nor did he seem to recognize my name when I telephoned him. At any rate, I told him only that we would need his services for about an hour or so in London, and to come to my hotel, the Royal Garden, where we would start.

Promptly at 9:00 P.M. Mr. Hearn presented himself. He is a dark-haired, soft-spoken young man in his early thirties, and he did not ask any questions whatever. With me were two New Yorkers, who had come along because of an interest in producing a documentary motion picture with me. Both men were and are, I believe, skeptics, and knew almost nothing about the case or the reasons for our visit to 69 Deane Street, Soho.

It was just a few minutes before ten when we jumped out of a taxi at a corner a block away from the Gargoyle Club. We wanted to avoid Mr. Hearn seeing the entrance sign, and he was so dazzled by the multitude of other signs and the heavy nightclub traffic in the street that he paid no attention to the dark alleyway into which I quickly guided him. Before he had a chance to look around, I had dragged him inside the Gargoyle entrance. All he could see were photographs of naked girls, but then the whole area is rich in this commodity. Nothing in these particular photographs was capable of providing clues to the historical background of the building we had just entered.

I immediately took Hearn up the back stairs toward the dressing rooms to see if it meant anything to him. It did.

"I've got a ghastly feeling," he said suddenly. "I

don't want to come up the stairs . . . almost as if I am afraid to come up and come out here. . . ."

We were standing on the roof now. Jimmy Jacobs had joined us and was watching the medium with fascination. He, too, was eager to find out who was haunting his place.

"My legs are feeling leaden as if something wants to stop me coming out onto this rooftop," Hearn explained. "I feel terribly dizzy. I didn't want to come but something kept pushing me; I've *got* to come up!"

I inquired if he felt a "living" presence in the area. Hearn shook his head in deep thought.

"More than one person," he finally said. "There's a fight going on . . . someone's trying to get hold of a man, but someone else doesn't want him to . . . two people battling . . . I feel so dizzy . . . more on the staircase. . . ."

We left the chilly roof and repaired to the staircase, carefully bolting the "haunted door" behind us. We were now standing just inside the door, at the entrance to the dressing room where Cherry Phoenix had encountered the various phenomena described earlier. Unfortunately, music from the show going on below kept intruding, and Hearn found it difficult to let go. I decided to wait until the show was over. We went down one flight and sat down in Jimmy Jacobs' office.

Hearn took this opportunity to report a strange occurrence that had happened to him that afternoon.

"I had no idea where I was going tonight," he explained, "but I was with some friends earlier this evening and out of the blue I heard myself say, 'I don't know where I'm going tonight, but wherever it is, it is associated with Nell Gwyn.' My friend's name is Carpenter and he lives at 13, Linton Road, Kilburn,

N.W. 6. His telephone is Maida Vale 1871. This took place at 7:30 P.M."

My skeptic friend from New York thereupon grabbed the telephone and dialed. The person answering the call confirmed everything Hearn had reported. Was it a putup job? I don't think so. Not after what followed.

We went down into the third-floor theater, which was now completely dark and empty. Clouds of stale smoke hanging on in the atmosphere gave the place a feeling of constant human presences. Two shows a night, six days a week, and nothing really changes, although the girls do now and then. It is all done with a certain amount of artistic finesse, this undressing and prancing around under the hot lights, but when you add it up it spells the same thing: voyeurism. Still, compared to smaller establishments down the street, Jimmy Jacobs' emporium was high-class indeed.

We sat down at a table to the right hand of the stage, with the glaring night light onstage providing the only illumination. Against this background Ronald's sharp profile stood out with eerie flair. The rest of us were watching him in the dim light, waiting for what might transpire.

"Strange," the psychic said, and pointed at the rotund form of proprietor Jimmy Jacobs looming in the semi-darkness, "but I feel some sort of psychic force floating round him, something peculiar, something I haven't met up with before. There's something about you, sir."

Jimmy chuckled.

"You might say there is," he agreed, "you see I'm psychic myself."

The two psychics then started to compare feelings.

"I feel very, very cold at the spine," Jimmy said, and his usual joviality seemed gone.

He felt apprehensive, he added, rather unhappy, and his eyes felt hot.

"I want to laugh," Hearn said slowly, "but it's not a happy laugh. It's a forced laugh. Covering up something. I feel I want to get out of here, actually. I feel as though in coming here *I'm trapped.* It's in this room. Someone used to sit here with these feelings, I've been brought here, but I'm trapped, I want to get out! It's a woman. Voluptuous. Hair's red. Long and curled red hair."

We sat there in silent fascination. Hearn was describing the spitting image of Nell Gwyn. But how could he know consciously? It was just another nightclub.

"Fantastic woman . . . something in her one could almost love, or hate . . . there's a beauty spot on her cheek . . . very full lips, and what a temper. . . ."

Hearn was breathing with difficulty now, as if he were falling into trance. Jimmy sat there motionless, and his voice seemed to trail off.

"Do you know where the Saddlery is?" Jimmy mumbled now, before I could stop him. I wanted one medium at a time.

"Below here," Hearn answered immediately, "two floors below."

"Who'd be in the Saddlery?" Jimmy asked. I motioned him to stay out of it, but he could not see me.

"John," Hearn murmured.

"What's his rank?" Jimmy wanted to know. It

was hard to tell whether Jimmy Jacobs, medium, or Jimmy Jacobs, curious proprietor of the Gargoyle Club, was asking.

"Captain," Hearn answered. He was now totally entranced.

"Who was this Captain John?"

"A friend of the King's."

"What did he serve in?"

"Cavalry," the voice coming from Hearn's lips replied.

Jimmy nodded assent. Evidently he was getting the same message.

"What duty?" he asked now.

"In charge of the guard."

Hearn's own personality was completely gone now, and I decided to move in closer.

"Brought here," I heard him mumble.

"Who was brought here?" I asked.

"They made me . . . to hide . . . from the King . . . jealous. . . ."

"For what reason?" The breathing was labored and heavy.

"Tell us who you are!"

"Oh God it's Car . . . Charles. . . ." The voice was now so excited it could scarcely be understood.

"Whose house is this?" I demanded to know.

"I. . . ." The communicator choked.

"What is your name?"

But the entity speaking through Hearn would not divulge it.

A moment later, the medium awoke, grimacing with pain. He was holding his left arm as if it had been hurt.

"Almost can't move it," he said, with his usual voice.

I often get additional information from a psychic just after the trance ends.

"Was the entity female or male?"

"Female."

"Connected with this house?"

"Yes, yes. She must have lived here, for some time at least."

"Is she still here?"

"Yes."

"What does she want?"

"She can't leave. Because she is ashamed of having caused something to happen. She felt responsible for somebody's death."

"Whose death?"

"It was her lover. Somebody was murdered. It has to do with the stairs."

"Is she here alone?"

"No, I think there is somebody else here. There was a fight on the stairs. Two men."

"Who was the other man?"

"He was sent . . . terrible, I feel like banging my head very hard. . . ."

Evidently Hearn was in a semi-trance state now, not fully out, and not really in, but somewhere in between.

"What period are we in now?" I continued the questioning.

"Long curls and white hats . . . big hats . . . Charles the First. . . ."

"Who was the other man who was killed?"

"I can't be sure. . . ."

A sudden outburst of bitter laughter broke through the clammy, cold silence of the room. Hearn was being seized by a spell of laughter, but it wasn't funny at all. I realized he was again being taken over. I asked why he was laughing so hard.

"Why shouldn't I?" came the retort, and I pressed again for a name.

"Are you ashamed of your name?"

"Yes," came the reply, "trouble . . . *my name was trouble* . . . always trouble . . . I loved too much. . . ."

"Why are you here?"

"Why shouldn't I be here? It is my house."

"Who gave it to you?"

"Charles."

"What do you seek?"

Mad laughter was my answer. But I pressed on, gently and quietly. "Oh, no . . . you could pay, love . . . but the King wouldn't like it. . . ." The voice was full of bitterness and mock hilarity.

"Are you here alone?" I asked.

"No. . . ."

"Who is with you?"

"He is . . . my lover . . . John."

"What is his name?"

"He has many names . . . many. . . ."

Evidently the communicator was having her little fun with me. "What happened to him?"

"He was killed."

"By whom?"

"The King's men."

"Which ones of the King's men?"

"Fortescue."

"What is his rank?"

"Lieutenant."

"Regiment?"

"Guards."

"Who sent him?"

"The King."

"How did he find out?"

"Sometimes . . . beyond talking. . . ."

"Did you cheat on the King?"

"Yes, many times." Great satisfaction in the voice now.

"Did he give you this house?"

"He did."

"Then why did you cheat?"

"Because he wasn't satisfactory. . . ." It was said with such disdain I almost shuddered. Here was a voice, presumably from the 1660s or 1670s, and still filled with the old passions and emotional outbursts.

"How many years since then?" I said. Perhaps it was time to jolt this entity into understanding the true situation.

"Oh, God . . . what's time? What's time?! Too much time. . . ."

"Are you happy?"

"No!!" the voice shouted, "No! He killed my lover!"

"But your lover is dead and should be with you now? Would that not give you happiness?" I asked.

"No," the entity replied, "because my lover was the same cheat. Cheat!! Oh, my God . . . that's all these men ever cared about . . . hasn't changed much, has it? Hahaha. . . ."

Evidently the ghostly communicator was referring to the current use to which her old house was being put. It seemed logical to me that someone of Nell Gwyn's class (or lack of it) would naturally enjoy hanging around a burlesque theater and enjoy the sight of men hungering for girls.

"Not much difference from what it used to be."

"How did it used to be?"

"The same. They wanted entertainment, they got it."

If this was really Nell Gwyn and she was able to observe goings-on in the present, then she was a "free spirit," only partially bound to these surroundings. Then, too, she would have been able to appear both here and at her country house whenever the emotional memories pulled her hither or yon.

"Is this your only house?" I asked now.

"No . . . Cheapside . . . don't live there much . . . Smithfield . . . God, why all these questions?" The voice flared up.

"How do we know you are the person you claim to be?" I countered. "Prove it."

"Oh, my God," the voice replied, as if it were below her dignity to comply.

I recalled Jimmy Jacobs' view that the ghost was an imposter posing as Nell Gwyn.

"Are you an imposter?"

"No . . ." the voice shot back firmly and a bit surprised.

"Where were you born?"

"Why do you want to know? . . . What does it matter? . . ."

"To do you honor."

"Honor? Hahaha. . . . Sir, you speak of honor?"

"What is your name?"

"I used to have a name. . . . What does it matter now?"

She refused and I insisted, threatened, cajoled. Finally, the bitterness became less virulent.

"It is written," she said, "all over . . . *Nell* . . . *Nell* . . . God!!!"

There was a moment of silence, and I continued in a quieter vein. Was she happy in this house?

Sometimes. Did she know that many years had passed? Yes. Was she aware of the fact that she was not what she used to be?

"What I used to be?" she repeated, "Do you know what I used to be? A slut. A slut!!"

"And what are you now," I said, quietly, "now you're a ghost."

"A ghost," she repeated, pensively, playing with the dreaded word, as I continued to explain her status to her. "Why did they have to fight?" she asked.

"Did you know he was coming?"

"Yes."

"Why didn't you warn him?"

"What could I do? My life or his!"

"I don't understand—do you mean he would have killed *you?*"

"The King was a jealous man," she replied, "always quarrels . . . he was bald . . . bald . . . hahaha . . . with his wig. . . ."

"Why are you in this part of the building? What is there here for you?"

"Don't I have a right?"

I explained that the house belonged to someone else.

"Do I—disturb—?"

"What are you looking for here?"

"I'm not looking for anything. . . ."

Again, the name Fortescue came from the entranced lips of the medium. "Where did this Fortescue do the killing?" I asked. Almost as if every word were wrought with pain, the voice replied,

"On the stairs . . . near the top. . . ."

"What time was that?"

"Oh, God, time! It was the autumn. . . ."

"Was there anyone with him?"

"Outside."

"Where did you yourself pass over?" I said as gently as I could. There was a moment of silence as if she did not understand the question. "You do know you've passed over?" I said.

"No."

"You don't remember?"

"What is there to remember, nobody cares. Why do they use this house, these people?" she demanded to know now. I explained it was a theater.

"Is there any other place you go to, or are you here all the time?"

"I think so. . . ."

"What are those noises for? What do you want?"

"Do you want me to stop the fighting, you hear them fighting on the stairs? . . ."

"What was John's full name?"

"Molyneaux."

"He was a lieutenant?"

"Captain . . . in the Guards."

"And Fortescue, what was he?"

"Lieutenant . . . King's Guards. He was sent by the King."

"What was the order?"

"Kill him. . . . I was terrified . . . fight with swords . . . I was below . . . the salon. . . ."

"What can I do to help you find peace?"

"What is peace?"

"Do you know Salisbury Hall?" I decided to see what the reaction would be.

"You want to know I was his mistress . . . I was there . . . sometimes. . . ."

I demanded to have further proof of her identity, but the visitor from beyond demurred.

"Let me go. . . . Why have you come here?"

Again, following Jimmy Jacobs' suggestion, I accused her of being an actress impersonating Nell Gwyn. But the entity did not budge. She was Nell Gwyn, she said, and would not discuss anything about her family.

In retrospect I feel sure she was speaking the truth.

Shortly after, Ronald Hearn woke up. He seemed tired and worn out, but could not recollect anything that had come through him the past hour or so. At any rate he stated he didn't, and while I can never objectively *prove* these absences of a medium's true self, I have no reason to doubt their statements either. We left, and Hearn was driven back to his home in the suburbs.

On September 24, I came back to the Gargoyle Club with Trixie Allingham. It was the end of a very long day which we had spent at Longleat, the ancestral seat of the Marquess of Bath, and I didn't expect too much of Trixie, as even mediums get tired.

But time was short and we had to make the best of our opportunities, so I took her quickly upstairs to the same spot where we had brought Ronald Hearn, a table in the rear of the clubroom.

Trixie looked at the somewhat seedy surroundings of the old place in astonishment. It was clear she had never been in or near anything like it. After all, she was originally a nurse who had turned professional psychic later in life when she discovered her great gift. This wasn't her kind of place, but she was willing to have a go at whatever I wanted of her. It was late afternoon, before the club was open for business, and quite dark already. She did not realize where she was, except that it was some Soho nightclub, and she wanted to get out of it as soon as possible!

There was a curiously depressing atmosphere all around us, as we sat down in the empty club, breathing stale air mixed with the smoke of the previous night.

"There's a man and a woman concerned," she said immediately, "there's a tragedy . . . the one she loves is killed." She then continued, "She's tall, rather lovely, dark eyes, pale face."

I wanted to know how she died, but Trixie does not like direct questions as it throws her off her thought track. So I decided to just let her get into the atmosphere of the place by herself, as we watched her intently.

"I'm conscious of a stab . . . a knife goes through me . . . there's some triviality here to do *with a garter."* The King of England, of course, was the head of the Order of the Garter, which is considered a royal symbol. Trixie's psychometry was working fine.

"There's something to do with a triangle here," she continued, "also something to do with money . . . *initial R* . . . some people looking at a body on the ground . . . stabbed . . . she is most unhappy now, tears pouring down her face. I think she said 'marry'. . . . Why on earth am I seeing a bear?!"

While Trixie wondered about the bearskin she was seeing, one of my companions, the American writer Victor Wolfson, commented that the Royal Guards wear a bearskin. I don't like to have any information disclosed during an investigation, but I thanked him and requested that he hold back any comments until later.

Meanwhile I asked Trixie to press the girl ghost for some proof of her identity, and further personal data.

"Some extraordinary link with the Palace. . . . Does that sound crazy?" Trixie said, hesitatingly, for her logical mind could not conceive of any connection between a Soho striptease club and Whitehall. I reassured her, and let her continue. "That's what I'm getting . . . something in French . . . my French is so poor, what did you say, dear? Someone is to guard her . . . I'm going back in time for this picture . . . two men to guard her . . . darkish men, they've got European dress on, band of silk here. . . ." She indicated the waistline. "Can't quite see them . . . turbans . . . *M* . . . link with royalty . . . acting and royalty . . . and heartache . . . someone linked with her at the time was ill . . . Harry . . . *clandestine meetings* . . . real love . . . betrayal . . . two men fighting . . . castle is linked with all this . . . I hear the words, 'Save for the world . . . passion . . . save and deliver me!' "

We were all listening very quietly as the drama unfolded once again.

"It was nighttime," Trixie continued in a halting voice as if the memory were painful. "There was a fog outside . . . C . . . *Charles* . . . now I'm seeing a prior coming into the room from that door and he is saying, 'Time this was remedied! I've called you here.' . . . now I'm seeing a cherub child leading her away and I hear the prior saying, 'Go in peace, you have done what was necessary.' " Trixie put her head into her arms and sighed. "That's all I can give you. I feel so sick."

Since so much of her testimony had matched Ronald Hearn's, and as it was obvious that she was at the end of her psychic day, I felt it would do no harm to try to stimulate some form of reaction with material obtained by Hearn in the hope that it would be further enlarged upon by the second medium. "Does the name Fortescue mean anything to you?" I asked casually. Her facial expression remained the same. It didn't mean anything to her. But she then added,

"If it's got to do with an *Ancient House,* then it's right. An ancient lineage."

On later checking I found that the Fortescue family was indeed one of England's oldest, although the name is by no means common or even well-known today.

Trixie explained the girl was now gone, but the prior was still around and could be questioned by her psychically.

I asked about Salisbury. Just that one word, not indicating whether I was referring to a man or a place.

"A tall and rather grim-looking place," Trixie commented, "isolated, cold, and gray . . . dreary. . . ."

The description did indeed fit Salisbury Hall at the time Charles II bought it.

I asked the prior to tell us who the girl was.

"Some link here with royalty." Trixie answered after a moment, presumably of consultation with the invisible priest, "She came and she went . . . some obscure . . . linked up with this royal . . . setup . . . she rose . . . then something happened . . . she was cast off . . . that caused this tragedy . . . beautiful person, dark, I don't mean jet-black, but dark by comparison with a blonde, and curls . . . down to her shoulder . . . N . . . *Nell . . . this is Nell Gwyn!*"

To a man, we rose and cheered. Everything Trixie had said made sense.

Having shot her bow, Trixie now almost collapsed, mumbling, "I'm sorry, that's all I can do. I'm tired."

The spirit had left her in more ways than one, but it was no longer important. Gently we led her downstairs, and one of us took her home to the suburbs where she lives a respectable, quiet life.

On examination of the tapes, it struck me at once how both mediums hit on many similar details of the story. Since neither medium had had any foreknowledge of the place we were going to visit, nor, on arrival, any inkling as to why we were there, nor any way of knowing of each other, one cannot help but assume that both psychics were tuning in on the same past.

There were a number of extraordinary details not otherwise stressed in conventional history.

Both mediums described a triangle, with two men fighting on the roof—where all the hauntings had been observed—and one man going down in death. King Charles, also mentioned by name, had sent one of them, because someone had told him his mistress Nell was deceiving him.

Hearn had described the two men as Captain John Molyneaux of the Cavalry or Royal Guards (who were horseguards), and a Lieutenant Fortescue, also of the Guards. Captain John was the lover, who lived below in the Saddlery, and whose job it had been to guard her for the King. Instead, he had fallen in love with her. Lieutenant Fortescue (sometimes the name is also spelled Fortesque) was dispatched by the King to avenge him and kill the unfaithful officer at the house of his mistress. No first name is given for Fortescue by medium Hearn, but medium Allingham refers to the initial R. Trixie had added that money was involved, and I assumed that the murderer had been promised a bounty, which would seem natural in view of the fact that the killing was not the sort of thing a court of law would condone even if it were the King who had been cuckolded. Thus the need for an inducement to the young officer who did Charles' dirty work!

Evidently, Nell and John had planned to elope and marry, but were betrayed by someone to the King, who took revenge in the time-honored fashion of having the rival killed and the ex-mistress disgraced. We do know from the records that Nell fell into disfavor with the King during her heyday and died in modest circumstances. The plot became very clear to me now. Nell had seen a chance at a respectable life with a man she loved after years as the King's mistress. That chance was brutally squashed and the crime hushed up—so well, in fact, that none of the official or respected books on the period mention it specifically.

But then, who would know? In the dark of night, a troop of horsemen arrives at the house in the suburbs; quickly and quietly, Fortescue gains entrance, perhaps with the help of the servant who had tipped off the Palace. He races up the narrow stairs to Nell's apartments, finds John Molyneaux there and a duel to the finish ensues, up the stairs to the roof. The captain dies at his woman's feet, sending her into a shock that lasts three centuries. The murderer quickly identifies his foe, perhaps takes an object with him to prove that he had killed him, and departs to collect his bounty money.

Behind him a woman hysterical with grief awaits her fate. That fate is not long in coming. Stripped of all her wealth, the result of royal patronage, she is forced to leave the house near the Deanery and retire to more modest quarters. Her health and royal support gone, she slips into obscurity and we know little about her later years.

But I needed objective proof that Nell Gwyn really lived at that house and, more importantly, that these two men existed. If they were officers, there would have to be some sort of records.

Inquiry at the British Museum revealed that Nell lived in a house at the junction of Meard Street and the Deanery. This is the exact spot of the Gargoyle Club. As far as Fortescue and Molyneaux are concerned, I discovered that both names belonged to distinguished Royalist families. From Edward Peacock's *The Army Lists of the Roundheads and Cavaliers* I learned also that these families were both associated with the Royal Cavalry, then called Dragoons. During the Royalist expedition against Ireland in 1642, under the King's father, Charles I, the third "troop of horse," or cavalry regiment, was commanded by Sir Faithful Fortescue. With him served a younger member of the family by the name of Thomas Fortescue, a cornet at the time, but later most likely advanced to a lieutenancy. I didn't find any "R" Fortescue in the regimental records. But I reread the remark Trixie Allingham had made about this person, and discovered that she mentioned R as being present to identify the body of a slain person! Very likely, the murderer, Fortescue, had wanted to make sure there was no doubt about Molyneaux's identity so he could collect his bounty. Also, Molyneaux came from a family as prominent as his own, and he would not have wanted to leave the body of the slain officer unattended. No, the thing to have done would have been to call in a member of Molyneaux's own family, both to provide identification—and burial!

Was there an R. Molyneaux?

I searched the records again, and in C. T. Atkinson's *History of the Royal Dragoons* I discovered that a Richard Molyneaux, being head of the family at that time, had raised two regiments for Charles II. I also found that the name John was frequently used in the Molyneaux family, even though I haven't located a John Molyneaux serving in the Royal Guards at the exact period under discussion. Was his name stricken from the records after the murder? The King could order such drastic removal from official records, of course.

I should emphasize at this point that linking the family names of Molyneaux and Fortescue with Charles II and his time is highly specialized knowledge of history, and not the sort of thing that is taught in schools or found in well-known books about the period.

Thus we knew who the ghostly woman at the Gargoyle Club was and why she could not find rest. We knew the cause of the tragedy, and had discovered an obscure chapter in the life of not-so-Good King Charles.

In the process of this investigation, a royal trollop had turned into a woman who found love too late and death too soon.

Judging from similar investigations and the techniques employed in them, I can safely say, however, that Nell and her John are at last united in a world where the Royal Guards have no power and even

King Charles can walk around without a wig, if he so desires.

When I last visited the place in 1988—or rather, tried to—I discovered to my dismay that the club was no more.

But the building still stands: offices now occupy the upper floors and a disco is in the basement. I wonder how Nell feels about all this: but then having been an actress, perhaps she can live with the disco.

Encountering the Ghostly Monks

WHEN KING Henry VIII broke with Rome as the aftermath of not getting a divorce, but also for a number of more weighty reasons, English monastic life came to an abrupt halt. Abbeys and monasteries were "secularized," that is, turned into worldly houses, and the monks thrown out. Now and again an abbot with a bad reputation for greed was publicly executed. The first half of the sixteenth century was full of tragedies and many an innocent monk, caught up in the turmoil of a new wind in matters religious, was swept to his doom.

The conflict of the abolished monk or nun and the new owners of their former abode runs through all of England, and there are a number of ghosts that have their origin in this situation.

The "act of dissolution" which created a whole new set of homeless Catholic clerics also created an entirely new type of haunting. Our intent was to follow up on a few of the more notorious ghosts resulting from the religious schism.

I should be happy to report that it was a typically

glorious English fall day when we set out for Southampton very early in the morning. It was not. It rained cats and dogs, also typically English. I was to make an appearance on Southern TV at noon, and we wanted a chance to visit the famed old Cathedral at Winchester, halfway down to Southampton. My reason for this visit was the many persistent reports of people having witnessed ghostly processions of monks in the church, where no monks have trod since the sixteenth century. If one stood at a certain spot in the nave of the huge cathedral, one might see the transparent monks pass by. They would never take notice of you; they weren't that kind of ghost. Rather, they seemed like etheric impressions of a bygone age, and those who saw them re-enact their ceremonial processions, especially burial services for their own, were psychic people able to pierce the Veil. In addition, a rather remarkable report had come to me of some photographs taken at Winchester. The *Newark Evening News* of September 9, 1958, relates the incident:

> Amateur photographer T. L. Taylor thought he was photographing empty choir stalls inside Winchester Cathedral, but the pictures came out with people sitting in the stalls.
>
> Taylor took two pictures inside the cathedral nearly a year ago. The first shows the choir stalls empty. The second, taken an instant later, shows 13 figures in the stalls, most of them dressed in medieval costume. Taylor swears he saw no one there.
>
> Taylor's wife, their 16-year-old daughter Valerie, and a girl friend of Valerie's said they were with him when he took the pictures. They saw nothing in the stalls. "It gives me the creeps," Valerie said.
>
> Taylor, a 42-year-old electrical engineer whose

hobby is photography, is convinced that the films were not double exposed. He said his camera has a device to prevent double exposures and the company which made the film confirmed the ghosts were not caused through faulty film.

As I already reported in *Ghost Hunter*, I take psychic photography very seriously. Not only John Myers, but others have demonstrated its authenticity under strictest test conditions, excluding all kinds of possible forgery or deception. The camera, after all, has no human foibles and emotions. What it sees, it sees. If ghostly impressions on the ether are emotionally triggered electric impulses in nature, it seems conceivable that a sensitive film inside the camera may record it.

My own camera is a Zeiss-Ikon Super Ikonta B model, a fifteen-year-old camera which has a device making double exposures impossible. I use Agfa Record film, size 120, and no artificial light whatever except what I find in the places I photograph. I don't use flash or floodlights, and I have my films developed by commercial houses. I wouldn't know how to develop them myself, if I had to.

When we arrived at Winchester, it was really pouring. My wife and I quickly jumped from the car and raced into the church. It was eleven o'clock in the morning and the church was practically empty, except for two or three visitors in the far end of the nave. Light came in through the high windows around the altar, but there was no artificial light whatever, no electricity, only the dim light from the windows and the faraway entrance gate. The high wooden chairs of the choir face each other on both sides of the nave, and there are three rows on each side. Prayer books rest on the desks in front of each seat. The entire area is surrounded by finely carved Gothic woodwork, with open arches, through which one can see the remainder of the nave. There wasn't a living soul in those chairs.

The solitude of the place, the rain outside, and the atmosphere of a distant past combined to make us feel really remote and far from worldly matters. Neither of us was the least bit scared, for Ghost Hunters don't scare.

I set up my camera on one of the chair railings, pointed it in the direction of the opposite row of choir chairs, and exposed for about two seconds, all the while keeping the camera steady on its wooden support. I repeated this process half a dozen times from various angles. We then left the cathedral and returned to the waiting car. The entire experiment took not more than fifteen minutes.

When the films came back from the laboratory the following day, I checked them over carefully. Four of the six taken showed nothing unusual, but two did. One of them quite clearly showed a transparent group or rather procession of hooded monks, seen from the rear, evidently walking somewhat below the present level of the church floor. I checked and found out that the floor used to be below its present level, so the ghostly monks would be walking on the floor level *they* knew, not ours.

I don't claim to be a medium, nor is my camera supernatural. Nevertheless, the ghostly monks of Winchester allowed themselves to be photographed by me!

We left Southampton after my television show, and motored towards Salisbury. South of that old city, at Downton, Benson Herbert maintains his "paraphysical laboratory" where he tests psychic abilities of various subjects with the help of ingenious apparatus. One of his "operators," a comely young lady by the name of Anne Slowgrove, also dabbles in witchcraft and is a sort of younger-set witch in the area. Her abilities include precognition and apparently she is able to influence the flickering of a light or the sound of a clock by willpower, slowing them down or speeding them up at will. A devoted man, Benson Herbert was introduced to me by Sybil Leek, medium and "White Witch" of the New Forest. We witnessed one of his experiments, after which we followed his car out of the almost inaccessible countryside towards our next objective, Moyles Court, Ringwood.

The ghostly goings on at Moyles Court had come to my attention both through Sybil Leek, and through an article in the September issue of *Fate* magazine.

The original house goes back to the eleventh century and there is a wing certainly dating back to the Tudor period; the main house is mostly sixteenth century, and is a fine example of a large country manor of the kind not infrequently seen in the New Forest in the south of England.

Lilian Chapman, the author of the *Fate* article, visited the place in 1962, before it was sold to the school which now occupies it. The Chapmans found the house in a sad state of disrepair and were wondering if it could be restored, and at what cost.

Mrs. Chapman, wandering about the place, eventually found herself seated on the windowsill near the landing leading to the second floor, while the rest of the party continued upstairs. As she sat there alone, relaxing, she felt herself overcome with a sense of fear and sadness:

> As I looked toward the doors which led to the Minstrels Gallery, I was amazed to see, coming through them, a shadowy figure in a drab yellow cloak. There seemed more cloak than figure. The small cape piece nearly covered a pair of hands which were clasped in anguish or prayer. The hands clasped and unclasped as the apparition came towards me. I felt no fear, only an intense sorrow. And I swear I heard a gentle sigh as the figure passed me and drifted to the end of the landing. From there it returned to go down the stairs, seeming to disappear through a window facing the chapel.

I, too, have sat on that spot, quietly, relaxed. And I have felt a chill and known a heaviness of heart for which there was no logical reason.

The Chapmans did not buy the house, but the Manor House School did at the subsequent auction sale. Unknown to Mrs. Chapman at the time, Dame Lisle, one-time owner of the manor house, was tried and executed at nearby Winchester by the notorious "hanging judge" Jeffreys in 1685. The sole crime committed by the aged lady was that she had given shelter overnight to two fugitives from the battle of Sedgemoor. The real reason, of course, was her Puritan faith. As described by Mrs. Chapman in detail, it was indeed the apparition of the unfortunate lady she had witnessed.

I contacted the headmistress of the school, Miss V. D. Hunter, for permission to visit, which she granted with the understanding that no "publicity" should come to the school in England. I agreed not to tell any English newsmen of our visit.

When we arrived at Moyles Court, it was already five o'clock, but Miss Hunter had left on an urgent errand. Instead, a Mrs. Finch, one of the teachers, received us.

"What is the background of the haunting here?" I inquired.

"Dame Lisle hid her two friends in the cellar here," she said, "where there was an escape tunnel to the road. There were spies out watching for these people, they discovered where they were, and she was caught and tried before Judge Jeffreys. She was beheaded, and ever since then her ghost was said to be wandering about in this house."

"Has anyone ever seen the ghost?"

"We have met several people who had lived here years ago, and had reared their families here, and we know of one person who definitely has seen the ghost at the gates of the house—and I have no reason to disbelieve her. This was about twenty-five years ago, but more recently there has been somebody who came into the house just before we took it over when it was covered in cobwebs and in a very bad state. She sat in the passage here and said that she had seen the ghost walking along it."

"How was the ghost described?"

"She has always been described as wearing a saffron robe."

"Does the ghost ever disturb anyone at the house?"

"No, none. On the contrary, we have always heard that she was a sweet person and that there is nothing whatever to be afraid of. We've had television people here, but we don't want the children to feel apprehensive and as a matter of fact, the older children rather look forward to meeting the ghostly lady."

I thanked Mrs. Finch, and we were on our way once more, as the sun started to settle. We were hoping to make it to Beaulieu before it was entirely dark. As we drove through the nearly empty New Forest—empty of people, but full of wild horses and other animals—we could readily understand why the present-day witches of England choose this natural preserve as their focal point. It is an eerie, beautifully quiet area far removed from the gasoline-soiled world of the big cities.

We rolled into Beaulieu around six o'clock, and our hosts, the Gore-Brownes, were already a bit worried about us.

My contact with Beaulieu began a long time before we actually arrived there. Elizabeth Byrd, author of *Immortal Queen* and *Flowers of the Forest,* introduced us to the Gore-Brownes, who had been her hosts when she spent some time in England. Miss Byrd is keenly aware of the psychic elements around us, and when she heard we were going to visit Beaulieu—it consists of the manor house itself owned by Lord Montague and known as the Palace House; "The Vineyards," a smaller house owned by the Gore-Brownes; and, of course, the ruins of the once magnificent Abbey and gardens—she implored me to have a look from a certain room at "The Vineyards."

"When you go to Beaulieu please ask Margaret to take you up to 'The Red Room'—my room—and leave you alone there a while. It is not the room but the view from the window that is strange. If even *I* feel it, so should you have a very strong impression of static time. I have looked from that window at various seasons of the year at various times of day and always have sensed a total hush . . . as though life had somehow stopped. The trees are as fixed as a stage-set, the bushes painted. Nothing seems quite real. As you know, I am a late riser, but I was always up at dawn at Beaulieu when that view was nearly incredible to me—not just fog, something more, which I can only call permanent and timeless and marvelously peaceful. I would not have been surprised (or afraid) to see monks tending the vineyards. It would have seemed perfectly natural. If one could ever enter a slit in time it would be at Beaulieu."

The vivid description of the view given us by Elizabeth Byrd was only too accurate. Although it was already dusk when we arrived, I could still make out the scenery and the ruins of the Abbey silhouetted against the landscape. My wife was rather tired from the long journey, so I left her to warm herself at the comfortable fireplace, while Colonel Gore-Browne took me down to the Abbey, to meet a friend, Captain B., who had been a longtime resident of Beaulieu. The Palace House, comparatively new, was not the major center of hauntings.

A modern Motor Museum had been built next to it by Lord Montague, and has become a major tourist attraction. I have no objections to that, but I do find it a bit peculiar to have a washroom built into an ancient chapel, with a large sign on the roof indicating its usage!

The Abbey itself had not been commercialized, but lay tranquil on the spot of land between "The Vineyards" and an inlet of water leading down to the channel called "the Splent," which separates the Hampshire coast from the Isle of Wight. Here we stood, while the Captain looked for his keys so we could enter the Abbey grounds.

"What exactly happened here in the way of a haunting, Captain?" I asked, as we entered the churchyard surrounding the ruined Abbey walls.

"A young lady who lived in Beaulieu was walking across this little path toward what we call 'the parson's wicked gate,' when she saw a brown-robed figure which she thought was a visitor. She had been walking along with her eyes on the ground and she raised them when she got near to where she thought the man would be so as not to run into him—but he just wasn't there!"

We were now standing in the ruined "garth" or garden of the Abbey. Around us were the arched walls with their niches; back of us was the main wall of what is now the Beaulieu church, but which was once the monks' dining hall or refectory.

"Has anyone seen anything here?" I inquired.

"Well, there were two ladies who lived in the little flat in the *domus conversorum.* One of them, a retired trained nurse of very high standing, told me that one Sunday morning she came out onto the little platform outside her flat and she looked, and in the fifth recess there she saw a monk sitting reading a scroll."

"What did she do?"

"She watched him for a minute or two, then unfortunately she heard her kettle boiling over and she had to go in. When she came out again, of course, he was gone."

"Did it ever occur to her that he was anything but flesh and blood?"

"Oh, yes, she knew that he couldn't have been flesh and blood."

"Because there are no monks at Beaulieu."

"Yes."

"Was she frightened?"

"Not in the least."

"Are there any other instances of ghosts in this area?"

The Captain cleared his throat. "Well, old Mr. Poles, who was Vicar here from eighteen eighty-six to nineteen thirty-nine, used to talk of meeting and seeing the monks in the church, which was the lay brothers' refectory and which is now behind us. He also used to hear them as a daily occurrence."

We walked back to the church and entered its dark recesses. The interior is of modern design hardly consistent with its ancient precursor, but it is in good taste and the mystic feeling of presences persists.

This was the place where the Vicar had met the ghostly monks.

"He not only heard them singing," the Captain said, "but he also saw them. They were present."

"Has anyone else seen the ghostly apparitions in this church?"

"A few years ago," the Captain replied in his calm, deliberate voice, as if he were explaining the workings of a new gun to a recruit, "I was waiting for the funeral procession of a man who used to work here, and two ladies came into the church. We got to talking a little, and one of them said, 'When I came to this church about thirty years ago, with my friend, she saw it as it was.'

"I didn't quite understand what she meant and I said, 'Oh, I know, the church was completely altered in eighteen forty.'

" 'Oh, no,' she said, 'I mean—we both saw it—as it was, *when the monks had it.'*

"I questioned her about this.

" 'We came in,' she said, 'and we saw the church laid out apparently as a dining room. We were rather surprised, but we really did not think anything very much of it, and then we went out. But when we got home, we talked it over, and we came to the conclusion that there was something rather extraordinary, because we hadn't seen it as a parish church at all. Then we made inquiries and, of course, we realized that we had seen into the past.' "

The ladies had evidently been catapulted back in time to watch the monks of Beaulieu at supper, four hundred years ago!

I walked out into the middle of the nave and in a hushed voice invited the monks to show themselves. There was only utter silence in the darkened church, for it was now past the hour when even a speck of light remains in the sky.

As I slowly walked back up the aisle and into the present, I thought I heard an organ play softly somewhere overhead. But it may have been my imagination. Who is to tell? In that kind of atmosphere and having just talked about it, one must not discount suggestion.

Others have heard the ghostly monks in the garden, burying their own. Burial services are very important to a monk, and King Henry had deprived them of the privilege of being laid to rest in the proper manner. Where could the dead monks go? The Abbey was the only place they knew on earth, and so they clung to it, in sheer fear of what lay Beyond the Veil.

Quite possibly, too, the ghostly brothers cannot

accept the strange fact that their sacred burial ground, their cemetery, has never been found! There is a churchyard around the Abbey, but it belonged and still belongs to the people of Beaulieu. The monks had their own plot and no one knows where it is. I have a feeling that there will be ghostly monks walking at Beaulieu until someone stumbles onto that ancient burial ground, and reconsecrates it properly.

The massive manor house, or Palace House, also incorporates much of the abbot's palace within its structure. Monks have been seen there time and again. When I appeared on the Art Linkletter program in January of 1964, I was contacted by a Mrs. Nancy Sullivan, of the Bronx, New York, who was once employed as a cook at Palace House.

"Palace House used to have a moat all around," she explained, "and a spiral staircase running down from the top to the bottom. It was claimed Mary Queen of Scots escaped down that staircase, and a man was waiting in the moat in a boat, making good her escape. Some say her ghost still runs down those stairs!

"The help had their rooms on the top floor; there were five girls then, and every night we heard someone walking down those stairs, although we knew that the doors were safely locked, top and bottom. We were scared stiff, so much so, we all moved into one room."

Whether it was Mary Stuart getting away from Beaulieu, or perhaps an older ghost, is hard to tell. What is interesting is that the steps were heard where no one was seen to walk.

Television cameras have overrun Beaulieu in

quest of the supernatural. When all has quieted down, I intend to go back and bring a good trance medium with me. Perhaps then we can find out directly what it is the monks want.

Bloody Mary's Ghost

SAWSTON HALL lies a few miles south of the great English university town of Cambridge, and can be reached from London in about two and a half hours. When I heard that reliable witnesses had seen a ghost in this old manor house, I contacted the owner, Captain Huddleston, about a visit. The Captain's nephew, Major A. C. Eyre, wrote back saying how delighted they would be to receive us. Like so many British manor houses, Sawston Hall is open to the public at certain times and, of course, I wanted to avoid a day when the tourists were sure to interfere with our quest. Although I usually avoid getting secondhand information on hauntings, and prefer to talk to the witnesses directly when I see them, I like to know the general background of a haunted house before I approach it. This gives me a better idea as to what I might encounter in the way of atmosphere, mementos, and such. As a trained historian, I have no trouble finding my way around English history. I picked up one of the little booklets the Major had prepared for the visitors, to familiarize myself with the history of Sawston Hall while the car, driven by the imperturbable Mr. Brown, rolled quietly through the picturesque countryside. The booklet read:

> Sawston Hall has been the home of the Huddleston family for over 400 years and is noteworthy for being one of the few old manor houses in Cambridgeshire built out of stone. In 1553 Edward VI was ailing and entirely dominated by the ambitious Duke of Northumberland. The King was already dead, when his half sister, Princess Mary, afterwards Queen Mary Tudor, who was living in Norfolk, received a message purporting to be from him, begging her to come to him. Mary immediately set out for London and at Hoddesdon she received word that the message was a trap. On her way back, she accepted the hospitality of John Huddleston, the then Squire of Sawston, and spent the night at the Hall. During the night, however, the Duke's supporters from Cambridge who learnt she was there, set out to capture her. John Huddleston just got her to safety in time by disguising her as a dairy maid.

When we arrived at Sawston Hall, it was already four o'clock, a little late for tea, but our gracious hosts, the Huddlestons, had waited tea specially for us, and a delicious English brew it was. By now the light was not quite so strong as I would have liked it for the sake of my motion-picture camera. But I never use artificial lighting, only the available light.

We started up the stairs, and Mrs. Huddleston explained the treasures of the house to us. We admired, but quickly passed through the imposing Great Hall with its magnificent portrait of Queen Mary Tudor, the drawing room with its harpsichord in perfect playing condition, as if Queen Mary were about to use it, and proceeded past the Little Gallery and a paneled bedroom into the Tapestry Bedroom, so called because its walls are hung with a set of Flemish tapestries showing the life of King Solomon. Dominating this room is a four-poster bed in which Queen Mary is said to have slept, back during the dark days of 1553 when she was running for her life. To the right of the bed, there is a small marble fireplace and farther down the wall an oaken door opening onto a passage which ultimately leads to the priest's hiding hole. I think these connections are of some importance if the ghost is that of Queen Mary, who was Catholic.

We stood in front of the four-poster, when I started my examination.

"Tell me, Mrs. Huddleston, what are the facts about the hauntings here?"

Mrs. Huddleston, a soft-spoken, well-organized lady in her middle years, smiled a friendly smile. "Something always seems to take place in this room we're standing in. The original story is that in the middle of the night you suddenly hear three slow knocks at the door, and the door slowly swings open and a lady in gray slowly floats across the room and disappears into that tapestry. A great many people have slept in this room and there are a great many different stories of various things that have happened to them."

"What sort of things?"

"One girl woke up in the night very frightened, because she heard someone next to her in the bed breathe very heavily."

"What did she do, scream?"

"No, she just crawled to the bottom of the bed and tried to forget all about it."

"I can't say that I blame her under the circumstances. Did anyone else have trouble in this bed?"

"Well, there was a young man who was sleeping in this room, and he wasn't very well when he went to bed. When he came down to breakfast the next morning, he said, 'You know I was quite all right last night, you needn't have bothered to come to see me.' So I said, 'But I didn't.' He insisted, 'Oh, yes, you did; you knocked on the door three times, and rattled on the latch, and I got awfully frightened, and kept saying, "Come in, come in," and nothing happened, and I suddenly felt really, really frightened, so I crept down to the bottom of the bed and tried to forget all about it.' "

"Seems habit-forming," I said, "that bottom of the bed business. Of course, it *is* a huge bed."

"Well, he insisted, 'it must have been you; you must have come to see me,' but I told him, 'No, I'm sorry. I never came near you; you weren't nearly sick enough.' That was that."

"How long ago did this take place?"

"Four years ago."

"Did you yourself ever hear or see anything unusual?"

"When I was first married and came here as a bride, I heard distinctly some very tinkly music rather like a spinet or virginal, and I asked my husband who it was, and he said, oh, he had heard nothing and that it was all nonsense. However, I heard it again the next night and again a little later. He kept telling me this was all rubbish, so I felt very triumphant when about a month later a visitor came down to breakfast, and said, 'Do tell me, what is this music I keep hearing.' "

"Who do you think is playing the instrument?"

"The general opinion is that it is Queen Mary Tudor herself."

"You mean her ghost?"

"Yes. Of course, you know she slept in this bed and was very fond of this house. But the reason I think that it is really she is that she was a very good performer on the virginal, in fact she was so good that her father, Henry VIII, had her brought down from the nursery as a child to play for the Flemish ambassadors when they came over."

"And you are sure you heard the music?"

"Absolutely. It was quite clear."

"Has anyone else had psychic experiences in this room?"

"Oh, yes; quite a few, really," Mrs. Huddleston said with typical English understatement. To her, a ghost was no worse than a famous actor or politician in the family. In England, one need not be looked at askance just because one believes in ghosts. It is rather respectable and all that.

"One day I was taking a rather large group around the house, and when we were in this room an old lady suddenly stepped forward, and said, 'You know, I knew this house long before you did! You see I was employed here as a young girl, as a house maid. Once I was kneeling down, attending to the fire, and suddenly I felt very cold, looked up, and I saw the door slowly opening and a gray figure swept across the room and disappeared into the tapestry there. I was so frightened I flung myself out of the room and fell headlong from the top to the bottom of the stairs and hurt myself so badly that I've never dared come back to this house until this very day.' "

"That's quite a story," I said. "Did you check on it?"

"Yes. You see, you can't see the bottom of the stairs, when you're upstairs, and so she must have been absolutely right in the way she remembered things, because when we'd finished the round, and were at the bottom of the stairs, she suddenly called out, 'Oh, that's the place, I remember it, that's where I fell!' "

"And there was such a place?"

"Yes, there was."

"Have there been any manifestations here lately?"

"Not long ago, Tom Corbett, the well-known psychic, slept in this bed. He reported a presence bending over him every hour of the night. His alarm clock, which he had set for seven o'clock, went off at one, two, three, four, five, six. When it did so this presence kept bending over him. Mr. Corbett had the impression the ghost was that of a night watchman with one eye, and a name that sounded to him like Cutlass or Cutress."

"Did this make sense to you?"

"Well, I thought it simply meant he was carrying a cutlass with him, but Tom Corbett insisted it was a name. I made inquiries after Mr. Corbett had left, and I found to my amazement there was a man named Cutress living in the village. I had never heard of him. But the people who did the research for me said, 'That can't possibly have any connection with the night watchman, since he's only just arrived from London.'

"About a month later, the butler here was standing next to a stranger in the local pub, and he said, 'What is your name?' The stranger replied, 'Oh, my name is Cutress, and I've just come here a short time ago.' The butler wondered why he had come to this rather out-of-the-way place. 'Oh,' the man replied, 'my family's lived in Sawston for generations. I wanted to come back to the old family place.' "

"Tom Corbett certainly hit the nail on the head on that one," I acknowledged. "Any other interesting witnesses to uncanny phenomena?"

"I was taking an old lady round, and it was broad daylight, and I was showing her the tapestries, and was so busy with that, I didn't notice the change that had come over her face. When I looked around at her, she looked simply terrible, as if she were going to pass out. I asked her if I should get a doctor, but she assured me she would be all right.

" 'It's really this room,' she explained. 'It's the ghosts in this room.' "

We left the haunted bedroom and went along the Long Gallery to the priest's hiding hole, which was ingeniously hidden in the thickness of the wall, barely large enough for a man to sit in, and accessible to the outer world only through a small trapdoor which could easily be covered during a raid.

I wondered if any hauntings had been observed in connection with the hiding hole, since so much tragedy and emotional turmoil adhered to the atmosphere around it.

"Not by the hole itself, but there is a nearby bedroom where there have been some ghostly experiences during the last few years. That room just above the staircase. A friend of ours, a well-known Jesuit priest, was sleeping in it, and he had so much disturbance during the night, knocking at the door, and noises outside, that he got up several times to see what was happening."

"Did he find anything or anyone?"

"No, of course not. They never do."

"Was there anyone else who experienced anything out of the ordinary around that staircase?"

"A lady from South Africa came here for a first visit. She arrived rather unexpectedly, so we put her into the haunted room, but the next morning she reported that she had had a good night and not been disturbed at all. Maybe the ghost had moved away? 'Anyway,' she bragged, 'I always know when there is a ghost around, because I get very cold and get goose pimples all up my arms.' So we forgot all about the ghost and started to show her around the house. But when she got to this same big staircase, which leads to this room I have just talked about, she suddenly gave a little scream and said, 'Oh, there's no doubt about it, *this* is where the ghost is!' I hurriedly looked at her arms, and she was, in fact, covered with goose pimples.

"Tom Corbett also went up these stairs and he distinctly felt someone walking after him, so much so, he turned around to speak to him, but there was nobody there."

There we had it.

The Gray Lady floating across the haunted bedroom, and the haunted staircase.

During the years of religious persecution, Sawston Hall was the principal refuge for those of the Catholic faith, including a number of priests and lay brothers. Many atrocities were perpetrated in those days in the name of the Reformed Religion, and the atmosphere at Sawston Hall is soaked with the tragedy and suffering of those martyrs.

Then, too, one must realize that Mary Tudor, later known as Bloody Mary, had found the old manor house her salvation when the Huddlestons saved her life by hiding her. Her ghost might, indeed, be drawn back there even though she did not die there. I don't think the Gray Lady is merely an etheric impression without personality; the behavior is that of a bona fide ghost.

Midland Ghosts

I HAVE written of Catherine Warren-Browne and her previous life as Catherine Parr, queen to Henry VIII, in an earlier book, *Born Again.* There is no doubt in my mind that her flashes and recurrent dreams of that period are genuine and that she was indeed the one happy wife of Henry VIII, although Mrs. Warren-Browne herself has maintained a healthy skepticism in the matter and has by no means claimed that she was Queen Catherine. In a chapter entitled "Tale of Two Catherines," I have shown why I am so convinced of the authenticity of her experiences. But it is not her reincarnation memories I wish to speak of here, for Catherine Warren-Browne is one of the few people who has had psychic experiences as well as reincarnation flashes. When she heard I was going to visit England and follow up on some of her ghostly adventures, she supplied me with all the necessary data and wrote me a note saying, "Remember me to the rivers, Severn and Wye, and Worcester Cathedral," as lovely a remembrance as anyone can wish. Mrs. Warren-Browne and her husband now live in a modest home near Los Angeles. Once the owners of a large estate, the Warren-Brownes found the battle with taxation too much and decided to quit and go to America. I met Mrs. Warren-Browne several times while I was in Hollywood. The extraordinary experiences which have left her convinced of the reality of her past and future started early, when she was only four years old.

"In 1924, when I was four years old," Mrs. Warren-Browne began, "I was sitting by the fire playing when I saw very vividly a picture of a house unknown to me at the time. I saw myself going to the door with my mother, a maid letting us in, and then I saw a huge stone fireplace with a fire burning in it, and a woman in a blue tea gown sitting on a window seat with slightly gray auburn hair. She kissed us, and the maid served tea." At that time Catherine's family lived near Daventry, Northamptonshire.

It was a year later, while her father, a high-ranking naval officer, was overseas with his ship, that her mother took Catherine and her brother to stay with an aunt, Mary McKeever, at Kirkland, Little Malvern, in Worcestershire.

"After Christmas Day," Mrs. Warren-Browne continued her narrative, "my aunt said she was taking us to tea with her old friend Francis Berrington. We went to the house for tea, and everything was as I had seen it in my vision a year before. I had never been to this county before, and Francis Berrington was a friend of my aunt's, not my mother's."

But the most chilling episode in her unusual life happened while she was still a little girl, living at Gloucester House, Malvern Wells, about a mile from her aunt. Not far from there is an artificial hill called the British Camp, also known as the Hereford

Beacon. It is situated on the main road from Malvern to Ledbury and is one of the higher hills in the area. The summit of it is terraced and is, in fact, part of the old Roman earthworks which were built in this area.

"I had a very fiery French governess named Chevalier. One afternoon we were walking on the Hereford Beacon and sat down to rest. I remember clearly the sound of sheep cropping the grass and that wonderful scent of juniper. Suddenly I heard the tramping of feet that grew heavier, and over the Malvern Hills to the Beacon came a long line of men marching. We were on the east side of the hill, looking down over the reservoir toward Eastnor Park. There were hundreds of men, some mounted cavalry with a standard-bearer and the rest foot soldiers. I was only six at the time and had not yet started history. The men wore what to me looked like skirts, but there were helmets with plumes and a standard-bearer with a huge bronze-colored eagle. I called to Mademoiselle to hurry and get out of the way and dragged her to one side. She was naturally very shaken, but the men vanished as they reached a certain point of the Beacon. I was fascinated but not afraid, as they seemed quite real. I was sure that we would be walked into, since they marched without breaking line or seeming to give way. But Mademoiselle did not see them. She yanked me home to my aunt's, and I was considered to be ill and was put to bed with aspirin."

Mrs. Warren-Browne's family is Roman Catholic, and the entire area around Malvern is one of the strongholds of English Catholicism. Evidently the family had discussed her strange behavior with a friendly priest, Dom Rodger Huddleston, of a distinguished Roman Catholic family. The following morning, Father Huddleston came to see the little girl.

"As we sat in the garden he talked to me quite casually about what I had seen," Catherine recalls, "and he told me I must have seen 'a picture in time,' for the Roman legions fought a big battle against the Britons and Saxons in this area. He also told me that Cederic, the Saxon leader, was often seen riding when war was about to break out, and that many people in the area had actually seen him."

In 1951, the Warren-Brownes bought a beautiful Cotswold house near the village of Sutton Benger in Wiltshire. Built in 1380, with Tudor additions and three acres of walled gardens, stables, a rose garden, and a pond, it was a most delightful home for them. Their son Giles was away at school in Malvern, daughter Anne was in Bath, and only three-year-old Penelope was with them at the house. After buying the house they brought some fine eighteenth-century furniture into it and hunted for additional pieces to fill odd corners. The house had eight bedrooms, a forty-foot-long lounge hall, a dining room with a perfect early Tudor hearthstone hood, and a very charming drawing room off the hall. Then came a back hall, a butler's pantry, a housekeeper's room in which Mrs. Warren-Browne kept her sewing and linen, and finally a breakfast room with a side door on the lane running alongside the wall where the house joins with the garden wall.

"On November 24, 1951," Mrs. Warren-Browne recalls, "my husband and I returned from Wales. I was five months' pregnant at the time. It was about seven-thirty when we got home, and I was tired. We garaged the car and went indoors. The daily maid, Mrs. Rose Gingell, who lived a mile away, had left supper laid and fires lighted and the heat on. I remember telling my husband, 'What a wonderful house this is; how lucky we are.' He went to get a bottle of wine for our supper, and I went upstairs to bathe Penny and put her to bed. But in spite of the cheerful house, the lights and the fires, there was a terrible cold at the top of the stairs, so I went along the corridor to the older wing to see if a window was open. But they were all closed. I became icy and got a stole to wear, thinking, 'Pregnant women feel odd at times,' but I was very well and happy. I started downstairs. I could hear my husband go from the hall to the dining room. The stairs were shallow oak but carpeted, and as an expectant mother I was particularly careful walking down stairs. So I was going slowly, holding the stair rail, when I felt a very violent push in my back, as if from a hand. I shot halfway down the stairs onto the hall floor, and I know I screamed, as my husband came rushing from the dining room. He helped me to the couch in the hall. I couldn't walk, and the pain was so great he sent for the doctor. It turned out that I had a fractured tibia, fibula, and ankle, and a month later I lost the baby.

"I came home from the hospital in February, after a long siege, but I had to return to the hospital later on for some more surgery. The night before I was due to return to the hospital, I crossed into the hall and saw a bright light on the stairs, sort of bouncing from step to step. The maid was just leaving, so I called out to her and asked whether she knew anything odd about the house. She looked rather uncomfortable and said, 'Well, there have been rumors, and the last two owners only stayed a total of two years each,' but she had seen nothing. A month later I was back home after a rough bout in the hospital. I loved working in the garden, planting new beds, pruning up the old rose garden, and keeping busy about the house. My husband's business sometimes took him away for a day or two. During that time, Penny, the baby, would run screaming from the landing on the stairs, and our son, home from school, reported seeing a woman crying on the landing."

On April 25, 1952, she found herself alone in the house, the children being away and the little one with her grandmother. She was getting better and becoming restless. Before she went home, Rose, the maid, had prepared supper and brought it up to her room and left a log fire burning. Mrs. Warren-Browne decided to read and listen to the radio and then go to sleep.

"I awoke at two in the morning and felt frozen, although the fire was still burning. I had a heating pad, but I was still icy and thought I would get some hot milk and put some brandy in it. Then my dog Towy, a Labrador, who always sleeps by the fire, began to growl and bristle. I got out of bed and drew the curtains, and the dog became frantic when I moved from the bed. The door onto the landing was open, but she would not go out, so I picked up our large ginger cat from the end of the bed and thought, If she goes out, I am going out too, and I tossed the cat into the foyer. It came flying back at me like a projectile, spitting and screaming. All the time the cold grew more intense, like an ice barrier. I shot into bed and stayed put. The next day I thought, How crazy. I must have been made nervous by the dog's growling.

"In June, Penny had tonsillitis, so she was put into the guest room, and I went in there to sleep with her. It was a lovely room with a vaulted ceiling. The second night she woke up at two A.M. I give her a drink and aspirin and she settled down. It was a lovely summer night, for once. I looked out the window and then went back to bed and read a little, and finally put the lamp out. Soon after, the dog began to howl. I sat up and a figure floated through the wall opposite me. I saw the bars of Penny's crib through it. It was luminous but had no real shape. The room was icy and I could feel a sense of awful depression. I thought perhaps it needed prayers, so I said the 'De Profundis.' Instantly, the figure vanished."

A few days later a friend named Duncan Reeves, who knew nothing of these strange happenings, was a guest at the house. Mr. Warren-Browne asked him to get a radio from the room upstairs, but the young man was gone so long that Mrs. Warren-Browne went up after him, wondering what had happened to him.

"When I opened the door, he was holding the bedpost and looking very pale. He said, 'You have an odd bedroom,' and explained he had seen a thing similar to what I had seen in the guest room, only it went upward and through the ceiling. After this I felt I was not crazy and told our doctor about it. Dr. Hicks suggested we call our parish priest. Father Hickey came and very matter-of-factly went through the exorcism ritual in the hope that it would end the matter once and for all. On asking around, it turned out that we had about the most haunted house in Wiltshire."

Apparently, the ghost was of the obstinate kind. A little later a Dominican priest from New Zealand, a friend of the family, noticed that there was something odd about the house and suggested blessing the house again. Not much later, the Warren-Brownes sold the house to a family from Yorkshire with eight children. Mrs. Warren-Browne was sure that the children would frighten the ghost away, but they only stayed one year. Eventually the house was turned into a hotel, and if the guests have seen the ghosts and vice versa, they haven't said anything about it.

Mrs. Lilly Raymond is in her early sixties and a retired secretary. She is, in her own words, "quite sane and not an imaginative person," but the experience she went through in 1966 has quite unsettled her. Two of her grandchildren, a boy of six and a girl of three, were staying with her at the time in her house in Essex and were sleeping in her front room. One particular night the boy seemed restless and came into Mrs. Raymond's bedroom at two o'clock in the morning and again at two-thirty. When she tried to take him back to bed, he was reluctant to leave her. He then complained that he had been hearing "funny music," and as he was telling her about it, he held her hand very tightly and said, "Listen!"

"I then heard for myself the strange tinkly sound of a piano on which five notes only were repeatedly played. Not wishing to alarm the child in any way, I told him that it was somebody in the road having a party, but he immediately said, 'This isn't party music, as it keeps playing the same thing over and over again.' I stayed in the room the rest of the night, and several times more I heard the same five notes so sadly repeated."

The following morning she talked to a neighbor and inquired about previous tenants of the house and in particular if anybody had ever played the piano. It was thus that she learned about a certain Mrs. McKay who had lived in the house fifty years before her. Mrs. McKay's husband was in the merchant navy and often away. One of her twin sons died rather suddenly at age ten, followed a few months later by the demise of the other in a bicycle accident. Mrs. McKay became a diabetic and passed away in the very same year. Mrs. Raymond also discovered that the woman living in the apartment above hers hears the music continuously at different times of the day. Apparently, the succession of tragedies in Mrs. McKay's life unhinged her mind to the point where she was unable to leave: it was her piano, long gone from the flat, that the ladies kept hearing.

A few years ago a ghost made local newspaper headlines by keeping a man from going to jail. The story concerned a certain William Haywood, in his twenties, of Dunstable, Bedfordshire, who was in court for repeated traffic offenses. He was about to be sentenced when his attorney stepped forward and explained that there were special reasons why this man should not be sent to prison. Apparently Mr. Haywood lived in a haunted house, and Mrs. Haywood was so terrified of the specter that she could not possibly be left alone in the two-hundred-year-old house.

Mrs. Valerie Haywood explained that she had seen the ghost many times. "He is an old man dressed in rustic black Victorian clothes, with a gold stud at his collar. He appears in the bedroom at seven or eight o'clock at night. He just stands there in the room; he doesn't look evil, but he terrifies me. Even our dog won't go into the room; she whimpers when she passes the room."

Since the Haywoods had a small baby, they did not feel like moving out of the house. An exorcism was held, but apparently it did no good. William Haywood has also seen the ghost and called him the "man in black." As a last resort, they simply moved out of the bedroom and closed it off from the rest of the house. They asked around the neighborhood and learned that the description of the ghost fit a man who used to live in the house who had gone insane in that very bedroom.

The magistrate appreciated the Haywoods' predicament and fined the husband instead of sending him to jail.

Longleat's Ghosts

LONGLEAT IN Somerset must be the most publicized haunted house in all of England. If it isn't, at the very least its owner, Lord Bath, is the most publicity-conscious man among British nobility I have ever met: a genial, clever, very businesslike Aquarian who happens to share my birthdate, although a few years my senior. Longleat and its ghosts were first extensively publicized by Tom Corbett, the British society seer, who went there in the company of a British journalist, Diana Norman, who then wrote a book on Corbett's experiences in various British houses called *The Stately Ghosts of England.* Mr. Corbett goes to great pains to explain that he is not a medium but a clairvoyant. He most certainly is not a trance medium, and it takes a good deep-trance medium to really get to the bottom of any haunting. All a clairvoyant can do is pick up vibrations from the past and possibly come into communication with a resident ghost or spirit entity, while it remains for a trance medium to allow the spirit or ghost to speak directly to the investigator.

I began to correspond with Lord Bath in the spring of 1964, but before I could fix a date for my first visit to Longleat, NBC television decided to include the magnificent palace in its itinerary of allegedly haunted houses which its documentary unit wanted to film.

The *Psychic News* of May 23, 1964, headlined, FAMOUS ACTRESS AND MEDIUM TO STAR IN PSYCHIC FILM —WILL CAMERA RECORD SPIRIT FORMS? The newspaper was, of course, referring to Margaret Rutherford, the grand old lady of the British theater, who happened to be interested in ESP phenomena, although by no means a medium herself.

The idea of filming at Longleat and elsewhere was the brainchild of producer-director Frank De Fellitta, who had read the Tom Corbett–Diana Norman tome on Britain's haunted mansions. The NBC team went to Longleat, and immediately after they had set up for the filming all sorts of difficulties arose. Cameras would be out of place, tools would disappear; it seemed as if the resident ghosts were not altogether happy at the invasion taking place. But it is hard to tell how much of the reported difficulty was factual and how much of it a product of the NBC publicity department. One fact, however, was blissfully ignored in its implications by both NBC and the producer. They had set up a time-lapse exposure camera in the haunted corridor at Longleat, a camera which records one frame of film at a time over a long period of time. Such a recording was made during the night when no one was around. On developing the film, a whitish flash of light was discovered for which there was no easy explanation. The flash of light could not be explained as faulty film, faulty laboratory work, or any other logical source. What the camera had recorded was nothing less than the formation of a spirit form. Had Mr. De Fellitta any basic knowledge of parapsychology or had he been in the company of an expert in the field, he might have made better use of this unexpected bonus.

The choice of Margaret Rutherford as hostess of the program was not dictated by psychic ability or her integrity as an investigator, but simply because she looked the part, and in television that is the most important consideration. And she had played the magnificently written comedy role of the medium in Noel Coward's *Blithe Spirit.* Even the austere *New York Times,* which has generally ignored any serious treatment of parapsychology, managed to give the project and Margaret Rutherford quite a bit of space. "Miss Rutherford and company will visit allegedly spirit-ridden mansions. She will give her personal impressions of the hauntings—how they occur, when they occur and, maybe, why they don't occur," wrote Paul Gardner. Nothing of the sort was either intended or delivered, of course, but it read well in the publicity releases.

My first visit to Longleat took place long after the hullabaloo and the departure of Margaret Rutherford and the film crew. However, the usual large number of tourists was still milling around, so we had arranged with Lord Bath to come at a time when the grounds were closed to them.

Longleat is in the west of England, about three hours from London by car, and truly a palace, rivaling some of the royal residences in both size and appointments. Lord Bath himself had long ago moved into more modest quarters at nearby Warminster, where he and his wife lived in a charming old mill.

Longleat itself is named after a river which runs through the grounds. It has been the home of the Thynne family for four hundred years. Sometime before 1580 Sir John Thynne, direct ancestor of the current Marquess of Bath, began to build Longleat. His successors enlarged the mansion until it assumed the proportions of a palace. To describe the art treasures that fill the palace from top to bottom would take volumes. Suffice it to say that some very important paintings hang at Longleat and among them, perhaps a peculiarity of the present Lord Bath, art work by both Sir Winston Churchill and Adolf Hitler. The latter are in the private portion of the house, however, on one of the upper floors.

The first person Lord Bath wanted us to meet was the old nurse, a certain Miss Marks, who was then in her seventies. At the time when she took care of little Caroline, she had several encounters with a ghost.

"I saw a tall, scholarly looking man," the nurse explained. "He was walking along and looked as if he might be reading something; I only saw his back, but he had a high collar, the wings of it distinctly standing out. I would say, 'I think perhaps that is Grandpa. Shall we hurry up and speak to him?' We would follow him across the room, but when we got to the door at the end, which was shut, he just wasn't there. I didn't think anything of it, because I saw him lots and lots of times, and in the end I thought, It isn't a person at all. I didn't discuss it with anyone, but I knew it was friendly to me. I loved seeing this person, even after I discovered it was *only a ghost.*"

From the nurse's description and that given by Tom Corbett it was clear to historians that the ghost was none other than the builder of Longleat, Sir John

Thynne. Thynne had been a banker in the time of Henry VIII and was known for his sharp business sense. The grounds upon which Longleat stands were a result of his business acumen, and he was very much attached to it in his day. His haunting ground, so to speak, is the Red Library on the ground floor, where he usually appears between seven and eight o'clock at night.

Lord Bath then took us up to the haunted corridor, which is now completely bare and gives a rather depressing feeling, ghost or no ghost. This long, narrow passage runs parallel to the sleeping quarters of some of the Thynne family, and it was here that Tom Corbett felt a ghostly presence.

"This is the corridor," Lord Bath explained in a voice that betrayed the fact that he had said it many times before, "where a duel was fought by one of my ancestors, the second Viscount Weymouth, because he found that his wife, Louisa Carteret, had been unfaithful to him. He discovered her in a state, unfortunately, in which he thought a duel ought to be fought with the man she was with. He fought this duel with the intruder and killed the man, after which he buried him in the cellar. His skeleton was accidentally found when the boiler was put in downstairs six years ago."

One would assume the unfortunate lover to be roaming the corridors at Longleat, seeking revenge, or at least, to frighten the survivors. But apparently he took his fate like a man and remained a spirit rather than a ghost. Not so with Lady Louisa: "People have seen what is assumed to be the ghost of Louisa Carteret," Lord Bath explained. "I haven't seen her myself, because I don't have that power. My mother has seen the ghost in the Red Library downstairs, but not this one." I asked about visitors. Lord Bath explained that visitors were never taken to the part of the house where we were, so there was no way of telling whether they had experienced anything. I took a good look at the portrait of Lady Louisa. She was indeed worth fighting over: lovely face, beautiful eyes, slim figure in a green dress.

Shortly afterwards we left Longleat with the firm promise to return someday with a trance medium so that we could have a go at contacting the resident ghosts. But it wasn't until two years later that the opportunity came along.

Eventually I brought the London medium and former nurse, Trixie Allingham, to Longleat, introduced her to Lord Bath, and proceeded to enter the palace in the hope of really coming to grips with the phantoms that had never been dislodged, nor indeed fully contacted before. For the next two hours, Lord Bath, my friends, and I went through one of the most fascinating and gripping sessions we'd ever experienced.

All along, Trixie, a frail lady, had been unhappy in the car, partly because it was a rough ride and partly because she sensed some great tragedy ahead which would shortly involve her personally. As we were rounding the last long curve of the driveway leading to the palace, Trixie turned to me and said, "I saw the painting of a fair young woman. I thought she had something to do with my visit here, and she showed me an opened window as if she were telling me that there had been a tragedy connected with that window. Either she was pushed out, or somebody she loved had flung himself out, and then the vision faded. Then another woman came to me, rather charming and of the same period. She was older and looked rather haughty for a moment. Then she faded."

I had not replied, for I did not wish to give her any clues. A few minutes later we arrived at the main gate to Longleat and got out of the car. I gave Trixie time to "get to herself" and to get the shaky ride out of her system. Then we entered the Red Library, and I asked Trixie to sit down in one of the large antique chairs at the head of the room.

Immediately she said in a quivering, excited voice, "A long time ago something very evil happened here, or someone had a devilish temptation in this room, looking out of that window." She pointed at one of the several large windows on the far side of the room. "I have a feeling that there is a French link here, that either the wife or the daughter was of French ancestry," Trixie continued. "There is some connection with the French Revolution, for I see a guillotine . . . good heavens!"

"Do you sense a ghost here, Trixie?" I asked.

"As a matter of fact, yes, I get a woman. She has a dress with long sleeves, and she walks as if her hip were bent. There is a crucifix around her neck and she's saying, 'Help me, help me, help me!' This is going back more than a hundred years; her gown is sort of whitish with a mulberry shade. From way back." Trixie paused for a moment as if getting her bearings. Lord Bath, not exactly a believer, was watching her seriously now.

"Now I see a horse and a man galloping away, and I see the woman in tears and I wonder what it means. She sees the man galloping away, and she thinks life is over, and now I see her dead. I feel there is a church nearby, where her effigy is in stone on top of some sort of a sarcophagus. She showed it to me."

I asked Trixie if the woman was the same one she had seen in the car driving up, but she couldn't be sure, for she hadn't yet seen the woman's face. Were there any other presences in the room?

"Yes," Trixie replied. "Very dimly over there by the door and holding the handle, there is a man with a big hat on, and he wears a collar around the neck. He goes back a long time, I think."

I glanced at Lord Bath: nobody had told Trixie about the apparition seen by the nurse—Sir John Thynne, a man wearing a strange old-fashioned collar! While Trixie was resting for a moment, I walked around the library. I noticed that the shelves were filled with French books and that some of the furniture was obviously of eighteenth-century French origin. Had Trixie simply picked up the atmosphere of the room?

Trixie suddenly said in a rather challenging tone of voice: "Henry—is there a Henry here?" Almost like an obedient schoolboy, Lord Bath stepped forward. Trixie eyed him suspiciously. "You're Henry?"

"I'm the only one."

"Well, they said, 'Go talk to Henry.' "

"Who told you to talk to Henry?" Lord Bath inquired.

"I don't know. It is a man, a very unhappy man. He passed over a long time ago. He killed three people, and I don't mean in battle."

The story was getting more interesting. "How did he kill them?" I demanded to know.

"I look at his hands, and there are brown stains on them which he can't seem to wipe off. The letter H seems to be connected with him, and I have the feeling he did it in vengeance. I see a friar come up to him, and him trying to get absolved and being unable to. The friar is haughty, arrogant, and then the prior comes in and I see this unhappy man on his knees, and yet he does not get absolution, and that is why he comes back here."

"Can you possibly speak to him, Trixie?" I asked.

"I am speaking to him *now*," Trixie replied impatiently, "but he says, 'There is no hope for me.' I tell him we will pray for him. I hear him speak in Latin. I know a fair amount of Latin, and I'm saying it in English: 'Out of the depths I have called unto thee, O God, hear my voice.' Then the monk reappears, and there is also a tall lady here, by his side. I believe this is his wife; she's very slender and beautiful, and she's holding up one of his hands, saying, 'Pray, pray as you've never prayed before.' "

We left the Red Library and slowly walked up the staircase, one of the world's greatest, to the upper stories. When we arrived at the haunted corridor where the famous duel had taken place, Trixie sensed that something had happened around December or January of one particular year—not an ordinary passing. Immediately she explained that it had nothing to do with the haunting downstairs.

"The passing of this person was kept quiet. He was carried out in the dead of night in a gray shroud. I can see this happening. Five people are carrying out this ominous task. The whole situation was tragic and hushed up. He wasn't murdered and it wasn't suicide, but it was a person who came to an untimely end. Above all, they wanted no attention, no attention. He didn't live here, but he stayed here for a while. He came from Spain. I think he died from a wound in his side, yet it wasn't murder or suicide. He was about thirty-five years old. He says 'O my God, my God, to come to such an end.' He was a Catholic, he tells me. He was not shriven here after he passed. I see lanterns; he's not buried in sacred ground. Wait a moment, sir," Trixie suddenly said, turning to Lord Bath. "Is there a name like Winnie or something like that connected with your family?" Lord Bath's interest perked up. Winnie sounded a little like Weymouth.

"Francis, Francis," Trixie said excitedly now. "And I hear the name Fanny. She's just laughing. Did you know her?"

"Yes," Lord Bath replied, "a long, long time ago."

"Was she a very bright person?"

"Well, she was as a child. Her nickname was Fanny."

Evidently Trixie had gotten some more recent spirits mixed in with the old characters. "I see her as a younger woman, lovely, laughing, running along, and she tells me you have in your pocket a coin that is bent, out of order, not a normal coin. Is that true?"

"Yes," Lord Bath said, surprised.

"She just told me; isn't she sweet? Oh, and there is a lord chief justice here. Do you know him?"

"Peculiar," Lord Bath replied. "There *was* a lord chief justice upstairs."

For a moment Trixie seemed particularly sad, as she reported: "There is a child here named Tim, Timothy, but he died at the age of one and a half. Is this true?"

Lord Bath seemed to struggle with his emotions now. "Yes," he finally said in a low voice.

"He wants me to say, 'I am Tim,' and you should know he is still your son."

Lord Bath confirmed that his oldest son, Tim,

had died in infancy, but that the fact was known only to members of the family and had never been publicized.

Trixie then reported a servant woman, continuing to serve in her ghostly condition, and when I didn't show any particular interest, she went on to say that there was also a rather funny-looking man, "someone holding his head under his arm, walking, and I really shouldn't laugh at this sort of thing, but I saw this man with his head under his arm."

Since none of us were laughing, she assumed that it was all right to address the man with his head under his arm. "Can you tell me, sir, how you lost your head, and why?" She listened for a while, apparently getting an answer from the unseen headless specter. Nodding, she turned to us. "There is something about some rebels here; they are linked with France, and these rebels have come in strength. Somebody was being hounded, a person of high birth. He was hidden here, and I don't like it at all."

Lord Bath was visibly impressed. "During the rebellion of the Duke of Monmouth," he explained, "some rebels took refuge here. It is not at all unlikely that one of them was put to death on these grounds."

Trixie now exhibited unmistakable signs of weariness. Under the circumstances, we decided to call it a day and return in the morning. The following morning we started again in the Red Library. On entering, Trixie described a woman walking up and down wringing her hands and saying that her child had died. Trixie identified her as Christina and explained that this had happened no more than a hundred years ago. However, my main interest was in an earlier period, and I asked Trixie to try for full trance if she could. Again she seated herself in the comfortable chair at the far end of the Red Library.

"There is a link here with the tragedy I saw in part yesterday," she began. "I still see the horseman and the woman at the window, and I smell the tragedy. There is something about a rapier wound. Ron is murdered and a Helen is mixed up in this. The man I saw yesterday is still here, by the way, and he looks happier now."

"Ask him to identify himself."

"I get the initial R. He wears a cape and a lace collar."

"Why did he murder the three people?"

"I get the initial P. Someone was in a dungeon here." All of a sudden we weren't hearing Trixie's voice anymore, but a rough male voice coming from her entranced lips. I realized that the ghost had at last taken over the medium and was about to address us directly.

"Who put you into the dungeon?"

"S. Mine enemy, mine enemy."

"Is this your house?"

"Yes, of course."

"Did you build this house?"

"With bad money."

"What is your name, sir?" I insisted.

Suddenly the entity was gone again and Trixie was back. "He was a Catholic by birth," she said, "and he is showing me a very large ruby ring on his finger. His ankles hurt him. He must have been chained for a time, and I see a short dagger in his hand. Now he is fading again."

"Is he the victim or the murderer?" I almost shouted.

"He did it; he says, 'I did it, I have no peace.' He

was the owner of the house. He says, 'You will pray for me, you will pray for me.' " I assured the entity through the medium that we would all pray for him.

"He says someone owes him something."

"But he can be forgiven; tell him that."

"There is a little chapel here somewhere in this mansion. I can see the altar, and he wants Lord Bath to go there, to the chapel. 'If he will do it, he will give me peace; he will give me rest.' "

I promised that we would do it, without even asking Lord Bath, for I knew he would go along with it, although he was not a religious person.

"I can't do any more, I can't do any more," the medium said now, and she looked exhausted. I questioned her about what she remembered.

"I saw two men killed over a woman," Trixie recollected. "There is a lead coffin amongst all the others, one different from the others. It is away from the others. This man is in it, the one who murdered. I hear the name Grace, and someone was hung, hanged from the rafters."

Impressions seemed to hit her now from various directions, possibly getting different layers of history confused in the process. It was up to us to sort it out.

"Tom," Trixie now said firmly, and looked at me. I asked her to describe the man. "I see him very dimly; he is old and belongs to an earlier age." Lord Bath then informed me that we were in what used to be the chapel, although the floor had been changed and we were actually above it. Just as I had promised, we grouped ourselves around the spot where the altar once stood below, bowed our heads in prayer, and I said, "May Thomas rest free from worry, happy in his home. May he be free from any guilt or fear. Let us now have a moment of silent prayer."

In the silence I glanced at Lord Bath, a man who had told me before that he thought himself an agnostic. He seemed genuinely affected and moved.

"I don't know whether it was a bishop," Trixie said, "but I saw a man with a gold miter on his head make the sign of the cross and I heard the word 'progression,' and then something very odd happened. A feather was put on his shoulder, but I don't know what it means."

"Perhaps his soul is now light as a feather?" I suggested. Trixie then asked Lord Bath whether he knew of any jeweled crucifix in the mansion. Lord Bath could not remember such an item offhand. Trixie insisted, "It is a jeweled cross with dark stones, and it has to do with your people. I also see three monks who were here when you were praying. Three in a row. But now I feel peace; I feel a man who had a leaden weight on his shoulder is now without it. It was important that he be helped."

I have already mentioned that the name which the medium got in connection with the death of the thirty-five-year-old Spaniard in the haunted passage upstairs sounded very close to Weymouth, the man who killed him in a duel. The medium's description of this man's death as being neither death nor suicide is of course entirely correct: he was killed in an honest duel, which in those days was not considered murder. Trixie described the man's death as an affair that had to be hushed up, and so it was indeed, not only because a man had been killed, but also because the wife of the viscount had been unfaithful. A scandal *was* avoided: the body was interred underneath the kitchen floor, and, as Lord Bath confirmed, it had been found several years earlier and been given burial *outside* the house.

More fascinating is Trixie's account of the haunting in the Red Library. The man she described is obviously the same man described by the old nanny whom I interviewed in 1964, and the same man whom Dorothy Coates, former librarian of Longleat, had encountered, as well as a certain Mrs. Grant, former housekeeper in the greathouse.

In a somewhat confused and jumbled way, however, Trixie hit on many of the facts surrounding the ancient palace. I doubt that Trixie would have known of these family secrets, which are never found in tourist guides of Longleat or in popular books dealing with the Thynne family. They are, however, available in research libraries, if one tries hard enough to find the information. There exists, for instance, a contemporary source known as the "John Evelyn Diary," a seventeenth-century chronicle of the London scene. From this source we learned that Thomas Thynne, then already one of the wealthiest men in England and somewhat advanced in years, had fallen in love with a sixteen-year-old heiress by the name of Elizabeth Ogle. He married her despite the great difference in their ages, and after the wedding ceremony preceded her to Longleat, where Lady Elizabeth was to follow him in a few days' time. But Elizabeth never arrived in Longleat. Unwilling to consummate the marriage into which she felt herself forced by her family, she ran away to the Netherlands, where she continued living as if she weren't married. In the Netherlands, Elizabeth Ogle met a certain Count Koenigsmark and fell in love with this somewhat adventurous gentleman. Since divorce was out of the question, and Lady Elizabeth was legally married to Thomas Thynne, the young lovers decided to murder Elizabeth's husband so that she might be free to marry her count.

In view of Thynne's affluence and importance, such a plot was not an easy one to bring off. Koenigsmark therefore engaged the services of three paid murderers, a certain Lieutenant Stern, a Colonel Vratz, and a man named Boroski. The murderous foursome arrived in London and immediately set about keeping a close watch on their intended victim. One Sunday night Thynne left a party in London and entered his coach to be driven home. That was the signal they had been waiting for. They followed their victim, and when the coach with Thomas Thynne reached Pall Mall, which was at that time still a country road, the murderers stopped it. Lieutenant Stern, galloping ahead of the coach, put his hands onto the reins of the lead horse. As Thomas Thynne opened the door of the coach and stepped out, a volley of shots hit him in the face.

The restless ghost had called "mine enemy." Could this have been Stern?

The murder created a great deal of attention even in those unruly times. Count Koenigsmark and his henchmen were apprehended just as the count was about to leave England to join Elizabeth. According to John Evelyn, the trial, which took place in 1682, saw the count acquitted by a corrupt jury, but the actual murderers were condemned to death on the gallows. The hired assassins paid with their lives, but the man who had hatched the plot got off scot-free. No wonder the restless spirit of the victim could not find peace! But if one of the ghosts who contacted us through Trixie was indeed Thomas Thynne, the victim of the murder plot, why should he then grieve for the three people who had been put to death for his murder? Undoubtedly, Trixie, in reaching several levels of hauntings, had brought up bits and pieces of John, Thomas, and perhaps even his murderers—all presented in a slightly confusing but essentially evidential package.

Trixie also spoke of "one lead coffin, different from all others." According to the diaries, two weeks after Colonel Vratz had been put to death his body was still not decayed, owing to a new process of preservation which was being used for the first time. "He lay exposed in a very rich coffin lined with *lead,* too magnificent for so daring and horrid a murderer."

So it seems that at least four ghosts occupied the halls of Longleat: the Lady Louisa, who mourned her lover's death at the hands of her husband; the rebel from the Duke of Monmouth's army, who was caught and slaughtered; the builder of Longleat, Sir John Thynne, whose personal attachment and possibly feelings of guilt keep him from leaving his rich estate for greener pastures; and, of course, Thomas Thynne. I should think the latter has departed the premises now, but I am equally sure that Sir John is still around enjoying the spectacles his descendant, the present Lord Bath, is putting on for the tourists. Surely Sir John would have understood the need to install turnstiles in the cafeteria and a toilet downstairs, or to bring in lions for a zoo, and to do whatever was possible to raise revenue to keep the magnificent palace in prime condition; for Sir John, not unlike his descendant, was foremost a man of business and common sense.

The Ghost on Television

I HAD heard of two kinds of ghosts connected with television: those impersonated by actors and those caused by the interference of tall buildings. Now I was to learn of still another kind of ghost on television, this one being the real McCoy. It all started with a lecture I gave at the British College of Psychic Studies in London. After my lecture on ghosts, which was illustrated by slides of apparitions, I was approached by a tall, intellectual-looking lady who wanted to tell me about a very strange haunted house in East Anglia. This was my first meeting with Ruth Plant, who explained that she was a writer and researcher, with a background in social science. Her beliefs lay in the Spiritualist philosophy, and she had had any number of psychic experiences herself. I asked her to drop me a note about the house in East Anglia. I expected it to be just another haunted house, probably containing the usual complement of footsteps, doors opening or closing by themselves, or possibly even an apparition of a deceased relative. By *my* standards, that constitutes a classic, conventional haunting.

The following January, Miss Plant lived up to her promise. She explained that the house in East Anglia was called Morley Old Hall, and though it was principally of the Stuart period, it stood on much earlier foundations, going back to pre-Saxon times. It was situated near Norwich in the northeast of England and apparently belonged to a friend of hers who had bought it with a view to restoring it. It had been in lamentable condition and not suitable to be lived in. Her friend, by the name of Ricky Cotterill, was essentially a pig farmer; nevertheless, he and his young wife and their baby managed to live in the sprawling mansion, or rather in that part of it which he had been able to restore on his own funds, and the excitement of living with so much history more than adequately made up for the deprivations he was subjecting himself to. Miss Plant explained that the house was way off the beaten track and was, in fact, hard to find unless one knew the countryside. There were two moats around it, and archeological digs had been undertaken all over that part of the country for many years, since that part of East Anglia is one of the oldest and most historic sections of England.

At the time of her first communication with me, in January 1966, Miss Plant had not as yet undertaken any research into the background of the house or its surroundings. She thought the house worthy of my attention because of what had happened to her and a friend during a visit.

"I went to stay there with a Norwegian friend, Anne Wilhelmsen, whose father was a cultural attaché of Norway in London, and who was herself a university graduate," Ruth Plant explained. "This was two years ago at Easter. We had intended to stay at the local hotel, but Mr. Cotterill, the owner of the mansion, found that the hotel was entirely full."

Under the circumstances, the owner moved out of the room he had been occupying and let the two ladies use it for the night. As he knew of Miss Plant's interest in ghosts, he assured her that to the best of his knowledge there were no ghosts there, since he had lived there for three years and had seen nothing. As a matter of fact, the two ladies slept well, and in the morning Miss Plant got up and walked across the big room connecting the two wings with the kitchen, all of it being on the first floor.

"When I came back, I felt impressed to pause at the large window which looked down the front drive, in spite of the fact that it had no glass in it and the day was bitterly cold. I felt very peaceful and contemplative and I suddenly heard a Catholic prayer, the Hail Mary, and was sure that the 'presence' I felt was that of the lady of the house. After I had noted this, I went back into our bedroom and was surprised to find Anne sitting up in bed looking very worried. She said she had just heard the rustle of bedclothes and heavy breathing while she lay there. She had sat up in bed to listen more closely, and immediately the sound ceased, only to come back again when she lay down. We told our host about this over breakfast, but he could not enlighten us further. So I went into the village and in talking to people found out that several people who had lived in the house had experienced very much the same thing. One man had actually seen the lady quite clearly at the window, and others had heard her, like Anne."

The "Lady at the Window" fascinated Ruth Plant, especially as she didn't know her identity. As was her custom then, and is now, she decided to have a sitting with a reputable medium to see whether the medium might pick up something spiritual around her and possibly shed some light on the identity of the lady ghost of Morley Old Hall. This time she had a sitting with a certain Mr. Bogoran, one of the regulars sitting at the College of Psychic Studies, Queensbury Place. "I didn't mention anything about the ghost, but said I had a friend who was trying to restore a beautiful old Stuart house and I wondered if anyone on the Other Side could offer any helpful advice."

Instead of advice on how to restore the house, medium Bogoran described the house itself in minute detail and then added that he saw a ghostly lady standing at one of the windows. This of course came as a surprise to Miss Plant, but even more of a shock was in store for her: Mr. Bogoran volunteered two additional statements of interest. One, that the owner of the house, her friend, would be on television within a few weeks, and two, that there was another ghost in the house, a monk who was attached to the house, not because he had been happy there like the ghostly lady, but because he had been involved in a killing.

Since Mr. Cotterill, the owner of the house, had absolutely no connection with television, the first statement evoked nothing but doubt in Ruth Plant's mind. Picture her surprise when several days after her sitting with Mr. Bogoran, Ricky Cotterill telephoned to tell her that he had been approached by a local television station to have an all-night session at the house which would be filmed for television. The reason for his call was to invite her to Norwich to appear as part of the program. In the excitement of this development, Ruth Plant forgot all about the ghostly monk.

When she arrived at the Hall, she met Tony Cornell, a psychic researcher from Cambridge. Ruth and Mr. Cornell did not see things the same way: she sensed him to be skeptical and negative and suspected his presence in the house was more to debunk the ghosts than to find them. It turned out later that Mr. Cornell was, as the program producer put it, "Our handiest accredited psychic investigator," called into the case not necessarily because of his commitment to the reality of ghosts, but because his offices were not too far away, and time was of the essence. Ruth brought along a sound tape of her sitting with Mr. Bogoran, but it was not used in the film. She gave the required interview and thought no more about it. A few weeks later, the filmed report of Morley Old Hall went on the air. Ruth Plant saw it at a local hotel, where it was rather badly focused, and she could hardly recognize herself or anyone else. Nevertheless, something odd happened during that screening.

"During the performance, there was a loud bang on the set," Ruth Plant stated, "which seemed to have no normal cause. My basset hound, who had been fast asleep with her back to the screen, jumped up in great apprehension and stood gazing at the screen as though she saw *someone we could not see.*"

A few days later Ruth Plant telephoned Mr. Cotterill, and it was only then that she heard the amazing results of the televising of the film. It appeared that no fewer than twenty-three people from the general public had written into the broadcasting station and asked who the bearded monk was, standing behind Mr. Cornell while he was speaking!

Now no one had mentioned anything about a ghostly monk, but everyone connected with the venture knew that a ghostly *lady* had been observed by a number of witnesses. Consequently, she would have been on the minds of those participating in the experiment, if a mind picture could indeed find its way onto a television film.

The idea of a ghost appearing on television naturally excited me. Immediately I got in touch with Michael Robson, producer of the documentary and one of the executives of Anglia Television. Michael Robson, who had been to Morley Old Hall many times before the documentary was made, offered to let me see the actual film when I came to England. "Our film unit had an all-night vigil in the Hall," he explained in a statement dated September 2, 1966, "with the chairman of the Cambridge Psychical Research and Spontaneous Cases Committee, Mr. Tony Cornell. Various things of interest occurred during the night, in particular a moving tumbler, but what caused all the excitement was this: Mr. Cornell and I were discussing the Hall on film by a mullioned window as dawn was breaking. No sooner had the film been transmitted than a great many people wrote in asking who the figure was that appeared between Mr. Cornell and myself. All their descriptions were the same: the face and trunk of a monkish-type figure looking between us. Mr. Cornell and I examined the film closely afterwards ourselves and saw nothing: but in view of the large number of people who claimed to have seen the figure, Mr. Cornell thought it an interesting example of collective hallucination, and took away the letters for closer study."

It turned out that Mr. Cornell was not a parapsychologist with an academic connection, but merely an interested ghost-fancier. With the help of Miss Plant, and considerable patience, I managed to obtain the letters which Mr. Cornell had taken with him and examined them myself. His explanation of the phenomenon as a "mass hallucination" is, of course, an easy way out of coming to grips with the problem itself—a genuine psychic phenomenon. But the twenty-three witnesses are far more eloquent in their description of what they experienced than any would-be scientist could possibly be in trying to explain away the phenomenon.

Mrs. Joan Buchan of Great Yarmouth wrote: "My husband and I saw a figure of a monk with a cowl over his head and with his hands clasped as though in prayer. It could be seen quite clearly, standing quietly in the window. It didn't appear to be looking at the men conversing, but behind them."

"I saw the figure of a man which appeared to me to be that of a monk; he had on a round hat, a long cloak, and his hands were together as in prayer," observed Miss A. Hewitt of Southrepps.

"I saw the figure quite distinctly, considering I only have a twelve-inch screen and the sunlight was pouring into my room. The figure appeared behind the profile of the man who was talking, as if looking through the window," stated L. M. Gowing. "I thought perhaps it was due to the light, but the man talking moved and seemed to partly cover it. When he went back to his former position, it was there clearer than before."

"Both my daughter and myself certainly saw the outline of a priest to the right of the speaker and to the left of the interviewer," wrote Mrs. G. D. Hayden of Bromham. Not only did Mr. and Mrs. Carter of Lincolnshire say, "It was very clear," but Mrs. Carter sent in a drawing of the monk she had seen on the television. From Norwich, where the broadcast originated, came a statement from a viewer named Elviera Panetta, who also drew the bearded monk, showing him to have a long, haggard face. "Both my mother and I saw the monk looking through the window; he is cowled, bearded, and his hands are slightly raised." One viewer, Miss M. C. Grix, wrote to the station inquiring whether "it was a real person standing in the window just behind the man who was talking, dressed in black and looking as if he had his hands together in prayer," to which Nora Kononenko of Suffolk added, "It first looked to me like a skull with a hood, and then, as the gentlemen went on talking, it seemed to come forward and peer in. At that moment it distinctly changed into a gaunt-looking face, with a horrible leer upon it." The station decided to run the film again, as testimonies kept pouring in. After the second run, even more people saw the ghostly monk on the screen.

"Your repeat of the alleged haunted house shook me considerably," wrote Mrs. A. C. Mason, "Not because of what I had seen in the original broadcast, but because your Mr. MacGregor gaily quipped, 'Well, did you see anything?' I was astonished that anyone else *couldn't* see what was so clear to me. I did see the monk both times." Some viewers sent in simple statements, unsolicited and to the point. "I saw the monk in the window just as plain as could be. It was there at the time and I can assure you I did not imagine it," wrote Mrs. Joan Collis of Suffolk.

"He didn't seem to be hooded but had long hair and was bearded," stated Mrs. Janet Halls of Norwich, and Mrs. F. Nicolaisen of Cambridge volunteered that "I had seen the figure on the previous showing but didn't mention it for fear of being laughed at. This time I traced it out for my husband, but he still couldn't see it, much to my annoyance."

If all these people were suffering from mass hallucination, it is certainly strange that they hallucinated in so many different ways, for many of the reports differed in slight but important details. "Towards the end of the showing, my sister and I distinctly saw an image of a cowled monk from head to waist," wrote Miss W. Caplen of Lowestoft. Probably Mrs. J. G. Watt of Cambridge put it best when she wrote, "I had no idea what sort of ghost I was expected to look for, and I saw nothing until the two men were discussing the house. But outside the window I then saw clearly, behind them, the figure of a monk. He wore a monk's habit and was bare-headed, with the monk's haircut associated with the monks of olden days, bald patch with fringe, either fair or gray hair. His face was that of a young man and he had a very serene look on his face. His arms were hanging down in front of him, with his right hand placed lightly on top of his left. I saw this all very plainly and naturally and I thought everyone else would be able to, so I thought the television people were having a game with the viewers, and I thought it was all a hoax. Next day a friend told me of Anglia TV's purpose of rerunning the film, and I realized it was serious. The strange thing is that our television set is not what it used to be, and we don't get a good picture—and yet I saw this monk very clearly."

By now it was clear to me that twenty-three people—or at last count thirty-one—had actually seen or thought they had seen the figure of a monk where none was supposed to be. Many others, if not the majority of viewers, however, did not see the monk. Obviously, then, it was on the film, and yet visible only to those with psychic gifts. This raised interesting questions: while we know that ghosts appear only to those capable of seeing them, can apparitions also be photographed selectively, so that they can be seen only by those who are psychic, while others not so gifted will not be able to see them in the photograph or film? Also, was the case of the ghost on television unique, or are there other such instances on the record?

According to the *London Express* of December 19, 1969, five shop girls saw a ghostly figure on a closed-circuit TV set. "The girls and customers watched fascinated for forty-five minutes as the figure of a woman in a long Victorian dress stood at the top of the stairs in the boutique in High Street, Kent, occasionally waving her hand and patting her hair. Several times the figure walked halfway down the stairs and then went back up again to the upper floor of the boutique, which had been converted only a few months ago from an old house." The first one to see the ghostly apparition on the closed-circuit television setup was eighteen-year-old Sally White, who pointed her out to her colleague, Janet Abbs, saying, "You've got a customer." But Janet Abbs walked right through the figure. One of the other girls, Andree Weller, said "As the figure went upstairs it disappeared into a sort of mist and then reappeared again." The incident happened at lunchtime, and though five girls saw the woman, when they walked upstairs where they had seen her, they found the place empty. When they returned downstairs and looked at the screen, there was the ghost again. Unlike the monk of Morley Old Hall, who appeared for only a few seconds on screen, the Victorian lady of High Street, Chatham, Kent, stayed for a whole hour, apparently enjoying her performance hugely.

However, what none of the viewers who had written in had pointed out was the fact that the figure of the monk was not in proportion to the size of the two flesh-and-blood people talking on the screen at the time: the monk seemed considerably smaller than they were. Ruth Plant found the emergence of the second ghost most exciting. She decided to consult two other London mediums, to see whether they might pick up something concerning his identity. One of them was Trixie Allingham, who immediately "saw" a ghostly monk around the house and informed Ruth that he had been attacked by someone who came in while he was praying. The monk had defended himself by striking the intruder with a chalice. She felt that the priest, with the help of a soldier, had later buried the body and the chalice. George Southhal, primarily a dowsing medium, volunteered that there was a chalice buried on the premises and described a set of cups, the largest of which was reserved for a man of importance. He saw Morley as a place similar to a pilgrims' retreat. At the time of Miss Plant's sitting with George Southhal, neither of them knew as yet that it had been a little-known pre-Reformation practice to give a special chalice to a prior or bishop, since he was not supposed to use the chalice used by ordinary priests. All the mediums Ruth Plant sat with were emphatic about some buried treasure and secret passages leading from the house to a nearby church. The latter could be confirmed during later research. As for the treasure, it hasn't been found yet, but the effort continues.

I decided to arrange for a visit to Norfolk at the earliest opportunity. That opportunity presented itself in September of 1966 when a film producer offered to come with me to inspect potential sites for a documentary motion-picture. I suggested Morley Old Hall and notified Ruth Plant to get everything ready: arrange for a visit to the Hall, suggest a suitable hotel nearby, notify Anglia TV of our desire to see the controversial television documentary, and, finally, to make everybody happy, let the local press have a go at us—the American ghost-hunter and his entourage paying a call to the local ghost. Miss Plant was to serve as technical advisor to the film. (Unfortunately, the film was never made, because the producer and I could not see eye to eye on a treatment that would allow the story to be told in exciting but scientifically valid terms.)

We rode up to Norwich from London. The projected film producer, Gilbert Cates, who was a firm nonbeliever, could not see how such things as ghosts were possible, while the third member of the party, the distinguished motion picture scenarist Victor Wolfson, argued equally strongly that such things as spirits were indeed not only possible but likely. At one point the discussion got so heated that I began to worry whether we would ever arrive together in Norfolk. Finally, Victor Wolfson changed the subject. With a shrug, he commented, "I don't think I can convince Gil. He's underdeveloped." Gil, a good sport under all circumstances, smiled. As for me, I began to wonder about the wisdom of having brought my two fellow adventurers at all.

Ruth Plant had advised us to bed down for the night in Norfolk, but my producer friend was so eager to be close to the "action" that he insisted we stay at the little Abbey Hotel at Wyndmondham, which is very near to Morley. We arrived at the hotel, tired and dirty, just in time to have an evening meal.

Waking early, I looked out onto the church and cemetery below my windows. It seemed very peaceful and far removed from any ghostly encounters. I took a look at a local map supplied to me by Ruth Plant. The city of Norwich, where we would view the television film, was nine miles to the east, while Morley Old Hall was a little over twelve miles to the west.

The abbey church at Wyndmondham was an impressive edifice for a village of this small size. Early in the twelfth century, William D'Albini, who had been given the town and manor of Wyndmondham, which included Morley, for his help with the Norman invasion of England, established here a monastery consisting of a prior and twelve Benedictine monks. The Benedictines, wearing black habits, were the most aristocratic and wealthy of all the religious orders, and, because of that, frequently came into conflict with poorer, humbler religious orders. It also appeared that Richard, William's brother, was made Abbot of St. Alban's, in Hertfordshire, one of the largest Benedictine monasteries in England, and Wyndmondham was a sort of daughter house to St. Alban's.

"But the relationship between the two houses was never good, and the jealousies and rivalries between them only ceased when, in 1448, Wyndmondham became an abbey in its own right," writes the Reverend J. G. Tansley Thomas in his *History of Wyndmondham Abbey.* I had the occasion to study all this while waiting for the car to pick me up for the short journey to Morley Old Hall.

After twenty minutes or so, there appeared a clump of bushes, followed by tall trees—trees that showed their age and the fact that they had not been interfered with for many years. All sorts of trees were growing wild here, and as the road rounded a bend, they seemed to swallow us up. We rumbled over a wooden bridge crossing a deep and pungent moat. Directly behind it was a brick breastwork, overgrown by all sorts of plants. This was the second, inner moat, I was told later; the outer moat was farther back and scarcely noticeable today, although in Saxon times it was a major bulwark. The car stopped in front of the imposing mansion, built of red brick and topped off by grayish-blue shingles in the manner of the seventeenth century. Part of the surrounding wall was still standing, and there were two very tall trees inside the inner moat, which gave Morley Old Hall a particularly romantic appearance. The Hall rises three stories, and windows had been replaced in many of them, attesting to the owner's skill at restoring what he had bought as a virtual ruin. We walked up a beautifully restored staircase, to the second story, where the Cotterill family lived at the time. Much of the mansion was still uninhabitable. Some rooms consisted of bare walls, while others still had ancient fireplaces in them, staring at the visitor like toothless monsters.

Ruth Plant had managed to arrange it so that the principal witnesses to the phenomena at the Hall would be present for my interrogation, and so it was that we assembled upstairs in the library—not the magnificent Stuart library of old, but a reasonable facsimile. I first turned to Frank Warren, a man in his middle seventies who had once lived in the house, long before it passed into the present owner's hands. He had come from the nearby village to talk to me, and later I paid a courtesy call on his little cottage, adorned with beautiful flowers from one end to the other: Frank Warren was, and is, a dedicated gardener. Like so many people of the area, he is "fay," that is, psychic, and he recalls vividly how he saw and actually touched his pet dog two months after the animal had died. But the human ghost at Morley Old Hall was another matter.

"I was working in the garden," he began, "and the lady of the house said, 'I wish you'd clip around that window; those pieces annoy me.' So I started to clip. It was a beautiful day, with the sun shining. All at once, just like that, there appeared a lady in the window, as close to me as you are and she looked at me. She was tall, and I noticed every detail of her dress. She looked at me and the expression on her face never changed. Her lips never moved and I thought to myself, 'I can't stand it. I'll go and do some work in the vegetable garden.' When I returned she was gone, so I completed my job at the window. Well, I used to go and have a meal with the housekeeper. I said, 'There is something I'd like you to tell me: who is the other lady living in this house?'

" 'Well,' she replied, 'there is no other lady living in this house. You know exactly who is in this house.' I replied that I didn't, because I had seen somebody here I had never seen before."

Apparently the housekeeper was frightened by the idea of having ghosts about the place, for Lady Ironside, who was then the owner of the Hall, summoned the gardener about the matter. "I can't help it," he replied to her protestations. "I saw her with my own eyes." It was wartime and Lady Ironside was hard put to keep servants about the place, so she asked the gardener please to keep quiet about the ghost.

"Did you ever see the lady ghost again?" I inquired.

"A fortnight afterwards I went past the other window, on the opposite side, and there sat the housekeeper reading a book, and beside her sat the same lady. The housekeeper didn't see her. She wore a plain black dress, which seemed a bit stiff and went right to the ground, so I couldn't see her feet. I had a quarter of an hour to examine her, and I didn't see her feet."

Gordon Armstrong had come from London to talk to us at Morley Old Hall. "This is my second visit," he began. "I was here toward the end of July last year, 1965. I was working in London at the time and hitchhiked my way through the night and arrived at Morley in the small hours of the morning. Having walked up the road, I came into the house—it must have been somewhere around two o'clock in the morning—and at the time I had already heard of a ghost being there, or rumored to be there, so I was half expecting to see one. Of course, I had never seen a ghost before, so I was rather apprehensive. When I came up the stairs in the dark, with only a small flashlight to help me, I heard a sound that reminded me of a cat jumping from one landing to another. This was on the third-floor landing."

"Did you see a cat?" I asked.

"No, I didn't see a cat. I thought I was alone, that is, until I heard someone breathing in one of the rooms. Part of the floor was only rafters, without floorboards, so one could hear what went on on the floor below. It was one of the rooms on the second floor where the noise came from."

"What did the breathing sound like?"

"I thought I heard a man breathing rather heavily."

"What did you do next?"

"I was sitting up there on these rafters, and it was pretty dark. I didn't feel like meeting anyone, so I slept against a wall up there. I must have been asleep for a couple of hours. The wind was blowing, and I woke up once and went back to sleep again, and when I came to the second time it was just getting light. I went down and explored the house further and found the room where the noise had come from, and there was a sort of couch there, so I lay down for a bit and dozed off for another couple of hours. I looked at the room and realized that no one had slept there during the night."

Ruth Plant remarked at this point that the area where Mr. Armstrong had heard the heavy breathing was the same spot where her friend from Norway had also heard breathing, though she thought it could have been a woman, not necessarily a man.

Later on, the television people ran the controversial documentary for us. None of us saw the monk. We stopped action at the spot where thirty-one people said that they had seen the bearded monk, but all we could see were two men in conversation.

Nevertheless, the question of identifying the two ghosts at Morley intrigued me. This was one of the oldest and most fought-over spots in all of England, and the emotional imprint of many periods was undoubtedly still very strong. In antiquity the Iceni lived in this area. Their famous Queen Boadicea battled the Romans here in the first century. Later the Saxons made it a stronghold, and there is undoubtedly much undiscovered treasure in the ground. "A few years ago a ploughman turned up a wonderful collection of Saxon silver not far from Morley," Ruth Plant, ever the historian, explained. Scandinavian raiders had been there at an early stage: the word *mor* in Morley means mother in Norwegian. In 1066 a survey of all the land in England was undertaken. Known as the *Domesday Book,* it listed Morlea as belonging to one William de Warrenne. He was a wealthy Norman baron who took part in the Battle of Hastings. The *Domesday Book* also states that the land was let out to a priest and five freemen. Eventually the manor passed from the Warrenne family into the hands of the Morleys, and in 1545 it was sold to Martin Sedley, a Roman Catholic, whose family held it until 1789, when the direct line died out. It appears that the house fell into disrepair soon after, for, according to Ruth Plant, the Norfolk Directory of 1836 describes it even then as a "farmhouse encompassed by a deep moat." White's Norfolk Directory of 1864 named a certain Graber Brown as Lord of the Manor, and called Morley Old Hall "an Elizabethan house with a moat around it now used as a farmhouse." Eventually General Lord Ironside, World War I hero, bought it, but he passed on soon afterwards, and it passed into the hands of the Cotterills.

Since we could not stay on in Norfolk beyond the two days assigned to our visit, I entrusted further research to Ruth Plant. She concentrated on the monk and, whether through historical intuition or her psychic ability, shortly came up with some strange facts about one of the abbots of nearby Wyndmondham Abbey. "I unearthed the extraordinary fact that one of the abbots went completely mad and was so violent he was put into chains and died in them at Binham Priory. I believe I can find out more about this if I go to St. Alban's Abbey where the records are kept."

I encouraged Ruth to undertake that journey, and a few months later she contacted me again.

Ruth had managed to get hold of a rare book in a London library which contained a commentary on the records of St. Alban's Abbey done by an eighteenth-century vicar. It contained the story of a prior of Wyndmondham whose name was Alexander de Langley. "He went violently mad while in office at Wyndmondham and was recalled to St. Alban's," Ruth Plant informed me. "He lived around 1130 and died in chains at Binham Priory, about ten miles from Morley. I am sure Alexander de Langley, the mad prior, is the ghostly monk." In a further effort to throw light on the two ghosts at Morley, Ruth visited Lady Ironside, who resided at Hampton Court.

"I had agreed with Ricky Cotterill not to mention the ghostly side," Ruth Plant explained to me. "But she greeted me by remarking about 'that lovely Morley and the lovely lady who is seen standing at the window looking at the view.' She then asked me if I had ever visited it, making it quite clear she knew nothing of my psychic experiences concerning it. She added that many people have claimed to have seen her, though she didn't think that any of them would still be alive in the village to talk about it now."

But who *was* the ghostly lady at the window? Ruth Plant showed Lady Ironside the letters written to Anglia TV. One of the letters describes not a monk but a ghostly woman wearing a mantilla. Lady Ironside felt that the ghost must be Anne Shelton, daughter of one of the great supporters of Mary Tudor, which would account for the impression received by

Ruth Plant that the female ghost was Catholic, and for her hearing a Hail Mary.

"As regards the monk, Lady Ironside told me that when they went there, Frank Warren's brother Guy, who farmed the place, told them, 'There is an old monk about the place, but you have no need to take any notice of him.' But she knew nothing about the coffin lid mentioned by Frank Warren."

Apparently, when Frank Warren was first being interviewed by Ruth Plant, he recalled Lord Ironside's coming out of the house one day carrying the stone lid of a coffin saying, "This belonged to a monk."

"But Lady Ironside mentioned that men, while excavating, had found a square stone with the name ALBINI on it in Roman capitals. And since Wyndmondham was founded by Albini, the Norman baron who later became the Earl of Arundel and still later the Duke of Norfolk, the question is, was this the chapel of the Albinis, and was Morley a cell of Wyndmondham Abbey and of the Benedictine order?"

There you have it: a sixteenth-century Tudor lady, staying on forever in what was once her home, curiously looking out at a forever changing world; and a twelfth-century monk, gone mad, forced to die in chains ten miles from where he used to live. Perhaps he was drawn back to his house because it was there that he had committed his crime—killing a man, even if in self-defense, with a holy object as his weapon, thus compounding the crime. Was it the crime that had turned Alexander de Langley into a madman, or was it the madman in him that made him commit the crime?

The Ghosts at Blanchland

THE MOST obvious thing about Blanchland is its remoteness," writes G. W. O. Addleshaw in his short history of Blanchland. It wasn't as remote for us, because we arrived on a well-planned schedule, by private car, followed about two hours later by a busload of special tourists: participants in a Haunted Britain Tour arranged by Vision Travel, under the guidance of Andre Michalski, Polish nobleman and former orchestra conductor. Over the hills, into the dales, and over still another chain of hills we rode, shaken up all the while, but hopeful of eventually reaching our destination intact. By *we* I mean my wife Catherine and myself and London medium Trixie Allingham, whom I had invited to participate in a rare and unusual experiment. She hadn't the slightest idea why I was bringing her up north. All she knew was that I was on a ghost-hunting expedition, that she would have a quiet room that night and be brought back to London the following day.

When we left the airport at Newcastle, I had no idea that I would soon be in the heart of the Middle

Ages, in a small market town so perfectly preserved that it gave one the impression of being in the middle of a motion-picture set in Hollywood. The square commons was reached through a city gate, turreted and fortified, and to the left was a solid-looking gray stone building with a colorful sign dangling from the second story. The sign read "Lord Crewe Arms." This was the unusual hotel which was once a sixteenth-century manor house, which in turn had been converted from a twelfth-century monastery.

The Abbey of Blanchland had been founded by Premonstratensian monks, a strict offshoot of the Benedictines. The land which gave the abbey its income was originally part of the old earldom of Northumbria, expropriated by Henry I for the Norman de Bolbec family. The family itself added some of their own lands in 1214, and it was then that the name Blanchland, which means white land, was mentioned for the first time. Most probably the name is derived from the white habits of the Premonstratensian monks. Up until the middle nineteenth century, the area around Blanchland was wild and desolate, very thinly populated and cut off from the outside world. This was, in a way, most fortunate, because it prevented Blanchland from being embroiled in the political struggles of the intervening centuries and allowed the monks to lead a more contemplative life here than in any other part of England. The monastery was dissolved under Henry VIII, as were all others, and in 1539 the remaining monks were pensioned off, leaving Blanchland Abbey after four hundred years of residence. At first a family named Radcliffe owned the estates and buildings of the dissolved abbey, but in 1623 the Forsters, an old Northumberland family, came into possession of

Blanchland. By now the church was in ruins, but a chapel still existed within the main building. Part of the abbey buildings were converted into houses for the village, and the abbot's residence became the manor house. When the last male of the line died, the property passed into the hands of Dorothy Forster, who had married Lord Crewe, Bishop of Durham.

When the owners of Blanchland got into financial difficulties in 1704, Lord Crewe bought the estates, and thus the name Crewe was linked with Blanchland from that moment on. Unfortunately for the family, they became embroiled in the Scottish rebellion of 1715, taking the Jacobite side. The estates eventually passed to a board of trustees, which rebuilt the damaged portion of the village.

A group of buildings, chiefly the kitchen and the prior's house, eventually became an unusual hotel, the Lord Crewe Arms, owned and operated by the Vaux Breweries of Sunderland. The stone-vaulted chamber of the house now serves as a bar. There is an outer stone staircase leading to the gateway and another one leading to what is called the Dorothy Forster Sitting Room, a room I was to know intimately.

We were welcomed by the manager, a Mr. Blenkinsopp, and shown to our quarters. Everything was furnished in eighteenth-century style. Our room, facing the rear, led onto a magnificent garden behind the house: obviously this was the monastery garden, or what remained of it. I understood from previous correspondence with the owner that the area is frequently plunged into sudden mists, but the day of our arrival was a particularly nice day in early August, and the sun was warm as late as seven o'clock at night. "Mrs. Holzer and yourself are in the Bambrugh

Room," the manager said, with a significant raising of the eyebrows, when I came downstairs after unpacking. Then, making sure that no one was listening to our conversation, he added, "This is the room in which most of the activities are reputed to have taken place, you know." I nodded. I had specifically asked to be put up in the "haunted room."

Our arrival had gone unannounced, by my request; however, I offered to give a press interview *after* we had done our work. While my wife and Trixie rested after the journey from the airport, I took a walk around the premises. The peaceful atmosphere of the place was incredible. It almost belied the rumors of a haunting. A little later we had dinner in the candlelit bar downstairs. My psychic tour had meanwhile arrived and been placed in various rooms of the inn, and they were eager to participate in what for them was a unique and exciting adventure: to witness an actual seance or make contact with an authentic ghost!

It was already dark when we repaired to the room in which we were to sleep that night. Things were a bit on the tight side, with fourteen people trying to squeeze into a double bedroom. But we managed to find everyone a spot, and then Trixie took to a chair in one corner, closed her eyes and leaned back, waiting for the spirits to manifest.

Immediately Trixie looked up at me with a significant nod. "There was a murder in this room, you know," as if it were the most natural thing to expect from a room that was to serve as our sleeping quarters for the night.

"Anything else?" I said, preparing myself for the worst.

"I saw three monks come along, and the odd

thing is one dropped his girdle—you know, the cord. It is all very odd."

I agreed that it was, but before I could ask her anything further, she pointed at the bed we were sitting on. "I see a woman lying on this bed, and she is dead. She has been murdered. This happened centuries ago. Now I see a little child running into the room, also wearing a dress of centuries ago. There is an unusual coffin leaving this room. I hear chanting. The coffin is black and shaped like a boat. I have the feeling this happened between the eleventh and thirteenth centuries. Also, I have a feeling of sword play and of a stone, a very special stone standing up somewhere outside."

At this point Trixie called for us to join hands to give her more power for what was to come.

Immediately her face became agitated, as if she were listening to something, something coming to her from far away. "I can hear somebody calling, 'Jesus, Jesus have mercy, Jesus have mercy,' and I see a monk wearing a dark habit, while the others are wearing a grayish white. But this man has on a dark robe which is extraordinary. He is a monk, yet he is really Satanic. I think his name is Peter. I don't know whether he committed this murder or got caught up in it. He has a hawklike face, and there is a very beautiful woman who was tied to this monk. I hear her crying, 'Help me, help me, help me!' "

"How can we help her?" I asked.

"Get on your knees and pray," Trixie replied. "She wants absolution."

"What has she done?"

"*Credo, credo*—what does it mean?"

Trixie seemed puzzled, then she handed me a key. "Go to my room and you'll find a crucifix there.

Bring it to me." I asked one of the tour members to get the crucifix from the room down the hall.

"This very beautiful girl died in childbirth, but it was not her husband's child," Trixie explained. "And now she wants absolution for what she has done. I hear 'Ave Maria.' She was buried stealthily outside this area, but she comes back here to visit this guilty love. Her progression is retarded because of her inability to clear her conscience, and yet one part of her wants to cling to the scene here. Wait a minute, I get 'Lord' something. Also, I wonder who was imprisoned for a time, because I see a jailer and rusty keys. It is all very much like looking at a movie screen—I'm getting bits and pieces of a picture. There is a great sense of remorse; this woman was married, yet she had this love for a monk. The child is lying on a bier. It is all tinged with murder. It seems she killed the child. Now I'm getting something about Spain and the Inquisition, but I don't understand why."

"Tell her she must divulge her name, so that she may be completely cleared," I suggested.

Trixie strained visibly to read the woman's name. "I get the initial F," she finally said.

"Can you get something about the period when this happened?"

"She said twelve hundred and sixty. She's beautiful; her hair is chestnut colored."

"What happened to the monk?"

"He was banished and died in misery, and she says, 'My fault, my fault!' "

I instructed Trixie to relieve the unhappy one of her guilt. Trixie took up the crucifix and intoned in a trembling voice, "You are forgiven and helped in Christ, the Savior!" I asked what was the name of the unlucky monk so that we could pray for him too. "F. F. F." Trixie replied. "He was a monsignor."

At this point, trance set in and Trixie turned more and more into the unhappy woman ghost. "I thought it would be some reparation for the misery I caused if I came back here. I am trying to impress my survival by coming from time to time. I do not see him now. Oh, we are separated from each other. I kneel in the church."

Trixie "returned," and the entity again spoke to her, with the medium relaying her messages to me. "When she was young, this house belonged to the earl." I offered to have some prayers said on her behalf in the church, but in whose name should they be said?

"Just pray for me. I shall know much happiness and I shall be free."

"Then go in peace with our blessings," I replied, and I could see that the entity was fast slipping away. Trixie came out of her psychic state now, visibly tired. While she was recuperating, I asked the others whether they had felt anything peculiar during the seance. One lady spoke up and said that there was a sort of electric feeling in the room; another admitted to having a strong feeling that she received the impression of a monk who wasn't a real monk at all. Trixie said, "Now I understand about the three monks and one of them putting down his cord. He was being defrocked!"

Mr. Hewitt, one of the managers, had been present throughout the seance, watching with quiet interest. I asked him for verification of the material that had come through Trixie. "It all makes sense," he said, "but the peculiar thing is that the times are all mixed up—everything is correct, but there are two different layers of time involved."

The part of the building where the seance had taken place was the only part of the abbey remaining from the very early period, the Abbey of the White Monks—the white monks seen clairvoyantly by Trixie at the beginning of our session. Mr. Hewitt could not enlighten us concerning the defrocked monk, and when I mentioned it, Trixie filled me in on some of the details of her vision. "It was a terrible thing to see this monk. There he stood in his dark robe, then the cord dropped off and his habit came off, and then I saw him naked being flayed and flayed —it was a terrible thing."

According to the manager, several of the villagers have seen the apparition of a woman in the churchyard and also in the church next door to the hotel. People sleeping in the room we were in had at various times complained of a "presence," but nobody had actually seen her. "She was absolutely beautiful with her rust-colored hair," Trixie said. "I could just see her vaguely, but she had on a light dress, very low, nothing on her head, and her hair was loose." The manager turned to me and asked whether he might bring in a picture of the lady whom they suspected of being the ghost. When Trixie looked at it, she said firmly, "This is the girl I saw." The picture was a portrait of Dorothy Forster—Trixie had named the woman F.—and it was this Dorothy Forster who had played an important role in the history of Blanchland. In 1715, Dorothy's brother Thomas was a general in the Jacobite army, although he was not really qualified for the post. He was captured and imprisoned at Newgate Prison. Three days before his trial for high treason, his sister Dorothy managed to enter the prison, disguised as a servant, get her brother out, and help him escape to France, where he eventually died. Also of interest is the reference to the initials F. F. F. by Trixie. In 1701 a certain John Fenwick killed Ferdinando Forster in a duel at Newcastle. As a result of this, the estate fell into debt and was later sold to Lord Crewe, the Bishop of Durham. He in turn married Dorothy Forster's aunt, also named Dorothy. "There still seems to be some confusion as to which of the two Dorothys haunts the village and the hotel," says S. P. B. Mais in a pamphlet entitled "The Lord Crewe Arms, Blanchland." "She is to be seen walking along the Hexham Road and opens and shuts doors in the haunted wing of the hotel. A portrait of the niece hangs in the sitting room which is named after her, and a portrait of the aunt hangs in the dining room alongside that of her husband, the Bishop of Durham."

I realized by now that Trixie had tuned in on two separate time layers: the grim twelfth and thirteenth centuries, together with the story of a monk who had done wrong and had been punished for it. This particular haunting or impression came as a surprise to the manager, because it had not been reported before. On the other hand, the ghostly presence of Dorothy Forster was generally known around the area. The question was, which Dorothy was the ghost? During the state bordering on trance, Trixie spoke of the house owned by the earl. This was in reply to the question of whose house it was when Dorothy was young. So the ghost could only be the niece, the second Dorothy, because Lord Crewe, the Bishop of Durham, had married her aunt, also named Dorothy. The younger Dorothy would have grown up in her aunt's house. But why was Dorothy Forster, the younger, seeking forgiveness of her sins? Here the mystery remains. On the one hand, Trixie identified the ghost from the portrait shown her by Mr. Hewitt; on the other hand, Dorothy Forster definitely had nothing to do with any monks, since in the eighteenth century there weren't any monks around Blanchland.

The following morning we left for Newcastle and a television interview. A reporter from one of the local papers, *The Northern Echo,* headlined the August 9, 1969, issue with "HAUNTED, YES—BUT WHOSE GHOST IS IT?"

Two psychic sisters from Dallas, Ceil Whitley and Jean Loupot, who had been on the haunted tour with us, decided to jot down their impressions in the haunted room immediately afterwards.

"Both of us feel that Trixie was mistaken in at least one of her impressions. Trixie felt the young woman was inconsolable because she had killed her newborn child, but both of us had the definite impression that she said, 'did away with,' meaning, not killed. We thought it was spirited away by the monks who delivered it. We are so sure of this impression that we do want to go back to Blanchland and see if we can pick up anything further."

Years later, the two ladies got in touch with me again. "When we were at Blanchland, Jean 'saw' a woman standing beside a wall at an open gateway. She was quite plump, approximately forty to forty-five years old, and dressed in a black, stiff, full-skirted, long-sleeved dress, nipped in at the waist. There was a laced scarf over her head, crossed in front and back over her shoulders. She stood with her arms crossed in front of her, and her face had a look of sad resignation, as though she were remembering some long-past sadness. We thought it was the girl we 'picked up' last summer, only she was showing us herself in middle age, though still suffering the loss of her child."

The Real Camelot

WAS THERE a Camelot?

Did King Arthur preside in its splendid halls over the Round Table and its famous knights amid medieval splash and chivalry?

Musical comedy writers Lerner and Loewe thought so when they created the Broadway musical *Camelot.* Basically, this version presents Arthur as the champion of justice in a world of corruption and violence. He and his chosen knights of the round table challenge the sinister element around them—and usually win. The religious elements are subdued, and Arthur emerges as a good man eventually hurt by his closest friend, when Lancelot runs off with Queen Guinevere. This treachery makes Arthur's world collapse. The major point made here is that breach of faith can only lead to disaster.

I have been fascinated by the King Arthur tradition for many years, wondering if there ever was a Camelot—if, indeed, there ever was a *real* King Arthur. Historians have had a go at all this material over the years, of course, and the last word isn't in yet, for the digs are still fresh and new evidence does turn up in forgotten or lost manuscripts. Also, reinterpretations of obscure passages shed new light on ancient mysteries.

Now, I stood in the inner portions of the ruined abbey of Glastonbury in the west of England. Near me was a bronze tablet neatly stuck into the wet soil. "King Arthur's tomb," it read, and a little farther on I found Queen Guinevere's tomb. I had not come to search for these tombs, however, but to see for myself the remnants of this "holiest spot in all Britain," which had been discovered through a combination of archaeological prowess and psychic gifts. A professional archaeologist named Bligh Bond had discovered that he was also psychic. Far from being incredulous, he did not reject this gift, but put it to a prolonged and severe test. As a result of this test, he received alleged communications from a monk who claimed to have lived at Glastonbury in the early Middle Ages. These communications came to Bond through automatic writing, his hands being guided by the unseen person of the monk. This, of course, sounds fantastic, and Bond was attacked for his lapse into what his fellow professionals thought was pure fantasy.

The location of Glastonbury Abbey was unknown then, yet Bond's communicator claimed that it was there, beneath the grassy knoll near the present town of Glastonbury. He even supplied Bond with exact details of its walls, layout, and walks. Eventually, Bond managed to have excavations started, and the abbey emerged from its grave very much as predicted by the ghostly monk.

As I said, though, I had not come to study King

Arthur's grave, but to look at Glastonbury Abbey. Yet the trail seemed to lead to Camelot just the same. Glastonbury is 12½ miles due northwest of the area I later learned was the site of Camelot. Originally a Celtic (or British) settlement, it is the Avalon of the Arthurian legends.

My interest in the subject of King Arthur and Camelot was temporarily put aside when more urgent projects took up my time, but I was suddenly brought back to it in 1967 when I was contacted by a man named Paul Johnstone, who had read one of my previous books.

Johnstone is a scholar who specializes in historical research and is also a free-lance writer. His articles on British history have appeared in *Antiquity* and *Notes and Queries,* his fiction in *Blue Book* and other magazines. His writing leans toward medieval historical subjects, and after twenty-five years of research, in 1963 he completed a book called *The Real King Arthur.* That year his mother passed on, and he felt that her spirit might want to communicate with him. Although Paul Johnstone is a rationally inclined individual, he had never discounted the possibility of such communications, particularly in view of the fact that as a youngster he had some ESP experiences. By means of a "fortune-telling board" he had purchased for his own amusement, he was able to come into communication with his late mother, and although at first he asked her only the most obvious questions, she eventually made it known to him that Artorius wanted to talk to him.

Now, the legendary King Arthur and his Camelot were merely fictional re-creations of old ballads, mainly French, which Sir Thomas Malory condensed into *La Morte d'Artur* in the fifteenth century. These ballads, however, in turn were only re-creations of older Welsh tales that, while not accurate, were nevertheless closer to the truth. According to Godfrey Turton in *The Emperor Arthur,* the medieval trappings "are completely inappropriate to the historical Arthur, who lived nearly a thousand years before Malory was born."

The only contemporary source extant from the late fifth century when Arthur lived is a book called *De Excidio Britanniae,* written by Gildas, a monk who later became an abbot. Arthur himself is not mentioned in this work, but according to *The Life of Gildas,* Gildas and Arthur had been enemies since Arthur had put the monk's brother to death for piracy.

In the ninth century a man named Nenius described Arthur's reign and victories in great detail. This Arthur was a late-Roman chieftain, a provincial commander whose military leadership and good judgment led him to be chosen to succeed the British chief Ambrosius as head and defender of post-Roman Britain. At this period in history, the Saxons had not completely taken over Britain and the Western part in particular was still free of their savage rule. Although the Romans no longer occupied Britain, centuries of occupation had left their mark, and Artorius was as much a Roman general as any of his Italian colleagues.

Because of Johnstone's twenty-five years devoted to research into King Arthur's life and times, he had evidently attracted the attention of the King's spirit, who now wished to reward him by conversing with him directly and setting the record straight wherever he, Johnstone, might have erred in his research. According to Johnstone's mother, Arthur had for years tried to tell Johnstone his side of the story directly, though Johnstone had not been aware of it. But now, with her arrival on the Other Side, a missing link had been supplied between Arthur and Johnstone, and they could establish direct communication.

I have examined the transcripts of these conversations, and since Johnstone himself is writing a book about his experiences with communicators like Arthur and others, it will suffice to say that they are amazing and detailed. The question of course immediately presents itself: Is this really King Arthur of the Britons speaking, or is it a figment of Johnstone's imagination, caused by his preoccupation with the subject and fed by the accumulated knowledge in his conscious and unconscious minds? That this also occurred to Johnstone is clear and he started the talks by asking the alleged Artorius a number of questions that had not been satisfactorily answered before, such as exact sites of battles and places mentioned in the records but not yet discovered. The answers came via the board in a mixture of Welsh, Latin, and modern English. Many of the names given were unknown to Johnstone, but he looked them up and found that they fit.

Paul Johnstone questioned the communicator calling himself Artorius extensively about the main events of his life, and thus was able to adjust or confirm some of his own earlier ideas about the period—ideas obtained purely archaeologically and through research, not psychically. Thus we have a date for Arthur's birth, A.D. 459, and another for the battle at Badon Hill, 503, where Arthur decisively defeated a coalition of Saxons and their allies, and established his kingdom firmly for twenty peaceful years.

To me it did not even matter whether Arthur spoke through Johnstone or whether Johnstone, the psychic, obtained factual information not previously known or confirmed. The knowledge was gained, one way or the other, through paranormal means. When I brought up this delicate point, Johnstone referred to a number of instances where his own knowledge and opinion had been totally different from what he received psychically from Arthur. For example, when he asked what Castle Guinnion was, he was told it was a refuge of the Picts. His own views had been that it was a British stronghold, assailed by the Picts.

All this correspondence came to a sudden climax when Johnstone informed me that new digs were going on at what might or might not be the true site of Camelot.

Now the question as to where Arthur's famed stronghold was situated—if there was indeed a Camelot—has occupied researchers for centuries. The Tourist Board insists it is Tintagel Castle in Cornwall. Arthur spent his boyhood there, according to Mr. Johnstone, and there was a monastery on the spot, but the castle itself is many centuries later than Arthur. Cadbury Hill, west of Ilchester, was a more logical choice for the honor. This hill fort in Somerset overlooks the plains all the way to Glastonbury, which one can clearly see from its ramparts. Johnstone suggested it as the site of the true Camelot when he wrote his book in 1963. His opinion was based on archaeological evidence, but the "establishment" of professionals rejected this possibility *then.* The Cadbury Hill ruins were considered pre-Roman, and any connection with Arthur's fifth-century Britain denied. It was the opinion of Leslie Alcock of the University of Wales, one of the men digging at

Cadbury, that in Arthur's time warfare did not use fortified positions of this size. But after digging at the site in the summer of 1966, he expressed a different view in the March 1967 issue of *Antiquity*: Cadbury was a vital strongpoint in Arthur's time.

What Johnstone suggested to me was simply this: Why not take a good medium to Cadbury and see what she can get? Let us find out, he asked, if Cadbury Hill is Camelot. He himself would not come along with us, so that no one might accuse my medium of being influenced by knowledge in his mind or subconscious. But he was willing to give me exact instructions on how to get to the site, and to a few other sites also connected with the Arthur-Camelot lore, and afterward help me evaluate the material I might obtain on the spot.

I enthusiastically agreed to this, and made arrangements to visit Britain with Sybil Leek serving as my psychic bloodhound.

Our plans would be made in such a manner that Sybil could not guess our purpose or where we were headed, and I would take great pains in avoiding all sensory clues that might give away our destination. Thus I made my arrangements with the driver whenever Sybil was not within sight, and confined our conversations to such innocent topics as the weather, always a good one in uncertain Britain.

Paul Johnstone had given me two sites to explore: Cadbury Hill, allegedly the true Camelot, and a point in Hampshire where he thought England was founded. If his calculations were correct, then the latter place would be the actual site of Cardic's barrow, or grave, a spot where the first king of Wessex, precursor of modern England, was buried.

"It's at Hurstbourne Priors in Hampshire," he

wrote, "halfway between Winchester and Salisbury, but closer to Andover. But there is a drawback to this one. Nobody seems to know the exact site."

Since Cardic was one of the local rulers Arthur fought at Badon Hill, I felt we should include the visit, especially as it was not out of our way to Camelot.

Johnstone was able, however, to give me one more clue, this one not archaeological, but psychic:

In 1950 he had had a strange dream about Cardic's grave. He saw that a nineteenth-century church had been erected over the site, on the hill where the barrow was. Cardic's grave, called Ceardicesbeorg in the original tongue, had escaped even so renowned an archaeologist as Professor O. G. S. Crawford, the founder of *Antiquity,* and a man whose home territory this was, as he lived in nearby Southampton.

Thus armed with a meager clue and the story of a strange dream, we set out from London on September 22, 1967. Sybil Leek was to meet us at the Andover railroad station.

I had with me an ordnance map of the area so that even the smallest piece of territory could be quickly explored. Our driver had long realized we were no ordinary tourists (by "we" I mean Catherine and myself, and now, Mrs. Leek).

We left Andover and drove three miles northeast to the little village of Hurstbourne Priors. In fact, we drove right through it, several times, actually, before we realized that we were going too fast. As we turned the car around once more, I spotted a narrow country lane, covered by the shadows of huge old trees, opening to our left. And at the bottom of the lane, a church—our church. We had found it, exactly as Paul Johnstone had dreamed it in 1950!

Johnstone had never visited Europe, nor did he have access to the fact that an early nineteenth-century-type church would stand there at the end of this country lane. But there it was, and we piled out.

Built in the traditional Church of England neo-Gothic style, this church had earlier beginnings, but its essence was indeed early nineteenth century. It stood in the middle of a romantic churchyard filled with ancient gravestones, some still upright, but the majority leaning in various directions due to age. Farther back were a number of huge trees. Suddenly the busy country road we had just left did not intrude any longer, and we were caught up in a time warp where everything was just as it must have always been. It was close to noon now, and not a living soul around.

We entered the little church and found it the very model of a country chapel.

The driver stayed outside near the car while we started to walk around the soft green grounds.

"The church is not important here," Sybil said right away, "it's the ground that is."

We stood near the biggest of the trees now.

"We should be on a hill," she said, "a small hill, a rise in the ground that has been utilized for a practical purpose."

I became interested and moved in closer. The funerary bowers of old were just that.

"There is some connection with a disease . . . people congregating here because of a disease. . . . I expected to find the hill here."

Considering the changes possible in the course of fifteen centuries, I was not at all surprised that the hill no longer existed, or at least that it was no longer prominent, for there was a rise in back of the cemetery.

"Why is this hill important?" I asked.

"A long time ago . . . comes in in flickering movements, but I can see the hill distinctly. There is a male dominance here. This is not a local thing. I can't quite see his legs. He dominates, though there are other people. He has a tall rod, which he is holding. There is a bird on the rod. It's not a flag, but it's like a flag. The hill is important to him . . . J . . . initial J. This is in connection with the flag thing. I can see his face and his head."

"Is there anything on his head?"

"Yes, there is, a headgear—it is related to the thing he is holding. I can't see it very clearly. The bird is also on his headgear, swept up from it. An outdoor man of great strength. *He is a soldier.* A very long time ago."

"What period are we in with him, would you say?" I asked softly. Nothing in the appearance of the place related to a soldier. Sybil was of course getting the right "vibrations," and I was fascinated by it.

"So far back I can't be sure."

"Is he an important man?"

"Yes. I'm looking at letters. C-Caius . . . C-a-i-s . . . Caius. He is very important. The hill is connected with him, yet he is foreign. But he needs the hill. He faces west. West is the road he has to go . . . from east to west is the journey. . . ."

"What has he done?"

"The thing in his hand is related to his position. Coins . . . trading . . . a lot of people in one spot but he dominates. . . ."

Sybil felt at this point that we should move back

farther for better "reception" of the faint waves from the past. She pointed to the two oldest trees at the extreme end of the churchyard and remarked that the strongest impression would be there.

"Kill . . . someone was killed between those two trees," she now asserted, "he was chased, there is an old road beneath this cemetery. He had to go this way, make the way as he went. Not just walk over. Almost on this spot, I have the feeling of someone meeting sudden death. Violent death. And yet it was not war. More like an attack, an ambush. There is a big connection with the west. That's what he wants to do, go west. This man was very dominant."

We were now in the corner of the old cemetery. The silence was unbroken by anything except an occasional jet plane soaring overhead. There is an airbase situated not far away.

"There ought to be a clearing where you look out to a hill," Sybil insisted. "This man was here before those trees. The trees are at least a thousand years old."

I did some fast arithmetic. That would get us back to about the ninth century. It was before then, Sybil asserted.

With that, she turned around and slowly walked back to the car. We had lots more mileage to cover today, so I thought it best not to extend our visit here, especially as we had found interesting material already.

When I saw Paul Johnstone in St. Louis in February of the following year, I played the tape of our investigation for him. He listened with his eyes half closed, then nodded. "You've found it, all right. Just as I saw it in my dream."

"What exactly did you dream?"

"I was there . . . I was looking at the hill . . . there was a church on the hill, not a particularly ancient church, and there was a bronze memorial of a British soldier in it . . . then I was looking at a book, a book that does not exist, but it was telling of Cardic of Wessex, and that he was buried on this hill where stood this nineteenth-century church. The church had obliterated the traces of his grave, that is why it had not been found. I simply wrote this dream down, but never did anything about it until you came along."

The reference to Cardic's grave goes back to the tenth century, Johnstone pointed out. I questioned him about the name CAIUS which Sybil tried to spell for us.

"In his own time, Cardic would have spelled his name C-a-r-a-t-i-c-u-s. . . . Mrs. Leek got the principal letters of the name, all right. The long rod with the bird on it is also very interesting. For in the Sutton Hoo find of ancient British relics there was a long bronze spear with a stag atop it. This was a standard, and Cardic might well have had one with a bird on it. This founder of Wessex undoubtedly was a "dominant personality," as Sybil put it—and again some interesting things fall into place. Cardic's father was a Jut, as were most of his people—remember the letter, J, that Sybil used to describe him and his kind?"

Johnstone then went on to explain the role Cardic played in history. I had not wanted to have this knowledge before, so that Sybil could not get it from my mind or unconscious.

Both Cardic and Artorius served as officers of British King Ambrose, and when Ambrose died in A.D. 485 Cardic went over to the Saxon enemy. In 495 he invaded Hampshire with his Jutes, and ruled the country as a local chieftain. In 503, when Arthur fought the Battle of Badon Hill against the Saxons and their allies, Cardic's people were among those allies. According to Johnstone, he arrived a little late and made his escape, living on to 516, at which time he might have been ambushed at the barrow site and buried there with the honors due him. This site was very close to his western frontier, and the ambushers would have been Britons from Ambrose's old kingdom, based at Salisbury, rather than men from the distant Camelot. Johnstone does not think Arthur could have ordered Cardic murdered: They had been friends for years, and though their kingdoms were close to one another, there was no war between them between 503 and 516, a pretty long time of peace in those days. Arthur could have crushed Cardic's kingdom, which was based at what is now Winchester, yet he chose for some reason not to do so. But Ambrose's heirs might not have felt as charitable about their neighbor, and it is there that we must look for the killers of Cardic.

Johnstone also suggested that the long rod with the eagle on top and the helmet might very well have been Roman, inasmuch as Roman culture was still very dominant in the area and Cardic certainly trained as an officer in that tradition.

The name Cardic itself is Welsh, and Johnstone suggested that Cardic's father, Elesa, was of Anglo-Jute origin, his mother Welsh, and he himself a native of Britain, perhaps the reason for his divided loyalties in those turbulent times.

I questioned my expert concerning the remark, made by Mrs. Leek, that the man wanted to go west and had come from the east.

"As a Saxon commander, he naturally came from the east and wanted to extend his power westward, but he was fought to a standstill," Johnstone replied.

It seemed fitting to me to visit the last resting place of the man who had been Arthur's counter-player, and yet a friend once too, before proceeding to Arthur's lair, Camelot, some two hours' driving time farther to the southwest.

Finding Cadbury Hill proved no easier than discovering Cardic's bower. We passed through South Cadbury twice, and no one knew where the excavations were to be found. Evidently the fame of Cadbury Hill did not extend beyond its immediate vicinity. It was already the latter part of the afternoon when we finally came upon the steep, imposing hill that once held a succession of fortified encampments from the dawn of history onward—including, perhaps, the fabled Camelot?

A twisting road led up the hill, and we decided it best to leave the car behind. After crossing a wooded section and passing what appeared to be remnants of old stone fortifications, we finally arrived on the plateau. The sight that greeted our eyes was indeed spectacular. Windswept and chilly, a slanting plateau presented itself to our eyes: earth ramparts surrounding it on all four sides, with the remnants of stone walls here and there still in evidence. The center of the area was somewhat higher than the rest, and it was there that a team of volunteer archaeologists had been digging. The sole evidence of their efforts was a criss-cross network of shallow trenches and some interesting artifacts stored in a local museum, most of it of Roman or pre-Roman origin, however, which had led to the assumption that this was nothing more than a native Celtic fortress the Romans had taken over. Was this the great palace of Camelot with its splendid halls and the famed Round Table?

At the moment, a herd of cows was grazing on the land and we were the only bipeds around. The cows found us most fascinating and started to come close to look us over. Until we were sure that they were cows and that there were no bulls among them, this was somewhat of a nerve-wracking game. Then, too, my tape recording of what Sybil had to say was frequently interrupted by the ominous and obvious sounds of cow droppings, some of which came awfully close for comfort. But the brave explorer that I am stood me in good stead: I survived the ordeal with at least as much courage as did Arthur's knights of old survive the ordeal of combat. There we were, Catherine in a wine red pants suit, the driver somewhere by himself looking down into the village, and Sybil and I trying to tune in the past.

If this was indeed the true Camelot, I felt that Mrs. Leek should pick up something relating to it. She had no conscious notion as to where we were or why I had caused her to walk up a steep hill in the late afternoon, a hill evidently given over to cows. But she saw the trenches and diggings and may have assumed we were looking at some ancient Roman site. Beyond that I honestly don't think she knew or cared why we were here: She has always trusted me and assumed that there is a jolly good reason.

After walking around for a few moments, I cornered her near the diggings and began my questioning.

"What do you think this place is?" I began.

"I think it's a sanctuary," came the odd reply, "a retreat. A spiritual retreat."

"Can you visualize what stood here?"

"As I was coming up the hill I had the feeling of a monastery, but I am not thinking in terms of pure religion—more like a place where people come to contemplate, a spiritual feeling. I see more the end of the period than the buildings."

"How did it end?"

"The breaking up of a clan . . . a number of people, not in a family, but tied by friendship. . . ."

"How far back?"

"I'll try to get some letters. . . ." She closed her eyes and swayed a little in the strong wind, while I waited. "G-w-a-i-n-e-l-o-d. . . ."

My God, I thought, is she trying to say "Camelot"?

"A meeting place," Sybil continued, gradually falling more and more into trance, "not a war place, a good place, friendship . . . this place has had for many years a religious association. A very special one."

"Is there some leader?" I asked.

"Abbot *Erlaile* . . . not of necessity in the same period."

"When were these people here?"

"A long, long time ago. Not much power behind it, very diffuse. I can only catch it from time to time. There are many Gwaine letters, a lot of those."

"You mean people whose names sound like that or start with Gwaine?"

"Yes."

"Are they male?"

"Not all male. But the friendship is male. Coming up from the sea. This was their sanctuary."

"Who were these men?"

"Gwaine is one."

"Who ruled over them?"

"It's a very mixed thing . . . not easy to catch . . . *thirteen people* . . . tied together by friendship. . . ."

"Do they have any name as a group?"

"Templars."

Later, when I examined the evidence, it became clear to me that Sybil was getting more than one layer of history when she made contact with the imprint left upon these storied rocks.

Paul Johnstone, my Arthurian expert friend, assured me later that Camelot was derived from the Welsh *Camallt,* meaning crooked slope, which is a pretty good description of the place at that.

In his psychic contact with the historical Arthur, Johnstone, using his dowsing board, established the name as *Cambalta,* which is pretty close to the modern Welsh form. But on an earlier occasion, again using the board, Johnstone questioned his communicator (as he describes it in an article, "News from Camelot," in *Search* magazine, March 1968) about the ancient name of the hill at South Cadbury. This time the answer differs.

"Dinas Catui," Johnstone quotes his informant, and explains that it means Fort of Cado. But he also gives an alternate name: Cantimailoc. Thus, even the "horse's mouth" wasn't always sure what the name was, it would seem. Unless, of course, there was more than one name. This is precisely what I think. As its owner changed, so the name might have changed: When Cado was king, perhaps it was Dinas Catui, which would be the post-Latin form, or Cantimailoc, the local Welsh form. Then when Arthur succeeded his erstwhile colleague, the name might have left out the reference to King Cado and become Cambalta, referring to the geographical peculiarity of the place, rather than incorporating Arthur's name, a modesty quite consistent with the character of the historical Artorius. But when Gwaine became prominent in the area, he might not have held such modest views as Arthur, and thus the fortified hill might have become known as Gwaine's slope or Gwainelot.

Mrs. Leek, getting her impressions at the same time and with varying degrees of intensity, could not possibly distinquish between the various layers that cling to the place. Certainly, from what I heard, there were at least two sixth-century layers, that of Artorius himself and that of Gwaine, and a third layer not directly connected either in time or relationship with the two earlier ones, but somehow also concerned with the over-all aspects of the site. This strange discrepancy would require some sorting out, I thought immediately, but surely there must be a connection. I knew enough of Mrs. Leek's work to take nothing lightly or dismiss any bit of information obtained through her as unimportant.

After our return, I went over the tapes very carefully to try to make sense out of what had come through. To begin with, the sanctuary and Abbot Erlaile and the Templars would certainly have to be much later than the thirteen men tied together in friendship, and the man she called Gwaine, and yet there might have been a strong link.

Gwainelod—was that a contemporary name for Camelot? Gwaine himself was the son of a northern chieftain whom Arthur had taken under his wing. Sometimes styled Gawain, this historical knight with the Welsh name actually lived in the early sixth century, and shows up also as a fictional hero in the medieval Arthur legend, where he is called Sir Gawain. The many people with names beginning with Gwaine to which the medium referred might very well have included Queen Gwainewere, better known as Guenevere, Arthur's first wife. According to Johnstone, the one who did most of the things the medieval Guenevere was supposed to have done was not this queen, who died after a short time, but her successor, Arthur's second queen named Creirwy.

Now the Knights Templars belong to a much later period, that of the Crusades. Strangely, the legend of the Holy Grail is set during that latter time, incorporating much of the Arthurian traditions. Was there a connection somewhere between a post-Roman local ruler and a Christian mystical upholder of the faith? Was Camelot reoccupied long after its fall and destruction by Arthur's nephew Mordred, in the Saxon period by a group of monks who established a sanctuary there, linking the Arthurian traditions with their early medieval Christianity? In other words, did a group of monks during the early Crusades occupy the hill at Cadbury, and found upon the ruins of Arthur's sanctuary and palace a new sanctuary dedicated to the revived belief in the Holy Grail of nearby Glastonbury?

All these thoughts came to me much later, when I sifted the material back in New York.

At the moment we were standing atop Cadbury Hill, and the air was getting chilly as the sun started to disappear behind the horizon.

"There was some link with the sea, but they were finished, they had to move . . . very suddenly . . . came here for sanctuary and tried to build up . . . the same meeting place . . . feeling. . . ."

"What was the place called then?" I asked with bated breath. "B-r-y-n-w- T-o-r," Sybil answered.

"Brynw Tor?" I repeated. Nearby Glastonbury

Tor came to mind. A tor is a high, craggy hill that in England usually has a temple on it.

"What was here actually?" I pointed to the ground.

"The home of. . . . I see a face lying down . . . with gray things hanging . . . *chains.* It's a good man, in chains. Loss of freedom must cause suffering . . . tied here."

Later I wondered who the prisoner she felt might have been. I found that Arthur himself was thrown into prison by one of the sons of King Ambrose, after the king had died. Arthur had become embroiled in the quarrel among Ambrose's sons and successors. Eventually Arthur was freed by his men. Could Sybil be picking up this mental image of that event in the far past?

Again I asked, who was the leader here, and Sybil replied, she did not know. When I saw Paul Johnstone in St. Louis many months later, he informed me that he had had contact with Arthur, through his psychic board. Arthur had informed him that he had not been present when I came to look for Camelot, even though I had come to the right place.

"Do you sense any leader at all?" I insisted, and looked at Sybil.

"Two leaders. Two men."

This, I discovered later, was also interesting. Arthur ruled jointly with King Cado at Camelot when Arthur first came there. Later, Arthur became sole ruler. Cado is remembered today in the place name for Cadbury, site of Camelot.

"What does the place look like?" I continued my questioning.

"There is a circle . . . the circle is important

. . . building, too, but there must be a circle . . . the knights . . . brave men . . . Welsh names . . . *Monserrey.* . . ."

I was overcome with the importance of what we were doing and spoke in a subdued voice, even though I could have shouted and nobody but the cows would have heard me.

"Are we here . . ." I asked, "Is *this* Monserrey?"

"The place is here, but the cavity is not here."

"Where is the cavity?"

"West . . . toward the sun. . . ."

"What is in the cavity?"

"The chains."

"What is kept here?"

"No one must know. Not ready. Not ready for knowledge."

"Before the circle. . . ."

"Who is at the head of the circle?"

"He's dead. You should not look yet."

"What is the secret kept here?"

"I will not say the name."

The conversation was getting more and more into the realms of mysticism, I felt. What Sybil had brought through made sense although I would not be able to sort it out until afterward, on my return to New York. The circle could refer to the Round Table, the knights with Welsh names were certainly Arthur's men, but Monserrey (or Montserrat) belonged to the legend of the Holy Grail. Again, Sybil was fusing into one story two periods separated by many centuries.

The cavity containing the chains also interested me. Was she referring to a relic kept, perhaps, at Glastonbury? Was there something besides the cup and the sprig Joseph of Arimathaea had brought with him from Palestine? Were these chains of later origin? I was hardly going to get any objective proof for these statements, and yet the picture, although confused, was intriguing, especially so as Sybil had no way of connecting the windswept hill we were standing on with either King Arthur or the Holy Grail!

"Who is the communicator?" I demanded. I had the feeling it was not Artorius, and it wasn't Sybil any longer, and my curiosity was aroused: Who was it?

"Don't say communicator . . . communicant!"

"Very well, what is the communicant's name, then?"

"The King."

I was surprised, taken aback.

"I have to have proof."

"The name is not ready. . . . It is wrong to discover more than you can hope to learn. . . . I want to protect the secret with magic."

"What is your name?"

"*She* knows me. . . ." he said, referring to the medium, and all at once I, too, knew who my informant was, incredible though it seemed at that instant!

"I know you, too," I heard myself say, "and I'm a friend, you need not fear me."

"I'm a bird," the voice coming from Sybil's entranced lips said, a little mockingly.

Merlin! Of course . . . Merlin means "small hawk." How apt the name fit the wise counselor of Arthur.

Was there a Merlin?

Not one, but two, Paul Johnstone assured me, and one of them did serve as an adviser to Artorius. Whether or not he was also a magician is a moot question. But a historical figure Merlin (or Medwin) certainly was.

"Link between the sea and here . . . stranger . . . must come. . . . When will that be? When the hawk . . . when birds fly in the sky like me. . . . *Man flies in the sky. . . . The link is a bad one. . . .*"

"And who will the stranger be?" I asked.

"Erfino . . . a bird. . . ."

"Where will he come from?"

"From out of the earth."

"Inside the earth?" I asked incredulously.

"Out of the earth . . . will rise again."

"You speak in riddles."

"I know the answers!"

"Why not give them to me now?"

"You are a man. . . . There have to be *twelve others* . . . the *bird* is the secret. . . ."

I began to understand the implications of this prophecy, and, forgetting for the moment my mission here, said only, "Is there nothing I can do?"

But Merlin was gone.

Sybil was back.

The change in expression and personality was incredible: One moment ago, her face had been the wizened, serene face of a timeless wise man, and now it was Sybil Leek, voluble author and voluntary medium, merely standing on a hill she didn't know, and it was getting dark and chilly.

We quickly descended the steep hill and entered the car, the driver turned on the heat, and off we went, back to London.

But the experience we had just been through was not easily assimilated. If it was indeed Arthur's counselor Merlin, speaking for the King—and how could I disprove it even if I had wanted to?—then Sybil had indeed touched on the right layer in history. The implications of Merlin's prophecy also hit home: Was he speaking of a future war that was yet to come and that would drive the human race underground, to emerge only when it was safe to do so, and build once again the sanctuary?

The idea of a council of twelve is inherent in most secret doctrines, from Rosicrucian to White Brotherhood, and even in the twelve apostles and the esoteric astrologers' twelve planets (of which we know only nine presently) this number is considered important.

The prophecy of birds (airplanes) he calls hawks (warlike) that represent a bad link needs, I think, no explanation, and the subsequent destruction forcing man to live in caves was reminiscent of H. G. Wells' strangely prophetic *The Shape of Things to Come.*

But what was the meaning of the bird named Erfine, or perhaps Irfine, or some such spelling, since I only heard the word and did not see it spelled out?

When I confronted Paul Johnstone in his friend Dr. Saussele's offices in St. Louis in February of 1968, I questioned him about the Camelot material.

"I think Sybil got several periods there," he began. "The Templars were prominent in England in the 1200s, but that is of course seven hundred years after Arthur."

"Did Arthur build a sanctuary on the hilltop?"

"Not to my knowledge. He built a fortress and occupied a dwelling on the hilltop. Some invading Celtic tribes built a hilltop fort there around 200 B.C. Then the Romans came and chased these people away. The hill was semideserted for quite a while. Then Cado re-established himself there. Cado was a kinsman to Arthur, and around A.D. 510, after the victorious Battle of Badon Hill, he invited Arthur to share his kingdom with him, which Arthur did."

"Any other comments?"

"No, except to say that Sybil Leek was getting something *real.*"

Thus the real Camelot can no longer be sought at Tintagel, or in Wales or on the Scottish border: nowhere but atop the breezy hill at Cadbury near Ilchester. There are several other Cadburies in Somerset and Devon, but the one that once belonged to King Arthur lies at a spot marked Cadbury Castle on most maps. You can't miss it if you have an Ordnance map, and even if you don't, have Sybil Leek with you!

But to my mind Sybil had done more than merely establish via psychometry the reality of Camelot and the Arthurian presence at Cadbury. The puzzling dual impression of sixth-century Arthur and a twelfth-century Grail tradition *at this spot* seemed to me to point in a direction no other author has ever traveled: Could it be that the romantic, almost fictional Arthur of the Christian chivalry period was not merely the result of the continuous rewriting and distortion of ancient legends? Was there a kernel of truth in linking Artorius with the story of the Grail?

According to my psychic friend, Sybil Leek, the hallowed ground where Arthur tried to save Britain from the barbarians overrunning it at the time was later turned into another sanctuary by the Knights Templars. We know that the legend of the Grail became known about that period, when the monks of Glastonbury started to spread it.

So much of this part of the world is as yet underground, awaiting the spade of the archaeologist.

Perhaps some day in the not too distant future, additional digging will reveal tangible proof for what is now mainly information and deduction, but certainly not fantasy or make-believe.

The early Christian leadership of Arthur may very well have been the *example* the Templars wished to follow in their endeavor to found a sanctuary of their own in a period no less turbulent than Arthur's. In time, the two struggles might have become intertwined until one could no longer tell them apart. The thirteenth- and fourteenth-century authors merely picked up what they heard and uncritically embroidered it even further.

Unraveling the confused yarn is not an easy task, but through the talents of a psychic like Sybil Leek we could at least assure ourselves of a totally fresh and independent approach. There can be no doubt that Mrs. Leek picked up impressions out of the past at Cadbury, and not thoughts in my mind, for most of the material she obtained was unknown to me at the time of our expedition.

It probably matters little to the producers of the magnificent film that the *real Camelot* looks a lot less glamorous than their version of it; no matter, Arthur would have liked it, I'm almost sure.

Scotland

The Ghosts Around Edinburgh

I WOULD not be so familiar with some of the ghosts in and around Edinburgh were it not for the friendship and enormous help given me by Elizabeth Byrd, the author of *Immortal Queen,* and Alanna Knight, author of *October Witch* and many other books, and her husband, Alistair. These wonderful friends not only helped plan my recent visit to Scotland but spent much time with me as well. There is something very peculiar about the intellectual atmosphere of the Scottish capital: when you walk along the impressive eighteenth- and early nineteenth-century streets, you feel in the heart of things, yet also removed from the turbulence of the world.

I checked in at the George Hotel in the heart of Edinburgh. Shortly after my arrival, Elizabeth paid me a visit with detailed plans for the rest of my stay, pretty much in the manner of one of Napoleon's field marshals when the emperor was about to embark on a campaign. As my first official act on Scottish soil I presented Elizabeth with a large bottle of Scotch, imported from New York. Elizabeth had wanted to take me to one of the famous old hotels where she had had an uncanny experience in the ladies' room. There was some question on how to get me into the ladies' room and what to tell the manager. "Suppose I watched outside and barred any lady from coming in?" Elizabeth suggested. "Five minutes in there should suffice, should you feel any impression." I declined, explaining that I wouldn't mind going to a haunted men's room but then since there wasn't any at that particular hotel, I would pass. But my curiosity had been aroused, so I asked Elizabeth what exactly happened at the ladies' room at the —— Hotel.

"Well," Elizabeth replied in her well-modulated voice, "last year on December 8, which happens to be my birthday, I was in a very happy mood. I was in Edinburgh for business appointments and to celebrate. At noon, I happened to run into a book dealer who invited me for a drink. So we went to the —— Hotel. He ordered the drinks and I went upstairs to primp. The ladies' room is immaculate, new, and neon-lit. Absolutely nothing to frighten anyone, one would think. No one else was in there. I was there for about two minutes when a feeling of absolute terror came over me. Without so much as combing my hair, much less putting on lipstick, I just had to run."

"Did you hear or see anything?"

"No, just this feeling of terror. I went down two flights of stairs and was extremely glad to get that drink from the book dealer, who said, 'You look peculiar.' I kept wondering what had frightened me so. All I knew about the hotel was that it had been built around 1850. When I told a friend, Kenneth Macrae, what had happened to me in the ladies' room, he said, 'I know something about the history of the hotel.' He suggested I also check with *The Scotsman.*"

Elizabeth's greatest terror is fire, so she inquired whether there had been any disastrous fires at the hotel at any time. There had indeed been a fire in May of 1971 in which a woman was killed, and a chef had been found guilty of starting the fire and causing the woman's death. Earlier, in 1967, a fire had broken out in a club nearby and the hotel staff had been evacuated, but the fire had been quickly brought under control. The newspaper librarian regretted that there was no fire of any proportion at the hotel at any time. A little later Elizabeth went to London and while there she received a note from her friend Kenneth Macrae: "Dear Elizabeth, is it possible that your discomfort in the ladies' room was prophetic? A Welsh Rugby supporter was killed in a fire on February 3, 1973, in the hotel."

Miss Byrd thought that was the end of that, but then on April 29, 1973, a really disastrous fire broke out in the hotel, the result of which left two hundred people dead. "It must have been this really big fire I felt, long before it actually happened. I'm glad I wasn't in the hotel at that time."

But Alanna Knight had a different impression of the haunted ladies' room. "Elizabeth insisted on taking me there one day. I must admit I was very skeptical, but as soon as I opened the door I got my unfailing signal—that old, familiar scalp-crawl—and I knew that despite the modern decor, and bright lights, there was something terribly wrong. Luckily we had the place to ourselves for the moment, although I must admit if Elizabeth had not been there, I would have taken to my heels at once!

"I felt immediately that she was mistaken about

thinking it had anything to do with a fire. I got an impression of a woman, thirty-five to forty, sometime about 1910, who had suffered such a tragedy that she took her own life in that room. It was a particularly gruesome end, and the room absorbed it. My impression of her was that she was neat but rather shabbily dressed, a 'superior' servant, perhaps a housekeeper or a teacher or someone of that nature."

Because Elizabeth frequently visits the hotel where all this happened, she has asked I not give the hotel's name. She likes the bar, the dining room, and the lounge—everything, in fact, except the ladies' room. Therefore, when the call comes, there is but one thing for Elizabeth to do—leave.

The telephone rang. It was Ian Groat, who with his friend James Grandison, who would serve as the driver, was to take us to the outskirts of Edinburgh for a look at a haunted country house. During the ride from the center of town up into the hills surrounding it, I had an opportunity to interview Mr. Grandison.

"This happened in 1965, in a modern bungalow built in 1935, on the outskirts of Edinburgh," he began in a soft voice colored by a pleasant Scottish burr. "The place was called Pendleton Gardens, and there had not been anything on the spot before. I lived there for about two years without experiencing anything out of the ordinary, but then strange things started to happen. At first we heard the sound of wood crackling in the fireplace, and when we checked, we found the fire hadn't been lit. Sometimes this noise would also occur in other parts of the place. Then there was the noise of dogs barking inside the house. My wife used to hear it on her own, and I of course discounted the whole thing, saying that there must have been a dog outside. But eventually I began to hear it as well. There were no dogs outside, and I was able to pinpoint the direction whence the bark came. Added to this was the noise of a kettle boiling over on a stove, as if one had to run to the kitchen and turn off the kettle. Whenever we approached the entrance to the kitchen, the noise stopped instantly. While we were still wondering about this, other things began to happen. A door would suddenly slam in our faces, just before we got to it. Or I would go to the bathroom, and the bathroom door would be halfway open, and just as I reached the handle, it would slam violently open, wide open."

"In other words, whoever was causing it was aware of you?"

"Oh, absolutely, yes. Then we started getting knocks on the walls. We tried to communicate by knocking back, and sure enough this thing kept knocking back at us, but we weren't able to establish a code, and apparently this thing didn't have enough energy to carry on indefinitely. We tried to ignore the whole thing, but then something or someone started to knock on the back door. Whenever we answered the door, there was no one there. One day I was lying on the bed while my wife, Sadie, was in another room with my mother. Suddenly I heard the sound of heavy footsteps walking down the path to the back door and someone knocking on the door. It sounded like a woman's footsteps, but I can't be sure. Then my wife and my mother also heard the footsteps going down the path. We did nothing about answering the door, and after a moment the noise came again, but this time it was a thunderous knock, *bang-bang-bang*.

It sounded like someone was very annoyed at not getting in, and this time both my wife and my mother ran to open the door, and again there was no one there and no sound of footsteps receding up the path.

"We were in the habit of going away weekends then and coming back Sunday night. During our absence the house was well locked up, with safety locks on the windows and on the front door. The back door was barred entirely with bolts and quite impregnable; there was no way of getting in. The first time we did this, when we came back we found all sorts of things amiss: the hearth rug in the bedroom had been picked up neatly from the floor and placed in the center of the bed. An ashtray had been taken from the mantelpiece and put in the middle of the hearth rug. We had a loose carpet in the corridor running the length of the house. It was loose and not nailed down. After we got back from our weekend, we found this carpet neatly folded up end-to-end, and we had to unwind the thing again and put it back along the corridor. There was a large piece of wood in the living room, part of the back of a radio-phonograph. When we came back after the weekend, instead of lying against the wall, it was flat on the floor. So the following weekend, we put the piece of wood back against the wall and two chairs up against it so it couldn't possibly fall down. But when we came back, the wood was again right on the floor, yet the chairs had not been disturbed! Whoever it was who did it must have lifted it straight up over the chairs and slipped it out from behind them and placed it in the middle of the floor, as if they were saying, 'Look, I've done it again, even though you tried to stop me.' By now we were pretty sure we had a *poltergeist* in our house."

"What did you do about it?"

"While we were still trying to figure it out, there was an incident involving a cat. One day we clearly heard a cat purring in the middle of the kitchen floor. But our cat was sitting on a chair, looking down at this imaginary cat as if she could see it. We also heard a terrible crash in the living room, only to find nothing at all disturbed. Once in a while one would hear an odd note on the piano, an odd key being struck, but there was no one near it. This went on and on, gradually building up. At first it was perhaps one incident a week. Eventually it was happening every day. After two years it was getting really ridiculous, and we were beginning to worry in case the neighbors would hear dogs barking *inside* the house and things like that. Finally I asked a medium by the name of James Flanagan to come to the house."

"A professional medium?" I asked.

"It is a hobby with him, but he tells me that his work is his hobby, and the mediumship is his actual profession."

"What happened?"

"He brought another man with him, James Wright, and they had tape recorders with them. He informed us that he felt spirits all over the room, and that he could see them even though we couldn't. He told us it was the original owner of the house, an old lady; she had become strange and was put in a hospital, where she died. She didn't know that she was dead and insisted on coming back to her home. He described her as having reddish hair. Her husband had been a freemason."

"Did you check this out?"

"The person who had shown us round the house when we bought it," Mr. Grandison replied, "was a ginger-haired woman who turned out to have been the daughter of a lady who had died. Also we found a number of things in the attic having to do with freemasonry."

"What advice did the medium give you to get rid of the spook?"

"He asked us to get a basin of clean water and put it in the kitchen and to try to imagine his face in the basin of water after he had left. Also, in two weeks time the entire phenomenon would disappear —and much to our surprise, it did. Incidents were less frequent and eventually they ceased all together."

I had mentioned to Elizabeth Byrd that a certain David Reeves had been in touch with me concerning a *poltergeist* at his Edinburgh residence and expressed the desire to visit with Mr. Reeves.

"It all started at the beginning of 1970, when my cousin Gladys, her husband Richard, myself, and my wife Aileen were discussing the unknown and life after death," Mr. Reeves had stated to me. "We had heard of other people using a ouija board, so I drew one on a large piece of paper and placed it on the floor, then placed a tumbler in the center of the paper, and we all put our right forefingers on the glass. After a few minutes I experienced a cold shiver down my back and Richard said he felt the same. Then the glass started to move!"

They received no message, and Mr. Reeves was very skeptical about the whole thing. But the little circle continued using the ouija board, and eventually they did get evidential messages, from a spirit claiming to be Richard's grandfather. The message was succinct: Richard was to have a crash on his motorbike. A few weeks later he crashed his three-wheeler, which had a motorbike engine. Messages came to them now from different people. One night they received a message stating that the two men were to drink salt water(!) and to make their minds blank at precisely eleven o'clock.

"At eleven I 'fell asleep,' and what happened afterwards is an account told to me by the others," Mr. Reeves explained. In trance, through Mr. Reeves, an entity calling himself St. Francis of Assisi manifested. Since none of the group were Roman Catholics, this was rather surprising to them. The entranced David Reeves then got up, demanded that the light—which he called 'the false light'—be put out, and that the curtains be opened. This done, he demanded that everyone fall to his knees and pray. He himself then proceeded to pray in Latin, a language which neither Mr. Reeves nor any of those present knew.

Unfortunately, Mr. Reeves's cousin Gladys mistook his deep state of trance for illness and put the light on. Immediately he came out of his trance and complained of great pains in his hands.

"When I looked at them, they were covered by blood, and each hand had a hole in the center," Mr. Reeves said. "This was witnessed by everyone present. I quickly ran to the tap and washed the blood away. The holes then vanished."

But the holy tenor of their seances soon changed to something more earthy: Mr. Reeves was impressed with advance information concerning local horse racing and won quite a lot of money because of it. This was followed by what he described as a "distinct evil presence" in the circle, to the point where his wife refused to participate any longer. The other couple, Richard and Gladys, evidently took part of the presence to their own home: *poltergeistic* activities started and objects moved of their own volition. It was at this point that Mr. Reeves contacted me and wondered what they ought to do next. Unfortunately, I was unable to find him at the address he had given me. Had he been forced to move? I wrote him a note advising him to stay clear of ouija boards and to consider his experience in trance as a form of psychic hysteria: it could just be that a spirit who *wanted* to be St. Francis had taken over Mr. Reeves's body and expressed this unfulfilled desire for martyrdom.

The discussion of various ghostly events had made the time fly, and suddenly we halted at our destination, Woodhouse Lea. Ian Groat, a gunsmith by profession, had had an uncanny experience here and wanted me to see the place where it all happened. We were on a hill overlooking Edinburgh, and there were a stable and a modern house to our left. Farther up the hill, following the narrow road, one could make out the main house itself. According to my information, Woodhouse Lea had originally stood on another site, farther east, but had been transferred to the present spot. There was a local tradition of a "White Lady of Woodhouse Lea," and it was her appearance that I was after. It was a bitingly cold day for April, so we decided to stay in the car at first, while we sorted out Mr. Groat's experiences.

"In January of 1964 I went to Woodhouse Lea in the company of Mr. and Mrs. Peter London," Ian told us. "We waited for several hours in the basement of the house, which had been used to store fodder for horses."

"I gather you went there because of the tradition that a 'White Lady' appeared there?" I asked.

Ian nodded. "After about two hours, a fluorescent light appeared behind one of the doors, which was slightly ajar. It seemed to move backwards and forwards for about five minutes and then disappeared. All three of us saw it. The light was coming from behind that door. We were waiting to see whether anything would actually enter the room, but nothing did, and so we left."

"What was the house like at that point?"

"It was still standing, though several large pieces of masonry had fallen and were lying in front of it. The woodwork was in very poor condition and floorboards were missing, but part of the original grand staircase was still there. It was dangerous to walk in it at night, and even in daylight one had to walk very carefully."

The house could have been restored, if someone had wanted to foot the expense. For a while the monument commission thought of doing it, but nothing came of it, and eventually the owners pulled it down. The decision was made in a hurry, almost as if to avoid publicity about the destruction of this historical landmark. It was all done in one weekend. The masonry and what was still standing was pulled to the ground by heavy machinery, then stamped into the ground to serve as a kind of base for the modern chalet which the owners of the land built on top of it. It reminded me of some of the barbarous practices going on in the United States in pulling down old landmarks in order to build something new and, preferably, profitable.

Peter London was shocked at the sudden disappearance of the old mansion house, and he got to talking to some of the girls working in the stables at the bottom of the hill, also part of the estate. Several of them had seen the apparition of a woman in white.

The strange thing is that the British army had

invested seven thousand pounds in central heating equipment when they occupied the building. This was during World War II and the building was then still in pretty good shape.

"During the war there was a prisoner-of-war camp that bordered on the actual Woodhouse Lea Estate," Ian continued. "The sentries kept a log of events, and there are fourteen entries of interest, stretching over a three-year period. These concerned sightings of a 'woman in white' who was challenged by the sentries. Incidentally, the stable girls saw her walking about the grounds, *outside* the house, not in the house itself or in the stables."

I decided it was time to pay a visit to the area where the mansion last stood. Since there had been no time to make arrangements for my investigation, Mr. Groat went ahead, and to our pleasant surprise he returned quickly, asking us to come inside the stable office, at the bottom of the hill. There we were received by a jolly gentleman who introduced himself as Cedric Burton, manager of the estate. I explained the purpose of my visit. In Scotland, mentioning ghosts does not create any great stir: they consider it part of the natural phenomena of the area.

"As I know the story," Mr. Burton said, "her name was Lady Anne Bothwell, and originally she lived at the *old* Woodhouse Lea Castle, which is about four miles from here. Once when her husband was away, one of his enemies took over the castle and pushed her out, and she died in the snow. I gather she appears with nothing on at all when she does appear. That's the way she was pushed out—naked. Apparently her ghost makes such a nuisance of itself that the owners decided to move the castle and brought most of the stones over here and built the mansion house called Woodhouse Lea up on the hill. The last person I know of who heard a manifestation was a coachman named Sutherland, and that was just before electric light was installed. There has been no sign of her since."

"I gather there were a number of reports. What exactly did these people see?"

"Well, it was always the same door on the north side of the building, and on snowy nights there was a fairly vigorous knock on the door; and when someone would go outside to investigate, there was never anyone there—nor were there any footprints in the deep snow. That, I think, was the extent of the manifestations, which are of course tremendously exaggerated by the local people. Some say it is a White Lady, and one has even heard people coming up the drive. I've heard it said, when the old house was standing there empty, lights were seen in the rooms."

"Has the house ever been seriously investigated?"

"Some Edinburgh people asked permission and sat in the old house at midnight on midsummer's eve. However, I pointed out to them that she was only known to appear around seven in the evening and in deep snow. Midnight on midsummer's eve wasn't the most auspicious occasion to expect a manifestation. There was another chap who used to bring his dog up and stand there with his torch from time to time, to see if the dog was bristling."

"When did the actual event occur—the pushing out of the woman?"

"The house was moved to this spot in the early fifteenth century. It was originally built around the old Fulford Tower. It is a bit confusing, because up there also by the house there is an archway built from stones from an entirely different place with the date 1415 on it. This comes from the old Galaspas Hospital in Edinburgh."

"If Woodhouse Lea was moved from the original site to this hill in the early fifteenth century, when was the original house built?"

"Sometime during the Crusades, in the thirteenth century."

While the early history of Woodhouse Lea is shrouded in mystery, there was a Lord Woodhouse Lea in the eighteenth century, a well-known literary figure in Edinburgh. Many other literary figures stayed at the house, including Sir Walter Scott, Alan Ramsey, and James Hogg. Evidently Sir Walter Scott knew that *old* Woodhouse Lea was haunted, because he mentions it in one of his books, and Scottish travel books of the eighteenth century commonly refer to it as "haunted Woodhouse Lea." In 1932 control of the house passed into the hands of the army, and much damage was done to the structure. The army held onto it for thirty years.

"Have there been any manifestations reported in recent years?"

"Not really," Mr. Burton replied. "When the bulldozer pulled down the old house, we told people as a joke that the ghost would be trying to burrow her way out of the rubble. Some of the stones from the old house have been incorporated into the new chalet, built on top of the crushed masonry, to give it a sort of continuity."

The chalet is the property of George Buchanan Smith, whose family uses it as a holiday house. He is the son of Lord Balonough, and his younger brother is the undersecretary of state for foreign affairs in Scotland.

"The house has been talked about tremendously," Mr. Burton said. "It has even been described as the second most haunted house in Scotland. Also, Woseley is not too far from here, and it too has a nude white lady. She has been observed running on the battlements."

"Why did they move the house from the old site to this spot?"

"Because of her. She disturbed them too much."

"And did the manifestations continue on the new site?"

"Yes," Mr. Burton acknowledged. "She came with the stones."

He turned the office over to an assistant and took us up to the chalet. The owner was away, so there was no difficulty in walking about the house. It is a charmingly furnished modern weekend house, with a bit of ancient masonry incorporated into the walls here and there. I gazed at a particularly attractive stone frieze over the fireplace. Inscribed upon it, in Latin, were the words, OCCULTUS NON EXTINCTUS: the occult is not dead (just hidden).

Twenty-three miles from Edinburgh, in a fertile valley that was once the center of the mill industry but is now largely agricultural, there stands the town of Peebles. The surrounding countryside is known as Peebleshire and there are a number of lovely vacation spots in the area, quiet conservative villas and small hotels much favored by the English and the Scottish. One such hotel is the Venlaw Castle Hotel, standing on a bluff on the outskirts of town, seven hundred feet above sea level. It is open for summer guests only and does indeed give the appearance of a castle from the outside. Standing four stories high, with a round tower in one corner, Venlaw Castle represents the fortified house of Scotland rather than the heavy, medieval fortress. Access to the castle, now the hotel, is from the rear; behind it, Venlaw, the hill which gave it its name, rises still further. The present building was erected in 1782 on the site of an old Scottish keep called Smithfield Castle, one of the strong points of the borderland in olden days. One half of the present house was added in 1854, in what is locally known as the mock baronial style.

Venlaw belonged to the Erskine family and in 1914 Lady Erskine offered her mansion to the admiralty as a convalescent hospital for twelve naval officers. According to James Walter Buchanan's *A History of Peebleshire,* it remained an auxiliary Red Cross hospital to the end of World War I. The same author describes the present dwelling house as being "built on a commanding position with one of the finest views in the county. It is presumed that it occupies the site of the ancient castle of Smithfield, which was in existence until about the middle of the eighteenth century."

In 1949 the house passed into the hands of Alexander Cumming, the father of the present owner, who turned it into a small hotel.

In the summer of 1968 an American couple, Mr. and Mrs. Joseph Senitt, decided to spend a few days at Venlaw Castle. "The room we occupied was at the end of the middle floor with a little turret room which my daughter used," Mrs. Senitt had explained to me. "The very first night we were there, the room was ice cold even though it was July, and we couldn't wait to close the lights and go to sleep. Immediately upon getting into bed, I suddenly heard a long-drawn-out and quite human sigh! It seemed to be near the foot of my bed. For the moment I froze—I was afraid to move or even breathe. If it hadn't been for the fact that my husband was with me, I might have gone into shock. I said nothing to him, as he usually kids me about my ghostly beliefs, and I felt he was probably asleep, as he made no move and said nothing. However, after a moment I got the strongest feeling that if it was a ghost it was friendly, because I felt welcome."

When the Senitts left the castle a few days later, Mrs. Senitt finally mentioned the incident to her husband. To her surprise he confirmed that he too had heard the sound. He had attributed it to their daughter, sleeping in the small room next door. But Mrs. Senitt was sure that the sound came from in front of her, and the turret bedroom where the girl slept was off to a corner in back of the room and the door was closed. Also, the Senitts were the only people staying in that part of the hotel at the time.

It was still raining when we crossed the river Tweed and headed into Peebles. The castle-hotel was easy to find, and a few minutes later we arrived in front of it, wondering whether it would be open, since we had not been able to announce our coming. To our pleasant surprise a soft-spoken young man bade us welcome, and it turned out that he was the owner, the son of the man who had opened the hotel originally, and also that he was the only person in the hotel at the present time, since it was not yet open for the season. I asked him to show us the room on the middle floor with the turret bedroom without, however, indicating my reasons for this request. I merely mentioned that some American friends of mine had enjoyed their stay at Venlaw, and I wanted to see the room they'd occupied. As soon as we had entered the room, Alanna turned to me and said, "There is something here. I'm getting a cold, crawly scalp." While Alanna was getting her psychic bearings, I took Mr. Cumming aside, out of her earshot, and questioned him about the hotel. Was there, to his recollection, any incident connected with the house, either since it had been turned into a hotel or before, involving death or tragedy or anything unusual?

Mr. Cumming seemed a bit uneasy at this question. "There are things we don't like to speak about," he finally said. "We've only had one traumatic accident. About twenty years ago one of our guests fell from a bedroom window."

Alanna came over at this point and stopped short of the window. "There's something at this window," she said. "Somebody either threw himself out of this window or fell out." But Alanna insisted that the tragedy went back a long time, which puzzled me. Was she confusing her time periods, or did a second death follow an earlier death, perhaps caused by a possessing entity? Those are the kinds of thoughts that race through a psychic investigator's mind at a time like this. Actually, it turned out that the guest fell out of a window one flight higher than the room we were in. He was a miner who had become ill and somehow fallen out the window. His friends carried him back in, but he had a broken neck; they actually killed him by moving him.

Alanna shook her head. "No. What I feel has to do with this window in this room. It may have something to do with the original place that stood here before. I get the feeling of a fire."

"Well," Mr. Cumming said, "Venlaw Hill, where we are standing, was the place where, during the persecutions, witches were burned, or people accused of such."

"I have feelings of intense suffering," Alanna said, "and I sense some noise, the feeling of noise and of a great deal of confusion and excitement. I get the feeling of a crowd of people, and of anger. Someone either fell out of this window or was thrown out, and also there is a feeling of fire. But this is definitely a woman. I feel it not only in this room but down on this terrace below, which seems to have something to do with it."

I questioned Mr. Cumming whether any of his guests had ever complained about unusual phenomena. "Not really," he replied. "We did have a guest who complained of noises, but she was mentally disturbed. She was a resident here for some time in the 1950s. I didn't know her well; I was very young at the time."

"And where did this lady stay?" I asked.

"Why, come to think of it, in the room next to this one."

I thanked Mr. Cumming and wondered whether the lady guest had really been unhinged, or whether perhaps she had only felt what Mr. and Mrs. Senitt felt some fifteen years later in the same area.

The afternoon was still young, and we had two hours left to explore the countryside. We decided to cross the river Tweed once again and make for Traquair House, making sure, however, to telephone ahead, since this was not one of the days on which this private manor house could be visited.

Known as the "oldest inhabited house in Scotland," Traquair House at Innerleithen rises to five stories amid a majestic park, in a tranquil setting that gives the illusion of another century, another world.

It is now owned by Lord Maxwell Stuart, of a distinguished noble family, related to the royal Stuarts. There is a tradition that the magnificent gates of Traquair, surmounted by fabled animals, shall remain closed until a Stuart king is crowned again in London. This Jacobite sentiment goes back to the times when the earls of Traquair gave support to the Stuart cause, but the present laird, Peter Maxwell Stuart, is more concerned with the quality of the beer he brews. He's also the author of a magnificently illustrated booklet detailing the treasures at Traquair House. These include, in the king's room, the bed in which Mary Queen of Scots slept, with a coverlet made by her ladies in waiting. That she slept there is not surprising, since Lady Mary Seaton, the wife of the second earl, was one of Mary's favorite ladies in waiting. Also, the very cradle used by Mary Stuart for her son James VI of Scotland now stands at Traquair, and in the many rooms of the house there are displayed treasures, documents, arms, and fine furniture, all of them dating back to the sixteenth and seventeenth centuries, when this great house was at its zenith. Much as we loved the sight of this beautiful house, so romantic on a rainy day, with the fog just lifting, we had come not to admire the antiques but to find out about its ghosts.

The caretaker, Andrew Aiken Burns, who had been at the house since 1934, took us around, painstakingly explaining room after room.

"Have you ever had any psychic experiences here?"

"Yes," he nodded, as if it were the most natural thing in the world to be asked. "It happened in 1936 in the afternoon of a beautiful summer day. I was out with my horse, clearing the brush from the front of the house, near the old ruined cottage in the field. My horse was a chestnut named Ginger, and suddenly he flicked his ears and I looked up. I saw a lady coming down the grass, dressed in a Victorian dress. She walked slowly down through the gate and into the cottage and then through the wicket gate into the garden."

"What was so special about that? Could she not have been a visitor?" I asked.

"Well, I left my horse and went right up to see where this person had gone, and the wicket gate was shut. She had been through the gate, and still the gate was shut."

"Did you ever see her again?"

"No. But later someone showed me some old photographs, and I recognized one as the lady I had seen walking on the grass. It was Lady Louisa Stuart."

Lady Louisa Stuart died in 1875 at age one hundred. She is buried in a vault in the Traquair churchyard, right in back of the castle. Why would she walk the grounds? I wondered.

According to the twentieth laird, Traquair House goes back to the tenth century when a heather hut stood on the place. In 1107 King Alexander I granted a charter to the Traquairs, and he was the first of a long line of Scottish kings who stayed here. Incidentally, Traquair means dwelling on a winding river. In the thirteenth century the building was incorporated into a border peel, a defensive palisade, and it served as such during the long period of border strife. In 1491 James Stuart, the son of the Earl of Buchan, became the first Laird of Traquair, and from him the present family is descended. Over the centuries the building was largely altered and added to, to fit the changing times. What was once an austere border fortress became a Renaissance castle and eventually one of the finer residences in Scotland. During the Civil War in the seventeenth century, Traquair became what the present laird describes as "one of the great bastions of the Catholic faith in Scotland," because of marriages with Catholic ladies. Since Catholicism was not favored in this part of the country, Mass had to be celebrated in secret. To this day, there is a Roman Catholic chapel on the grounds, unfortunately decorated in the most gaudy modern style and totally at variance with the rest of the house. In 1688 the house was raided by a mob from Peebles, and all the religious articles found were destroyed. It wasn't until well into the nineteenth century that Catholicism was freely admitted into Scotland. During the rebellion of 1715, Traquair sided with Bonnie Prince Charles, which brought much misfortune upon the family.

When Charles Stuart, the fourteenth laird, died unmarried in 1861, the property passed into the hands of his sister, Lady Louisa, born in 1775. She also didn't marry and died in 1875 after spending nearly all her time on her estate. All her life she had carried on a love affair with Traquair House. She looked after the gardens, took great pride in keeping the house itself in perfect order, and, though she was the first female head of the family in many centuries, she had the full respect of the villagers and of her servants. When she died, the question of the inheritance had to be settled by the courts. Eventually, Traquair House passed into the hands of Lady Louisa's cousin, the Honorable Henry Constable Maxwell Stuart, who thus became the sixteenth laird. Perhaps Lady Louisa was not altogether happy with the turn of events, for she had been the last in the direct line to hold Traquair. Possibly, her spirit does not wish to relinquish her realms, or perhaps her long residence here has so accustomed her to Traquair that she is unaware of the fact that there might be another, better place for her to go.

"Has anyone else seen the ghost of Lady Louisa?" I asked the caretaker.

"Well, some other people have seen her, but they have only seen a figure and did not recognize her. Some have seen her farther up the road."

"Why is she called The Green Lady?" I asked. I understood from my friends that the legendary Lady of Traquair was referred to by that name.

"Well, the dress I saw her wearing," the caretaker said, "was kind of green, the color of a wood pigeon."

"Is there such a dress in existence?" I asked. Since so much of the old furniture and personal belongings of the family were preserved at the house, perhaps the original dress still existed.

"Well, it is a strange thing: one of the old foresters here—his wife's mother was Lady Louisa's dressmaker. They kept some of the clippings from which the dresses were made, and when I asked her, the granddaughter showed me the materials. I recognized the color and the material of the dress the lady had on when I saw her." Mr. Burns, the caretaker, admitted that he had some psychic abilities. Sometimes he knew things before they actually occurred, but paid it no great heed.

I asked Mr. Burns to take us to Lady Louisa's room. There, beautifully framed on the south wall, was the great lady's portrait. "She was friendly with Sir Walter Scott," the caretaker commented. The room was oblong, with a fireplace on one end. Wine-red chairs, two sofas, and a strange mixture of eighteenth-century and Victorian furniture gave the room a warm, intimate feeling. On one side, one could gaze into the garden, while the other overlooked the driveway, so that Lady Louisa would always know who was coming up to see her. Alanna hadn't said anything for quite a while. I found her standing by the garden windows. The rain had stopped, and the sun began to pierce through the clouds.

"Do you feel her presence?" I asked.

Alanna gave me a curious look. "Don't you?"

I nodded. I had known for several minutes that Lady Louisa Stuart was at home this afternoon, receiving *unexpected* visitors.

Shortly afterwards, we drove back towards Edinburgh. We crossed the river Tweed again, and the rain started up once more. It was as if fate had held it back for an hour or so to give us a chance to visit Traquair House at its best.

I wondered what it was that bound all British ghosts together. Then it struck me: whether Medieval or Victorian, Renaissance or Edwardian, they all had *style.*

Spectral Mary, Queen of Scots

BACK OF Holyrood Palace, Edinburgh, residence of Mary Queen of Scots and other Scottish monarchs, stands a little house of modest appearance going by the quaint name of Croft-en-Reigh. This house was once owned by James, Earl of Moray, half brother of Mary, and Regent of Scotland in her absence. Today, the house is subdivided into three apartments, one of which belongs to a Mrs. Clyne. But several years ago this was the official residence of the warden of Holyrood Palace. The warden is the chief guide who has charge of all tourist traffic. David Graham, the onetime warden, has now retired to his house in nearby Portobello, but fourteen years ago he had a most unusual experience in this little house.

"There were twelve of us assembled for a seance, I recall," he said, "and we had Helen Duncan, who is now dead, as our medium. There we were, seated quietly in the top floor of Croft-en-Reigh, waiting for developments."

They did not have to wait long. A figure materialized before their astonished eyes and was recognized instantly: Mary Queen of Scots herself, who had been to this house many times in moments of great emotional turmoil. Within a moment, she was gone.

On several occasions, Mr. Graham recalls, he saw the ghost of a short man in sixteenth-century clothes. "I am French," the man insisted. Graham thought nothing of it until he accidentally discovered that the house was built by an architect named French!

The Ghostly Monk of Monkton

WHEN ELIZABETH Byrd moved into a monastic tower at Old Craig Hall at Musselburgh nine miles outside of Edinburgh, she probably didn't figure on sharing the quarters with a ghost, much less a monk. If there is one thing Elizabeth Byrd doesn't want to share quarters with, it is a monk. As for ghosts, she has an open mind: to begin with, she has had ghostly experiences all through the years.

The monastic tower has two stories and is part of a larger complex of buildings which was once a monastery. Her landlord, who is also a good friend, lives in the main house, while Elizabeth is lady of the manor, so to speak, in her tower—an ideal situation for a romantically inclined writer, and she has been able to turn out several novels since moving into Monkton, as the place is called.

We had left my visit to Monkton for the evening of my second day in Edinburgh, and it turned out to be a foggy, chilly day. Alistair and Alanna Knight brought me in their car, and Ian Groat, the gunsmith whom I had met earlier, was also there.

One walks up a winding stair from the ground floor to the main floor, in which Elizabeth has made her home. The apartment consists of a living room with fireplace, a small kitchen and pantry to one side, and a bedroom to the other. I am sure that when the monks had the place, they did not do nearly so well as Elizabeth does now, so I can readily understand why a monk, especially a ghostly monk, would be attracted to the situation. We grouped ourselves around the fireplace with only a candle illuminating the room.

"I rented this cottage in February 1972," Elizabeth Byrd began the account of her experiences. "I found it beautifully peaceful and benign. I discovered that the cottage was built in 1459, across a courtyard from a fortified house, which goes back to the twelfth century. Not much is known about my cottage except that it was built by monks. They worked this as an agricultural area, and it was an extension of Newbattle Abbey near Dalkeith. It came to be called 'The Town of the Monks.' From this, the name Monkton developed."

"During the year and a quarter that you have lived here," I said, "have you had any unusual experiences?"

"Yes," Elizabeth replied. "Six months after I got here I was reading in bed one night with the light on when I smelled a marvelous juicy kind of baking of meat, or the roasting of meat, which seemed to emanate from the old stone fireplace. It actually made me hungry. Of course I wasn't doing any cooking. This happened three or four times in the subsequent weeks, but I took it in stride, just looked up from my book and said to myself, 'Oh, there it is again, that smell.' It wasn't the kind of meat that you get in the supermarket: it was more like standing rib roast—expensive, gorgeous meat."

Alanna took up the narrative at this point. "I stayed at this cottage about a year ago for the first time. Of course, I was rather apprehensive of what I might find, but I found nothing but this wonderful feeling of great happiness and content. The first time I stayed here with Alistair, we went off to bed and slept in Elizabeth's room, and she slept in her study; it was a Saturday night. I woke up early Sunday morning and there was the sound of bells ringing. It must have been about six o'clock in the morning and I thought, 'Ah, there must be a Catholic church somewhere nearby. This is obviously a call to early Mass.' So I didn't wake my husband, but soon I heard the sound of trotting horses, and again I thought, 'Oh, well, that is somebody out with their horses. After all it is in the country.' When we had breakfast, I asked my husband whether the sound of the bells didn't wake him around six o'clock. He said, 'What bells?' I didn't say anything, but when Elizabeth came in I asked her, 'Doesn't the bell wake you up on a Sunday morning? Where is your church near here?' She said, 'We don't have a church here.' Actually, the bell I heard was on the side of the house."

"The bell has never been heard by anyone except by Alanna. There is no church within miles," Elizabeth said.

"Last March I stayed here again," Alanna continued. "I slept in Elizabeth's room, and around eight in the morning I woke up to a wonderful smell of food and thought. 'Oh, good, Elizabeth is making something absolutely delicious for breakfast,' and it was the most gorgeous, juicy smell, a gamey smell. There was also the smell of lovely, fresh bread. I jumped out of bed and rushed into the kitchen. There was no sign of Elizabeth and nothing was cooking. It was all emanating from the bedroom."

Now it was Ian Groat's turn.

"In January 1973, I was asked to spend a few days' holiday here. On the first night I retired about four-thirty. Before falling asleep, I realized that I might see things, not because Elizabeth had told me of anything in particular, but because I suspected there was a good reason why she wanted me to sleep in this particular room."

"Did you, in fact, see anything unusual?"

"Yes," the gunsmith replied. "The first thing I saw was a trap door slightly to the left, in the floor, and a pair of steps leading to the basement. I saw the top of the trap door and a small monk appeared and looked at me. He had climbed the steps into the bedroom and was looking around, but he didn't seem to see me. Since he didn't see me at all, I allowed myself to relax completely. Then I saw a procession come in. One appeared to be a high dignitary of the Roman Catholic Church. He may have been a bishop. He was flanked by monks and they seemed to be chanting. I had a very good look at the bishop. He was clean-shaven, with a very serene face, and he looked very intelligent. The procession walked past me and more or less disappeared.

"Now another apparition appeared which caused me a great deal of confusion. I had decided I could see through the floor if I cared to exercise my faculty to do so. So I looked through the floor, and what I saw were bales of hay, and then I saw what appeared to be an opening in the wall, and through it came what I took to be either Vikings or Saxons. They were dressed in rough clothing. There were three of them

—an old man, bearded, with gray hair, and two others, younger and fair-haired, also bearded, and none of them had weapons. I thought them to be farmers. They came through this cavity in the wall and they raised their hands in a greeting sign, but not at me. I was more or less an observer. Then I decided, since I could see through the floor, that I could perhaps see outside the building as well, and I then viewed the building from a height. Now I appeared to be on a parallel which was outside this dwelling, looking down. I saw soldiers coming up the drive and around the corner, and they seemed to be of the middle seventeen hundreds, dressed in gray coats of a very superior material. The accoutrements seemed to be made of white webbing. They were playing their drums and keeping step with them as they marched. I gained the impression that I was seeing this standing in a tower, but there is no tower there. I tried to see more, but I didn't, so I decided to go to sleep."

"My landlord, John Calderwood Miller," Elizabeth Byrd added, "bought this property in 1956 and restored it. There is a reference to it in Nigel Trentor's book, *The Fortified House in Scotland.* I told Mr. Miller about Ian's experience of having seen the hole in the floor and the monk going down and the hay, and he said, 'That is extraordinary, because in 1956 there *was* a hole in the floor between where your beds are now, and we had to cover it over and make a floor.' There was an exit down to what had been the stables where there were indeed horses. Now it is a garage and sheds."

There was still another witness to the haunting at Monkton: Ian Adam, whom I had interviewed in London, the mediumistic gentleman who had been so helpful to me during my ghost-hunting expedition in

April. Originally of Scottish background, Ian liked coming up to Edinburgh. The morning of December 27, 1972, he arrived at three forty-five. Elizabeth Byrd remembers it clearly; not too many of her friends drop in at that hour. But he was driving up from Newcastle with a friend, and Elizabeth had gotten worried.

"It was a very cold night, and Elizabeth greeted us as only Elizabeth can," Ian told me. "Immediately we sat down in her sitting room, she asked, 'Do you feel anything here?' but even before she had said it, I had felt that it had a very peaceful atmosphere about it."

"Within ten minutes, out of the blue, Ian, who had never been here, said, 'What a strong scent of rosemary! This place is redolent of rosemary!' " Elizabeth reported Ian as exclaiming, but none of the others could smell it.

"The place was very lovely, really," Ian said, "and I told Elizabeth I was sure there was a woman there, a very industrious lady, perhaps of the fifteenth century. She appeared to me to be wearing a sort of off-white dress and was very busy cooking, as if she had an enormous amount of work to do. She seemed young, and yet old for her years, probably owing to hard work. There was a definite sense of tremendous activity about her, as if she had an awful lot of people to look after. I had a strong feeling that the place was one of healing. I saw a man sitting in a corner on a chair; his leg was being dressed and strapped, and he was being given an old-fashioned jug, or bottle, to drink from by another man. I think it had an anesthetic in it. I remember distinctly there was a great deal of good being done in this place, as if it were a place where people came for shelter and healing, if there were accidents or fighting. It was certainly a place of great spiritual power."

When I checked Ian's testimony with Elizabeth, who had written down his impressions immediately after he had given them to her, she changed the description of the woman ghost somewhat. According to Elizabeth's notes, the woman seemed between thirty and forty years of age, wearing pale gray, sort of looped up on one side.

"Was the impression of the man being helped and of the woman doing the cooking simply an imprint of the past, or do you think these were ghosts that you saw?"

"Oh," Ian said firmly, "they were ghosts all right." He couldn't hear anything, but he did smell the cooking.

"Did anything else happen during that night?"

"No. I had a very peaceful night, although I was absolutely freezing. It must have been the coldest night I've ever lived through. In fact, I got out of bed in the middle of the night and put a jersey over my head to protect myself from the intense cold."

There is one more witness to the haunting at Monkton. James Boyd, by profession a sales representative, but gifted with psychic and healing powers, once stayed overnight in the same bedroom Ian Groat slept in when he had his remarkable experience. This was in early April of 1972.

"In the morning he came to me," Elizabeth said, "and reported that there was a woman in a long, dirty-white dress who seemed to be very busy about the fireplace in the bedroom. The two fireplaces in the sitting room, where we are now, and the bedroom next door, were once connected. James Boyd also told me, 'She's very busy and tired because she works so hard.' He had, of course, no knowledge of Ian Adam's experience in the house."

Ian Groat spoke up now. "Two weeks after his visit here, James Boyd telephoned me and said, 'Ian, I have the feeling that there is a well in that courtyard. It is all covered up, but I think if you go down that well, about halfway down, you will find a cavity in the wall and in this cavity lots of silver, household silver that was hidden in times of danger.' I promised I would tell Elizabeth about it and I did."

"There is indeed such a well in the courtyard," Elizabeth confirmed, "but the tower that Ian Groat mentioned no longer exists. It was part of a peel tower, used for defense. When I told Mr. Miller about the well, he said, 'Now that is very extraordinary. About a year ago I went down into the well, about fifteen feet, and when I looked up, the light seemed far away.' Mr. Miller decided to go back up, as he didn't know what he might hit down in the depths. But he did have the feeling that there was a treasure somewhere and encouraged me and my friends to look for it."

Now that everyone had had his say, it was time to tell them of my own impressions. While the others were talking about the bedroom, I had the very distinct impression of a large, rather heavy monk watching from the doorway. He had on a grayish kind of robe, and there was a rather quizzical expression on his face, as if he were studying us. The name Nicholas rushed at me. I also had the feeling that there was some agricultural activity going on around here, with chickens and geese and supplies, and that in some way the military were involved with these supplies. These impressions came to me *before* the others had given their respective testimonies.

"The monk I saw had a gray robe on," Ian Groat confirmed, "and my impression was that I was seeing events that had occurred and not people who were present at that particular moment. It was like seeing a film from the past."

Well, if the monks and the lady at Elizabeth's Monkton Tower are film actors, they are one step ahead of Hollywood: you can actually *smell* the food!

Scottish Country Ghosts

CULZEAN CASTLE rises sheer from the sea on the Ayrshire coast.

Built by Robert Adam in the latter part of the eighteenth century, the castle has been associated with the Kennedy family, the Earls of Cassillis, and the Marquises of Ailsa, whose portraits are seen all over the house. Today it is administered by the National Trust for Scotland as a museum. Its main tower rises majestically four stories from the cliff, and one of the top floors contains an apartment given to General Eisenhower as a gesture of gratitude from Britain. He stayed there with his family from time to time.

We were cordially welcomed by the administrator of Culzean, Commander John Hickley.

"I'm afraid we don't keep a tame ghost in this castle," he said apologetically, as Mrs. Hickley served us tea.

I assured him that we enjoyed the visit just the same. Neither the Commander nor Mrs. Hickley had seen a ghost in this comparatively modern castle, nor had any of the help complained about any unusual visitors. But a British visitor to Culzean by the name of Margaret Penney was somewhat luckier—if seeing a ghost is luck.

According to an Associated Press report of August 9, 1962, Mrs. Penney was going through the castle just like any other tourist when she encountered the ghost.

> "She came down a corridor when I was visiting Culzean Castle recently," said Mrs. Penney, "and said to me—'It rains today.' "
>
> Mrs. Penney said the ghost was dark-haired and very beautiful.
>
> "She appeared to be in evening dress though it was only about five o'clock in the afternoon when I encountered her.
>
> "Anyway, I squeezed myself against the corridor to let her pass and told her, 'Not much room for passing when you're as plump as me.' "
>
> Mrs. Penney said the girl looked at her very sadly and answered, "I do not require any room nowadays."
>
> Mrs. Penney said her entire right side then went cold.
>
> "Suddenly I realized that she had walked through my side."

Was she one of the Kennedy ladies who had come to a sad end in the lonely house on the Fyrth of Clyde? Until I bring a medium to Culzean at some future date, we can only guess.

Another nearby haunted castle drew my interest because its current occupants are British nobility from Baltimore, Maryland. Sir Adrian and Lady Naomi Dunbar inherited the ramshackle estate and castle of Mochrum Park by virtue of being the nearest cousin to the last British baronet, who died in 1953.

The Americans found the house a shambles and the income of the estate far from grand. Nevertheless, they still live in it, having restored some of it, and they are making a go of their newly found position in life.

When the new owners arrived late in 1953 to take over their new home, the villagers at Kirkcowan, Wigtownshire, were wondering how the Americans would take to the ghost. This is the "White Lady" of Mochrum Park, allegedly the shade of Lady Jacobina Dunbar, who married the sixth baronet back in 1789, and whose portrait was found in the debris of the old house a few years before 1953.

The National Gallery of Scotland in Edinburgh now owns this valuable painting by Raeburn. Servants of the tenth baronet, Sir James Dunbar, who died in early 1953, always complained that the ghost portrait would always be found askew, no matter how often they straightened it out, as if someone were trying to call attention to something!

Elgin Fraser, chauffeur of the Dunbars for many years, twice saw the "white lady" standing at the foot of his bed.

Perhaps the saving of the valuable painting, which was in danger of being destroyed by the customary dry rot, has assuaged the fury of the ghost. No further disturbances have been reported, and when I asked the American-born Lady Dunbar about the ghost, she said, with a broad Baltimore accent, "Nonsense. It's all just imagination."

A fine thing for a ghost to be called—imaginary! Especially by an American.

Border Country Ghosts

THE DIVIDING line between Scotland and England is known as border country. It is wild and remote, and the roads are far from good. At night you can very easily get lost there, but it is well worth the drive down from Edinburgh to Hermitage Castle, which is located outside the town of Hawick.

The area has a long history of warfare, even in peacetime. When Scotland and England were not yet joined together as one kingdom, this area was filled with lawlessness, and raids in one or the other direction were common. The lords of the area had a nasty habit of throwing their enemies into dungeons and letting them die of starvation there. One of the more sinister places in the area, Hermitage was built in the early Middle Ages and has long been associated with the Soulis family. It was here that the Earl of Bothwell, who later became her husband, was visited by Mary Queen of Scots, in 1566.

From the outside the castle looks very much the way it did when it was built in the thirteenth century. It consists of two main towers built of rough stones connected in such a manner that the fortress could withstand almost any attack. The entrance gate was well above ground, to prevent enemies from crashing it. Inside, most of the subdivisions no longer exist; but enough of the castle has been restored so that one can walk about and view what was once a reasonably comfortable dwelling—by early medieval standards.

In those far-off days, nobody trusted his neighbors. Petty wars and family feuds were the rule among the nobles of Scotland. When a neighboring chief sent a group of goodwill ambassadors to Hermitage to propose cessation of their long feud, the lord of the manor promptly put the men into a small room without food or water. They died there miserably and their ghosts are said to be among the many who still stalk the ruins.

On another occasion, the ruling Lord Soulis invited a number of local chiefs and nobles to a banquet in honor of the marriage of one of his daughters. Access to the castle was one flight up, not on the ground level. This was a defense measure, so that the castle could be defended by simply pulling up the wooden stairs leading from the ground to the first floor. As soon as the guests had all arrived and were seated in the banquet hall upstairs, the ladder was withdrawn and the gate closed by previous arrangement. The plan was to feed the guests first and murder them afterward.

However, the ladder need not have been withdrawn. As an afterthought Lord Soulis had instructed his cook to put poison into the food of his guests and it worked so well they were all dead before the last course of the banquet.

Individual enemies were not fed first and killed later: they were simply taken below, to the dungeon at the cellar level, which had and still has a clammy, cold stone floor made of roughly cut rocks. The most frightening spot in the building is a small hole in the stone floor. Enemies were pushed through this hole into the dungeon below, never to see the light of day again. Even their remains were not removed.

I do not doubt that Hermitage is still covered with impressions from its cruel past. Not only are the unhappy spirits of the victims felt in the atmosphere by anyone sensitive enough to do so, but there is still another reason why Hermitage is considered different from ordinary castles. One of the owners, Lord Soulis, was a black magician and had committed a number of documented atrocities. Finally the people of the countryside got together and seized him. Taking their inspiration from Lord Soulis' own way of life, they dispatched him in a most frightful manner by tying him with lead bands and then boiling him over a fire. According to the *Blue Guide to Scotland:* "To the E. [of Hermitage] is *Nine Stane Rig,* a hill with a stone circle, where the cruel Lord Soulis is said to have been boiled alive by his infuriated vassals. In reality Lord Soulis died in prison at Dumbarton Castle." But according to local talk his ghost is in evidence still at the castle—especially on the anniversary of his death.

Hermitage Castle can be visited without difficulty or previous arrangement. There is a custodian on the premises, who for a small fee readily takes you on a guided tour. The house is now a kind of museum. There are no accommodations for sleeping in it, nor would I advise anyone to try.

Ireland

The Ghost on the Kerry Coast

IF YOU'VE never heard of Ballyheigue—pronounced just like Rodgers' and Hammerstein's Bali-ha'i—you've really missed one of the most poetic stretches of coastland still unspoiled by human greed. It isn't completely untouched by habitation by any means, but there isn't—as yet—that glass-and-concrete luxury hotel, the nearby airport, the chic clientele. Ballyheigue just sits there, a small fishing village and a majestic castle, looking out onto the Atlantic. This stretch of land used to swarm with smugglers not so long ago, as it was rather difficult for the revenue people to catch up with the wily Irish in the many bays and loughs of Western Ireland.

Now I wasn't looking for smugglers' coves or new sources of poteen, but the spirit that moved me to travel down the Kerry coast had been brought to my attention in a respectable magazine piece, published a couple of years ago in Dublin. The article, entitled "On the Trail of a Ghost," is the factual report of Captain P. D. O'Donnell, about his strange experiences at Ballyheigue in 1962. The magazine, *Ireland of the Welcomes,* is published by the Irish Tourist Board, but this piece is the only instance of a psychic adventure appearing in its pages. Here then is Captain O'Donnell's report:

"It all started during a normal vacation in Ballyheigue in the first, sunny half of June, 1962. Even on holidays, a part-time writer like myself is always on the lookout for new ideas, but on that vacation I was determined to get the most out of a heat wave, and to heck with writing. I relaxed in the quiet atmosphere of the almost deserted village, lazed on the lonely four-mile-long beach with the family, or joined in the beach games with the handful of visitors from the hotel.

"Then, one day—it was the 4th or 5th day of June, be it noted—I took a walk with my eight-year-old son, Frank, up the winding avenue above the cliffs to the burnt-out shell of Ballyheigue Castle. It was purely in deference to my interest in old castles, and to show my son the castle. I had only a vague idea of its history, but knew that from here the strong Crosbie family had once lorded it over most of the north of County Kerry. They left the country when the republicans burnt the castle to the ground during the 'troubles' of 1921.

"For a while we talked to an old man working nearby, and he told us the castle was never explored fully. Then with camera in hand we started. I am one for always trying different angles and unusual shots with a camera, so when our short tour among the ruins satisfied Frank, we started to take a few snaps for the record. The snap that mattered was taken inside the castle. Frank was placed standing against a wall at right angles to the front of the castle, and I stood back. It was shadowy inside the castle, but the sun was slanting strongly through a window on his right. In the viewfinder I was able to get Frank on the left and hoped also to get the view of the beach through the window on the right. The light of the sun coming through the window would be enough, I hoped—no light meters for my amateur photography.

"The story of the rest of the vacation does not matter, except to record that the days were filled with sunshine, battling the breakers, looking for Kerry diamonds on Kerry Head, enjoying the relaxation and joining in the hotel sing-song at night. What did matter, however, was when the color film came back from the developers. The snap which I have described appeared to have another figure in it, partly obscured by the square of light that was the window. This figure held a sword, and its legs were not trousered, but appeared as if clothed in hose or thigh boots! At first I thought this rather frightening, but my wife passed it off as a double exposure.

"However, when she and I examined the other snapshots, we both agreed that there was neither a double exposure nor any other negative which if it was superimposed on the 'ghost' picture could have produced the same effect. What then was the answer, we wondered. Was it really a ghost I had photographed?

"The events that followed, indeed, made the affair more extraordinary. I brought the snap into the office, and passed it around my friends. Two were more interested than the others, and asked to see the negative. When I went home for lunch I slipped the negative into the same envelope with the snapshot—much to my later regret—and they were suitably impressed. That night, however, I gave the envelope to a friend, forgetting that the negative was also inside—and would you believe it—the envelope disappeared most mysteriously. If it was only the snapshot, it would have been all right, but as the negative was with it, all was lost. At least I had twelve witnesses who saw both negative and print, so anyone who says I am a liar can call them liars too.

"Of course, I advertised in the newspapers, and even got leaflets printed offering a very good reward, but my 'ghost' picture never turned up. I was interviewed by a newspaper and on radio, and determined to look into the whole matter of recent Irish ghostly appearances and write a book on the subject. The news travelled, and shortly after, I had queries from Stockholm and from Copenhagen seeking to buy the Swedish and Danish rights of the photographs. They were offering sums from £25 to £30, and if I had the photo, I would probably have been the richer by much more, when other newspapers got interested.

"Why were the Danes so interested in a photograph of a 'ghost' from the wilds of Kerry? That story is extremely interesting. According to old Kerry records a Danish ship, the *Golden Lyon,* of the Danish Asiatic Company, en route from Copenhagen to Tranquebar, was wrecked on the strand at Ballyheigue on October 20, 1730. It had been blown off its course by a fierce storm, but the local story was that the Crosbies of Ballyheigue Castle set up false lights on horses' heads to lure the ship ashore. The ship's captain, thinking the bobbing lights ahead from other shipping, kept on course, only to become a wreck on the Atlantic breakers.

"The crew were rescued by Sir Thomas Crosbie and his tenants. Also salvaged were many bottles of Danish wine, clothing, equipment, *and* twelve chests of silver bars and coin. The last was for the purpose of paying for goods and labor in Tranquebar, and was the cause of six people meeting their deaths. Soon afterwards, Sir Thomas Crosbie died suddenly, by poison it was rumored, and his wife, Lady Margaret, claimed a sum of £4,500 for salvage and the loss of her husband. She said it was because of his labors and exertions on the night of the wreck that he died. The ship's master, Captain J. Heitman, opposed the claim indignantly, and moved the twelve chests of silver down into the cellar under the strong tower of the castle. However, delay followed delay, and by June, 1731, he still found he could not get the silver safely to Dublin, and home to Denmark, or on another ship.

"Then one night he was aroused by the sound of many voices outside the castle gates. Jumping up, he was left under no illusions that a raid was in progress. About fifty or sixty men with blackened faces stormed the gates, and attacked the tower. Lady Margaret then arrived and flung herself in front of the captain, saying he would be killed if he ventured outside. Meanwhile, the sentry on the door to the cellar rushed, bleeding from stab wounds, up to his comrades on the first floor of the tower. He told them that his two fellow sentries lay dead outside, and that the mob had disarmed him. As the other Danes had only one musket between them and little ammunition—another bone of contention between Heitman and Lady Margaret—they retreated to the top room of the tower and were spectators to the scene of the twelve chests of silver being loaded on farm carts. Then the shouting stopped and the carts vanished into the night.

"However, within three days, Sir Edward Denny,

the governor of Tralee, had nine men in Tralee gaol. One of the Danes had spotted a nephew of Lady Margaret's in the mob, and it soon became apparent that the whole robbery was planned by friends of the Crosbies. In the dispositions taken before the several trials, a number of the accused stated that four chests of the silver had been laid aside for Lady Margaret. These were never recovered. Lady Margaret denied knowing anything about the affair, and the Danes recovered only £5,000 out of a total of £20,000 in silver. Some of the raiders fled across the Shannon to Clare, others left for France in a fishing boat loaded with silver, while the majority simply went to earth and said nothing.

"Two Crosbies, relatives of Lady Margaret, were tried in Dublin and acquitted, but a third man, named Cantillon, a tenant of the castle Crosbies, was found guilty. One man hanged himself in Tralee gaol and another, who turned state's evidence, was found dead in his lodgings in Dublin. It was said he was poisoned, although the castle put it out that he died of typhoid and drinking too much. And the local tradition handed down the story that most of the gentry of north Kerry were involved. The castle at Ballyheigue was owned by the Cantillons, ancestors of the man found guilty, before the Crosbies arrived in Kerry. They were originally de Cantillons, who came to Ireland with the Norman invaders.

"Pieces of Danish china still exist locally, and in the cellars of Ballyheigue Castle lie some bottles with Danish crests, but of the missing silver there is still no trace. Some of the accused said it was buried in the orchard there, others that it was buried in an orchard three miles away near Banna Strand, and still others that it was buried behind Ballysheen

House. If you enquire today in Ballyheigue, you will surely find someone who will tell you that he knows where it is buried, that he and his forefathers were afraid to dig it up, and maybe he might let you into the secret!

"The Danes are naturally still interested. It would make great copy if the 'ghost' photo was of one of the Danish sailors, and besides there is the lost treasure in silver. Long ago in the time of King Brian Boru, Viking ships of Norsemen and Danes raided Ireland, established the cities of Dublin, Wexford and Waterford, and brought loot back to Scandinavia. It was probably a simple matter for those envious of the Danish silver to persuade the local farmers that the presence of Danish silver in Ballyheigue Castle was a chance to reverse the flow of loot, and besides there was the landlord's wife, who lost her husband saving the shipwrecked Danes. However, the affair of the ghost picture has a more interesting history.

"All these historical details were new to me, and I found it highly interesting to read that swordsmen did indeed flash their swords in the castle. What was almost fantastic, however, was a little detail that almost escaped my notice. Remember, I said I had come on vacation to Ballyheigue in June. I arrived on June 1st. The second week was wild and rainy and it was not possible to take any color pictures in that week. The first week, however, was heat wave weather, with sunshine for 15 hours every day. It was after the week-end of 1st/2nd of June that I began to take the second roll of color film, and I am reasonably certain that the 'ghost' picture was taken on the 4th or 5th of June. Now, the record states that the Danish Silver Raid took place at midnight on June 4, 1731! Coincidence? Or do swords flash in Ballyheigue

Castle on every June 4th when three Danish sailors died?

"You may bet I will be there next June 4th, with camera at the ready. Do I believe in this ghost? Well, it's a good excuse for visiting that charming spot again. Will I be afraid, while waiting there till midnight? Not on your life. I won't be alone, but somehow I don't believe we will see anything at night. The 'ghost' photo was taken in mid-afternoon with the sun slanting through the window from the west. Possibly, what I photographed was an imprint on the wall. But then again, the Danes were there, they were probably wearing seaboots, and there was swordplay there on the 4th of June."

So much for Captain O'Donnell's experience. The irony of losing his negative can be appreciated—for I too guard my psychic photographs, such as those of the ghostly monks at Winchester Cathedral, England, as if they were treasures, which in a way they are.

I made inquiries about the author of the article and was assured his integrity was the highest. As an officer he was not given to imagining things.

We had been visiting Listowel and decided to continue on to Ballyheigue. On the map it seemed an easy hour's ride, but it was almost sundown by the time we rounded the last hill and saw the sparkling sea before us.

Quickly passing through the village, we drove up to the gate of the castle. There was an old gatekeeper in a tiny house nearby and we had no trouble convincing her that we meant the castle no harm. We opened the old gate ourselves and then the car drove up the winding driveway towards the gray castle, the ruins of which loomed large over the landscape. The gentle slopes reaching from its ramparts to the sandy shore were covered by meadowland, which was moist, as so much of Ireland is. On the land were perhaps two dozen cows and many more mementos of their presence.

We avoided the cows and parked the car close to the castle walls. Then I started to film the scene, while our driver ate a belated luncheon. The cows did not seem to bother him.

The castle looked eerie even in the daytime, with its windows staring out into the country like the eyes of a blind man. Inside, the walking was hazardous, for wet soil had long filled in the rooms. The fire that had devoured the castle in 1921 had left nothing of the interior standing, and the totally gutted heart of the once proud house now looked like an ancient Roman ruin. We walked about the many rooms, and Sybil tried to pick up impressions. Naturally, she knew nothing whatever about the place.

Ultimately, we followed her into one of the first-floor rooms looking out to the sea—a room whence one could have easily observed the ships and all that came and went. Here she stopped and listened, as if from within. Her psychic voice was giving her directions and we waited quietly for her words.

"Sybil, what do you think happened here?" I decided to break the silence.

"Whatever happened here," she replied hesitatingly, "certainly happened at a much lower level than the one we're on. I have a feeling that there is an underground passage connected with the sea."

She did not, of course, know about the Danish sailors and how the silver was hidden.

"I don't think I'm going back more than 150

years," she added, "although I know there are influences here going back three hundred years."

I urged her on, as she hesitated.

"This passage leading to the sea, Sybil—who came through it?" I asked.

"The name I have in mind is Donald," she replied. "I have a feeling of three young men, possibly sons, connected with the house, but Donald was not. The house was a large family house, but the people who came through the passage were travellers . . . *seafaring folk.*"

Again I thought, how would Sybil know, consciously, of the Danish sailors coming here for refuge? She could not know this.

"Were they of local origin?" I asked.

"Foreign," she shot back, "probably coming from France. Lots of coming and going here."

"Why had these men come to the house?"

"Some connection with food," Sybil replied, not at all sure of her impression now, "food or something for the table."

"Any tragedy here?"

"Not those coming from France but the people living in the house."

"What happened?"

"There is the influence of a woman, the name is, I think, Emily, but the woman is connected with the house. The tragedy is through the woman. At first I had only the feeling of a man here, but now the woman is very strong."

"A man?"

"Men," Sybil corrected herself, and added: "The name Glen comes to me. The man's fate in the house . . . something to do with the food. Could it be poison? He was eating, when something happened."

One should realize at this point that Sybil had said several things that were pretty close to the true facts. Sir Thomas Crosbie, owner of the castle, was poisoned shortly after the Danish wreck had been salvaged. Was Lady Margaret as guilty of this sudden death as of the "raid" on the Danish silver staged later on?

Also, the raiders eventually fled to France by boat. Had Sybil felt this event somehow? But I wanted to hear more of what my psychic friend had to say here in the ruined drawing room of Ballyheigue Castle.

"I have a feeling of a man going down the passage. I think he was drowned because he disappears in the sea."

"Any fighting here?" I asked.

"I don't feel it now," Sybil said. "The woman is not constant to this house; she comes or goes away. The conflict is between the sea and the house. I think it could be a family feud. There is something else but I am not getting it as clearly as I am getting a foreign influence here."

"Other than French?"

"Also, there is a Northern influence. Many foreign visitors. Beyond Scotland, Sweden. Fair men, Nordic influence. Two periods."

Sybil, of course, knew nothing about the Danish sailors.

Who was Emily? Who was Donald?

Did Captain O'Donnell indeed photograph the Danish silver raid, when the Danish sailors died defending their property in Ballyheigue castle?

Not having examined the photograph, I cannot attest to its genuineness, but I have taken similar pictures elsewhere and know it can be done. Thus I have no reason to doubt the story so movingly told by the Captain.

The silver may still lie somewhere underneath the crumbled walls of the castle. The Danes, as we know, only managed to get a fourth of their treasure out of there in the long run. And there may well be an 18th-century swordsman defending it now as of yore.

It really does not matter. When you stand at the empty windows of Ballyheigue Castle and look out into the bay towards Kerry Head as the sun slowly settles behind the water line, you can well believe that the place is haunted.

As we rode back towards County Clare, it became chilly and the moisture in the air came down as light rain.

Nobody spoke much.

At one point, we almost took a wrong turn in the road, perhaps due to the darkness now settling around us, or perhaps we were all a bit tired.

Ballyheigue Castle had disappeared into the night by now and the Danish silver was safe once more.

Haunted Kilkea Castle, Kildare

FROM A distance, Kilkea Castle looks the very image of an Irish castle. Turreted, gray, proud, sticking up from the landscape with narrow and tall windows which give it a massive and fortified appearance, Kilkea Castle is nevertheless one of the most comfortable tourist hotels in present-day Ireland. Anyone may go there simply by making a reservation with the genial host, Dr. William Cade.

The castle is about an hour and a half by car from Dublin, in the middle of fertile farmlands. There are beautiful walks all around it, and the grounds are filled with brooks, old trees, and meadows—the latter populated by a fairly large number of cows.

Kilkea was built in 1180 by an Anglo-Norman knight named Sir Walter de Riddleford, and it is said to be the oldest inhabited castle in Ireland, although I have seen this claim put forward in regard to several places. Let there be no mistake: the inside has been modified and very little of the original castle remains. But the haunting is still there.

The castle has four floors, not counting cellars and roof. The rooms are of varying sizes and kinds. The haunted area is actually what must have been the servants' quarters at one time, and it is reached through a narrow passage in the northern section of the castle. The room itself is just large enough for one person, and if you should want to sleep in it, you had better make a reservation way ahead of time. All you need to do is ask Dr. Cade for the haunted room. He will understand.

The story of the haunting goes back to the early Middle Ages. Apparently one of the beautiful daughters of an early owner fell in love with a stableboy. Her proud father disapproved and threatened to kill them both if they continued their association. One night, the father found the young man in his daughter's room. In the struggle that followed the boy was killed, but we are not told whether the girl was killed or not. But it is the boy's ghost who apparently still roams the corridors, trying to get his sweetheart back.

In the course of rebuilding, this room became part of the servants' quarters. A number of people have reported uncanny feelings in the area. The owner of Kilkea himself, though skeptical, has admitted to witnessing doors opening by themselves for no apparent reason.

Locally, the so-called Wizard Earl is blamed for the happenings at Kilkea Castle, and there is even a legend about him. Apparently to please his lady fair, the earl transformed himself into a bird and sat on her shoulder. But he had not counted on the presence of the castle cat, who jumped up and ate the bird. The legend continues that the earl and his companions still ride at night and will eventually return from the beyond to "put things right in Ireland"—if that is necessary. The legend does not say what happened to the cat.

The Ghosts at Skryne Castle

ONE FINE day we started out from Dublin aboard one of the Murray cars one rents in Ireland if one doesn't have a car of one's own, and as luck would have it, we had a most pleasant and intelligent driver by the name of Guy Crodder, who understood immediately what we were after.

Passing the airport, we started to look for Mara Castle, a ruin James Reynolds had briefly mentioned in his Irish ghost books as being suspect from the ghost-hunting point of view. The suburban town of Newton-Swords was interesting and charming, but nobody there knew of Mara Castle. Since our schedule for the day was heavy, I decided to go farther north. We took some of the quiet back roads, but our driver had a good sense of direction, and by high noon we had arrived at our first destination.

County Meath is much less forbidding than the West of Ireland we had recently left, and the nearness of the river Boyne gave the land an almost Southern charm. Before us rose majestically the high tower of a ruined church, built in the 14th century and dedicated to St. Colmcille, one of Ireland's three most sacred saints. The tower, sixty feet high on a hill of about 500 feet elevation, dominates the landscape. But it was not this once magnificent church we were seeking out. The much smaller castle of Skryne or Screen, at the foot of the hill, was our goal.

What had brought me here was a brief story in James Reynolds' *More Ghosts in Irish Houses,* published in 1956. He tells of this castle, smallish as castles go, set back of the river Boyne woodlands, not far from Tara, which he visited when it was owned by a relative of the Palmerston family which had long owned the house.

According to Reynolds, the tragedy that led to the haunting at Skryne happened in 1740. At that time the occupants of the house were one Sir Bromley Casway, and his ward, a beautiful young girl by the name of Lilith Palmerston. Lilith had led a sheltered life here and in Dublin, and had had little contact with the world of society or men. During her long stay at Skryne, she met a country squire named Phelim Sellers whose house stood not far from Skryne and whose wife had died mysteriously, possibly as the result of a beating administered by the brutish man.

Lilith Palmerston instantly disliked the neighbor. He in turn became a frequent visitor at Skryne Castle, playing cards with her elderly guardian, but always having an eye for her. On one occasion, Reynolds tells us, Sellers attacked her but was thwarted in his design by the gardener. Now Lilith asked that they return to Dublin to escape the unwanted attentions of this man. Her guardian agreed and all was in readiness for their journey down to the city. The last night before their planned departure, Sellers got wind of Lilith's plans, broke into her room and murdered her. Later caught, he was hanged at Galway City.

A number of persons living at the castle have heard shrieks in the night, and seen a woman in white clutching at her throat run out of the house.

Sellers had killed Lilith by forcing foxglove fronds down her throat, thus strangling her.

So much for Reynolds' vivid account of the tragedy at Skryne Castle.

I had not announced our coming, but we were fortunate in that the castle was open. It so happened that the owners were tossing a wedding breakfast for someone in the area; thus the house was bustling with servants. It was even more fortunate that only the downstairs part of the old house was being used for the festivities, leaving us free to roam the upper stories at will.

The house stood across from a cluster of very old trees, and on the meadow between them a lonely goat tended to her luncheon.

Built in 1172, the castle had fallen into disrepair and was rebuilt in the early 19th century. I walked around the castle, which looked more like an early Victorian country house than a castle, despite its small tower rising above the second story. The house was covered with ivy from one end to the other. The windows were neat and clean and the garden in back of the house seemed orderly.

I managed to talk to one of the caterers in the house, a lady who had come here on many occasions and slept upstairs now and then. She was Kay Collier, and quite willing to talk to me even about so elusive a subject as ghosts.

"I've never noticed anything unusual myself,"

she began, "but there is a tradition about a ghost here. It's a tall man walking around with a stick, wearing a hard hat, and a dog with him. He's been seen outside the castle. Mrs. Reilly, of Skryne, she's seen him."

Since she could not tell us anything more, I made a mental note to look up Mrs. Reilly. Then I asked Sybil, who had been sitting quietly outside under the age-old tree, to join Catherine and me in the upstairs rooms of the castle. The salon to the left of the stairs was elaborately and tastefully furnished in early Victorian style, with mirrors on some of the walls, delicate furniture, couches, sofas and small antiques dressing up the room.

Sybil sat down in one of the comfortable chairs, placed her hand over her eyes and gathered impressions. For a moment, no one spoke. The silence, however peaceful on the surface, was forbidding, and there was, to me at least, an atmosphere of doom hanging rather heavily around us in this room.

"This room immediately attracted me," Sybil said now.

"You know I first turned right, then turned around and came straight to this room instead."

I nodded. She had indeed changed course as if led by some invisible force.

"I feel that this is where a woman has walked," Sybil said slowly, deliberately. "The mirrors have some significance; perhaps there was a door behind the mirror on the right hand side, because she comes from the right. Whether she comes from the garden. . . ."

Was Sybil making contact with the unlucky wraith of Lilith whose favorite spot the garden had been, the same garden where her battered body had been found?

Naturally I had never told her of the tradition surrounding the castle, nor of James Reynolds' account.

"Do you feel her now?" I asked.

"Very slightly," Sybil replied, and looked up. "I don't think that she has been seen for some time. Fifty-eight, fifty-nine. I don't think she has made her presence known for some time, *but she is here.*"

"Can you communicate with her?"

"I'm only conscious of her, but not directly in contact with her. Also, there seem to be two periods, and yet the woman should not be a 'period piece' ghost—and yet she has this link with the past."

"What period do you think she belongs to?"

"I have an early period, of 1624, but the feeling in this room is of a very feminine influence, two periods."

"What did you feel outside the castle?"

"The tree is very important to this house somehow."

"What did you feel by the tree?"

"There I felt conflict. There I felt death. A man. This is the early period. We should go back to the tree, I think."

"Anything else you feel here?"

"I think something happened here in 1959. Perhaps the lady walked. I think you will find a link, something running, not from the house but to the house. That's where the tree comes in. Running from the old place, the church tower to this house—not this house but the one that stood here then."

"Can you describe any figure you see or sense?"

"Here the woman I see has fair hair, arranged in

curls; she belongs to the early 1900s—twenty-two comes up—I keep seeing the number 22. Could be her age. Perhaps she is a descendant of the people in the yard."

"Any names?"

"I have the girl's name . . . there are two names . . . Mathilda, Mary . . . Madeleine . . . *Mathild* . . . something like that. . . ."

Was Sybil referring to Lilith? How close are the sounds of Lilith and Mathild? Was she repeating a whispered name from the faint lips of a long-ago murder victim?

We left the room now and walked to the tree opposite the castle. Here Sybil sat down again and listened to what her psychic sense would tell her. The tree must have been here centuries ago and its twisted, scarred branches must have witnessed a great deal of history.

"What do you get, Sybil?" I finally asked.

"This is connected with the early part of the house. As I see it, the original drive to the house would be just in front of this tree. Coming down the rough driveway I have the distinct feeling of a horseman. Sixteenth century. He is running away from soldiers, running to this house. The soldiers are not Irish. There is a foreign element here."

"Is the one who is running Irish?"

"He is not Irish, either. But he belongs to this area. The soldiers following him have nothing to do with the area. They're alien. This is the remnant of a battle. He is taking refuge, but he does not reach the house."

"What happens to him?" I asked.

"His stomach is injured. The soldiers come down to the house. His body is near this tree. The injury is because of a horse going over him, I think, and he is left here. He dies here—he does not reach the house."

"Is he a soldier or a civilian?"

"I think he is a civilian, but who is to know in these times. . . ."

"Anything about a name, or rank?"

"I only get a foreign name. It's a French-Italian name. Alien to this country although he lives here."

"Is he still here under this chestnut tree?"

"Yes, he is," Sybil replied. "He still has to reach the house; he is not aware that he is dead. He has the feeling he has to get to the house. But he can't do it."

"Does he wish to talk to us?"

"He has someone close to him, not a blood relation, perhaps a brother-in-law, in the house. This is the person he had to go to. Fian . . . F-I-A-N-M-E . . . Fianna. . . ."

"Anything we can do for him?"

"I think that he would have to have some relation here, he has to feel a link. To know that he can go to the house. He is bewildered."

"Tell him the house has changed hands, now belongs to a Mr. Nichols," I said, but Sybil shook her head, indicating the futility of communication at this point.

"It was a much bigger house, much rougher house," Sybil said, and of course the original Skryne castle was all that.

"A much straighter house," Sybil continued to describe what she saw in the past, "with the door more to the right than it is now. The door he is heading for. The little garden was part of the house."

I asked Sybil to reassure the ghost that we would help him.

Sybil told the ghost that he was safe from his pursuers, and not to worry about reaching the house.

"Now he is to my right," Sybil said, and a moment later, "I can't find him now. I can only hear this one word—FIANMA—"

I promised to deliver the message, whatever it meant, for him, and suddenly the ghost was gone.

"He's gone now," Sybil said quietly, "and now the house is gone."

We packed up and started back to the village of Skryne, to look for Mrs. Reilly.

Much later I consulted the material about Skryne and I found some interesting information.

A local historian, the Reverend Gerald Cooney, wrote:

"The ancient name of Skryne was Ochil or Cnoc Ghuile, meaning the Hill of Weeping. Following the death of Cormac mac Airt, who established the *Fianna,* his son Cairbre became Highking. The Fianna rebelled against their king and the battle of Gabhra (Gowra) was fought at the foot of the hill now called Skryne. The Fianna were utterly defeated but Cairbre was killed in the battle."

The Fianna were the partisans of parliamentary government in medieval Ireland. Had Sybil somehow mixed up her centuries and seen a ghost going back to this battle?

We did not have to drive far. Someone pointed Mrs. Reilly's house out to me and I walked down a little country road to her gate. The house was set back behind a well-kept wall, a neat, reasonably modern country house covered by flowers. I rang the bell at the gate and soon enough Mrs. Reilly came out to greet me. She was a spunky lady in her sunny years, and quite willing to tell me all about her ghostly experiences.

"I can't exactly tell you when it happened," she said with a heavy brogue, "but it was a long time ago. I know about it through an uncle of mine, also named Reilly. I'm Kathleen Reilly."

"What is the story then?" I asked. The Irish have a way of telling someone else's story and sometimes a lot gets lost in the transition—or added. I wanted to be sure the account was believable.

"The ghost, well he was a coachman, and he had a dog. He was seen several times about the castle. And then there was a ghost of a nun seen, too."

"A nun?" I asked.

"A long time ago, the castle was a monastery and there was a nun's room."

"Was there ever any battle around here?"

"The battle of Tara," she replied and pointed towards another hill. "That's Tara over there."

"Has anyone ever come from there and taken refuge in the castle?"

"Not that I ever heard of."

She took me up to the house where I could see across the wooded glen to Skryne Castle.

"You see the spire?" she asked. "Well, right underneath is the nun's room."

The room Sybil had felt the woman's presence in, I realized at once.

"Twenty years ago," Mrs. Reilly volunteered, "a man I know by the name of Spiro slept in that room. He saw the nun, and he would never go back into that room."

"Did anyone ever die violently in the castle?"

She was not sure. The house had been in the

same family until twenty-five years ago when the present owner, Nichols, bought it.

"The girls often heard noises . . . the rustling of clothes. . . . I thought I heard footsteps there one night when I was sittin' for the woman who has it now. I did hear footsteps, and there was no one in to my knowledge but myself."

"Where in the house was that?" I asked.

"The part where the nuns are supposed to be there," Mrs. Reilly replied. In other words, the upstairs salon where we had been, which was Lilith's room.

"Have you been there often?"

"Many times. I worked there three years."

"Are you ever afraid?"

"No, I'm not. When I heard the footsteps I was a bit afraid, but it went away."

I thanked Mrs. Reilly and pondered the business about the nuns. Had the witnesses merely drawn on their knowledge of a monastic background of the house to ascribe the rustling of clothes to nuns? Had the figure in a white bed robe seemed like a nun to them? And was it really Lilith's ghost they had encountered?

Puzzle upon puzzle.

Our driver suggested that we drive into the nearby town of Navan, also known in Gaelic as An Uaimh. Here we found a nice restaurant and had a warm meal. The hills of Tara were our next goal, and though I had no reason to suspect a haunting in Ireland's ancient capital, or what was left of it, I nevertheless felt it was a worthwhile excursion. One could always try to see if Sybil got any impressions. Enough mayhem had taken place here over the centuries to create disturbances.

We arrived on the hill where Tara once stood in little more than half an hour. The place is absolutely breathtaking. Except for a hut where a small entrance fee is paid to this national shrine, and a church on a tree-studded hill in the distance, the hill, or rather the hilly plateau, is completely empty. Ancient Tara was built mainly of wood, and not a single building is now above ground.

Here and there a bronze plaque on the ground level indicates where the buildings of the old Irish capital stood. Brian Boru held court here in the 11th century, and after him, the office of Highking fell into disrepute until foreign invaders made Ireland part of their domain.

As we looked around, the wind howled around us with unabating fury. The view was imposing, for one could look into the distance towards Dublin to the south, or towards Drogheda to the north, and see the rolling hills of Eastern Ireland.

"I don't think I have ever been so moved by a place since I was in Pompeii," Sybil said. "The tremendous Druidic influences are still around and I wish this place were kept in a better state so that people could come here and see it as it was."

As an archaeologist, I could only concur with Sybil. The ominous shapes under the soil surely should be excavated. But I learned that only part of the land on which Tara once stood was owned by the nation; a small portion of it was privately owned and therein lies so much of Ireland's trouble: they could not get together to allow for proper excavations, so none took place.

The Haunted Rectory

THE FIRST time I heard of the haunted rectory of Carlingford was when its owner, Ernest McDowell, approached me on the advice of an American friend who knew of my work.

"I own an old rectory which is haunted. If you are interested I will show you over the house with pleasure."

Subsequently, I ascertained that Mr. McDowell was a man of standing and intelligence, and his report was to be taken seriously. I arranged for us to go up to the Dundalk area in late July of 1966. By this time, two editors from the German fashion magazine *Constanze,* Mr. and Mrs. Peter Rober, had decided to join us for a firsthand report on my methods, and also to act as neutral observers and arbiters should my camera yield some supernormal photographs. For this purpose, an elaborate system of safeguards was devised by Mr. Rober. It consisted of his bringing from Hamburg the very sensitive film I normally use for the purpose and personally inserting it in my

Zeiss camera, which he kept in his own possession until we were ready to visit the house in question.

After he had filled the camera with film, he sealed it with string and red sealing wax, so that I could not possibly manipulate the camera or the film inside without breaking the seal. By this method he was in a firm position to attest to the fact that nobody had tampered with my camera and to further attest that if supernormal results were obtained, they had been obtained genuinely and not by fraud. I was happy to oblige the German editors, since an article in that materialistic country, dealing in a positive way with psychic phenomena, would be an important step forward.

The Robers arrived on a hot Saturday evening at Jury's Hotel, and the following morning we set out for Dundalk in one of those huge Princess cars that can seat six comfortably. We arrived at Ballymascanlon Hotel north of Dundalk by lunch time; I had chosen this comfortable inn as our headquarters.

The former Plunkett residence, now fully modernized and really an up-to-date hostelry in every sense of the word, has beginnings going back to the ninth century, although the house itself is only a hundred years old. This area abounds in "giants' tombs" and other pre-Christian relics, and was the center of the Scanlan family for many centuries. Later it belonged to the Cistercian monks of Mellifont, a ruin we had visited the year before when we crossed the river Boyne.

As soon as Mrs. Irene Quinn, the hotel's spunky owner, had settled us into our rooms, we made plans. I put in a telephone call to Ernest McDowell and a pleasant, well-modulated voice answered me on the other end of the line. He was indeed ready for the expedition; within an hour he had driven over from his own home, a farm south of Dundalk called Heynestown, and we sat down in the comfortable lounge of Ballymascanlon Hotel to go over his experiences in detail.

"Let us start with the history of the house, as far as you know it at this moment," I asked McDowell, a pleasant-looking, well-dressed young man in his fortieth year whose profession was that of a painter, although he helped his brother run their farm as required. By and large Ernest McDowell was a gentleman farmer, but more gentleman than farmer, and rather on the shy side.

"The house was built in the seventeenth century," he began. "It was then a private house, a mansion that belonged to the Stannus family, before it was bought by the Church of Ireland for a rectory. The builder of the newer portion was the grandfather of the celebrated Sadler's Wells ballerina Ninette de Valois. I bought it in 1960."

"Have you moved in yet?"

"I haven't really . . . the house is empty, except of course for the ghosts."

"Ah yes," I said. "How large a house is it?"

"Twenty-two rooms in all. Nobody has lived there since I bought it, though."

"When was your first visit to the house, after you had acquired it?"

"I went up there every week to see if it was all right."

"Was it?"

"Well, yes, but one summer afternoon, in 1963—it was early September, I recall—my brother and I were at the rectory. My brother was out cutting corn, and I was mowing the lawn. It was rather a hot evening and I thought I was getting a cold. I was very busy, though, and I just happened to look up, towards the door, when I noticed moving towards the door *a figure of a girl in a red dress.*

"The motor of the lawnmower was not in good repair and it had bothered me, and I was taken aback by what I saw. It was a red velvet dress she wore, and before I could see her face, she just vanished!"

"Did she look solid?"

"Solid."

"Did she cast a shadow?"

"No."

"Did she touch the ground?"

"Yes."

"Did you see her shoes?"

"There wasn't time. I started from the ground up, and the red dress was the first thing I noticed."

"About that face?"

"I couldn't make it out."

"What period would you say the dress belonged to?"

"It was Edwardian, long."

"What did you do after she vanished?"

"I looked towards the gate—the gate that lets you into the grounds from the road—and coming in the gate was a clergyman with a very high collar, and he vanished, too!"

"Do you recall anything else about him?"

"He wore a rather out-of-date outfit, and a hat."

"What time of day was it?"

"About five p.m."

I thought about this ghostly encounter of two restless spirits for a moment, before continuing my questioning of the chief witness.

"Did they react to each other in any way?"

"I should say there was some bond between the two; there was a connection."

"Did you see anything else?"

"No, just the two figures."

"Did your brother see anything?"

"No. But Canon Meissner, who lived at the house for some time, saw the same girl in one of the rooms. She appeared to him on a separate occasion."

"How long ago?"

"About twenty years ago. He described her as a young girl who appeared near his bed and then just disappeared."

"Disconcerting for a Canon, I'd say. What else can you tell me about the haunted rectory?"

"Helen Meissner, his daughter, was in the dining room one night, with the door open, alone, when the other door, on the other end of the room, suddenly started to vibrate as if someone were trying hard to push it open. It opened by itself and the dog with her stood and stared at whatever came through the door, its hackles rising, and then it ran for its life.

"Then, too, Mrs. Meissner, the Canon's wife, and Helen heard footsteps on the backstairs one night. The steps started on the bottom of the stairs and went right up, past them, as they were standing on both sides of the stairs; but they did not see anything. This was about fifteen years ago when Meissner was Rector and lived at the house with his family.

"My sister-in-law, who is very sensitive, went through the house only two weeks ago, and she claimed that the back part of the house gave her a very uncomfortable feeling. She owned a house in Kent, England, that was haunted and we both felt it. I suppose we are both psychic to a degree, since I've on occasion felt things."

"What sort of things?" I asked. I always like to get a full picture of my witnesses to evaluate their testimony. If they have had ghostly experiences prior to the one under investigation, it would indicate mediumistic faculties in them.

"My brother and sister-in-law had bought a house in Kildare and I stayed there one night, and for no reason at all, I sat up in bed from a deep sleep, and I clearly heard both locks on the doors in the room click. But I was quite alone."

"To your knowledge, is there any record of any unhappy incident in this house?" I asked, getting back to the haunted rectory.

"No, it has a very happy atmosphere. Only when I go into it sometime, I feel as if there were people in it, yet it is obviously empty. It seems alive to me. Of course, I have heard footsteps in the corridors when I was quite alone in the house. That was mainly upstairs. It's a passage that runs up one stairway and around the house and down the other staircase. The only thing smacking of tragedy I know of was the coachman losing a child in the gatehouse that burned down, but that was not in the house itself."

"Is there any tradition or popular rumor that might refer to the apparitions of the clergyman and the girl in the red dress?"

"None whatever."

Thus it was that all members of our party had no foreknowledge of any event connected with the haunted house, no names, or anything more than what Ernest McDowell had just told us. Sybil, of course, was nowhere near us at this point, since she was to join us only after the preliminaries had been done with.

The Germans took it all down with their tape

recorders, and it was for their benefit that I made the point of our total "innocence" as far as facts and names were concerned.

"What is the house called now?" I asked.

"Mount Trevor," Mr. McDowell replied. "It was originally built by the Trevors, a very well-known country family. They also built the town of Rostrevor, across Carlingford Lough."

"Are there any chairs in the house now?" I finally asked, since Sybil had to sit down *somewhere* for her trance. McDowell assured me he had thought of it and brought one chair—just one—to the otherwise empty house.

When we arrived at the house after a pleasant drive of about fifteen minutes, Peter Rober gave me back my camera, fully sealed now, and I took pictures at random downstairs and upstairs, and Catherine joined me in taking some shots also, with the same camera.

We entered the grounds, where the grass stood high, and McDowell led us into the house by a side entrance, the only door now in use, although I was immediately impressed that a larger door facing the other way must at one time have existed.

The house is pleasantly situated atop a knoll gently sloping down towards the water of Carlingford Lough, with trees dotting the landscape and sheep grazing under them, giving the place a very peaceful feeling. In back of the house lay a kitchen garden, beyond which the ruined towers of ancient Carlingford Abbey could be seen in the distance. Across the road from the garden gate was the Catholic church house of Carlingford.

The hall was rather small; to the left, the staircase mentioned in the ghostly accounts immediately led to the upper story, while to the right of the door a short passage took us into the large downstairs corner room, where we decided to remain. Large windows all around gave the room sufficient illumination, and there was a fireplace in the rear wall. Next to it stood the lone chair McDowell had mentioned.

Sybil joined us now inside the house and I hurried to get her first clairvoyant impressions as they occurred.

"Something connected with the period of 1836," she said immediately, poking about the rooms. "I have two names . . . as we came in the name *Woodward* came to me, and the other is *Devine or Divine.* Something like that. Peculiar name, I think."

"Please don't analyze it," I warned, "just let it come. *I'll* do the analyzing."

"Woodward and Devine," Sybil repeated. "These names have some meaning in this house. Also, a hall of imprisonment. Someone was imprisoned, I feel."

We followed Sybil, who slowly walked from room to room. Catherine helped me carry the tape recorder and camera, Ernest McDowell following behind looking excited, and three friends of his whose presence he felt might be useful. They were two ladies sharing a house at Ardee, both of them very psychic. Mrs. Bay John and Pat MacAllister had brought a young ward named Julian with them. I secretly hoped there weren't any *poltergeists* lurking about under the circumstances!

Later, Mrs. MacAllister mentioned seeing a face as if etched onto the wall in the very room upstairs where I took some psychic pictures, though of course I did not know they would turn out to be unusual at the time I took them. I never know these things beforehand.

We were still on the ground floor and Sybil was investigating the rear section, the oldest part of the house. There were some iron bars outside the window of the rather dank room, giving it a very heavy prison-like feeling. It was the original kitchen area.

"Someone was *made to* stay upstairs," Sybil said now, "and I have gooseflesh on my forearms now." We walked up the stairs and I confirmed the latter observation.

Finally we found ourselves in a room about the middle of the upper story, and Sybil came to a halt.

"I feel I want to run away from this room," she observed. "It's a panic-stricken feeling. Someone wants to get away from here; the name Devine comes again here. Someone is hiding here, and then there is imprisonment. Is there a prison somewhere here? Several people are held. This is away from the house, however."

"Is there a presence here?" I asked as I always do when we are at the center of uncanny activities.

"Yes, several. The period is 1836. The strongest presence is someone in brown. A man. There is a connection with business. There are three people here, but of the same period. There is no overlapping of periods here. The main person hiding in this room or forcibly kept here went from here and was hanged, with other people. This was a man. Perhaps we should go downstairs now."

We followed Sybil's advice and repaired to the downstairs parlor.

"Father Devine . . . should not have left the church for business," Sybil suddenly mumbled. "Someone says that about him. I feel him around, though."

Now I placed Sybil in the one chair we had and

the rest of us formed a circle around her as best we could. It was about the same time, five o'clock, as the time of the haunting and I was prepared for *anything.*

Presently, Sybil showed all signs of deep trance. My German friends were riveted to the floor, Mrs. Rober clutching the microphone and Mr. Rober taking dozens of pictures with his Rolleiflex camera. The tension mounted as Sybil's lips started to move, though no word came at first through them. Gradually, I coaxed the spirit to take firmer possession of my medium's body and to confide in us who had come as friends.

"Who are you?" I said softly. The voice now emanating from Sybil was hesitant and weak, not at all like Sybil's normal voice.

"Aileen," the voice murmured.

I could hardly hear her, but my tape recorder picked up every breath.

"Aileen Woodward," the ghost said.

"Is this your house?"

"We live here . . . where is he? Where is he? Robert!"

"Whom are you seeking?"

"Devaine . . . Robert Devaine . . . speak slightly . . . my husband . . . be quiet . . . where is he?"

I wondered if she wanted me to keep my voice down so that I would not give her away to some pursuers.

"Where is Robert?" I asked, trying to reverse the line of questioning.

"Where is he, where is he?" she cried instead, becoming more and more upset and the tears, real tears, streaming down Sybil's usually tranquil face.

I calmed her as best I could, promising to help her find Robert, if I could.

"When did you first come to this house?" I asked quietly, while the sobbing continued.

The faces around me showed the great emotions that seemed to have been transferred from the ghostly girl to the witnesses. Not a word was spoken.

At this point, the tape had to be turned over. Unfortunately, it slipped out of our hands and it was several seconds before I started to record again. During those moments I tried to explore her family connections more fully.

Who was Robert and who were his people? Who was Robert's father?

"In the Church," she replied, quieter now.

"Does he like you?" I wanted to know.

There was a moment of quiet reflection before she answered.

"No."

"Why not?"

"The Church must not marry!"

"Is Robert a priest?"

"Shhh!" she said quickly. "Don't speak!"

"I don't quite understand . . . how does religion enter the picture?"

"Changer," she mumbled, indicating that someone had changed his faith.

"Are you and Robert of the same religion?" I now asked.

"Don't ask it."

"Are you Catholic?"

Utter silence was my answer.

I pleaded with her for more information so I could help her locate Robert. In vain; she would not budge on this question. Finally, she confused me with her enemies.

"You took him . . . I'm going for a walk now . . . follow . . . down the hill . . . just a walk . . . to see if he comes. . . ."

"If I get you to see Robert again, will you promise to do as I tell you?" I asked.

"I promise nothing," the frightened ghost replied. "You betray him . . . how do I know you're a friend?"

"You have to trust me if I am to help you."

"I don't trust."

Now I gently told her the truth about herself, the time that had come and gone since 1836 and why she could not stay on in this house.

"Don't speak so loud . . . you drive me mad . . . I'm going for a walk in the garden . . ." she said, trying to ignore the light of truth piercing her self-inflicted prison. But it did not work. The door of reality had been opened to her. In a moment she was gone.

Sybil reopened her eyes, confused at first as to where she was. I then asked her to take some fresh air outside the house, since the rain that had come down during part of our séance had now stopped and the countryside was back to its glorious Irish freshness.

With Sybil outside, I turned once more to the owner of the house and asked whether he had ever heard the names Woodward, Aileen, and Devine or Devaine before in connection with the house or area.

"The only thing I know is that Canon Meissner told me that this house was once occupied by a French family named Devine. Since Canon Meissner had the house from 1935 onward, this must have been before his time."

"The girl speaks of a clergyman, and you saw a clergyman ghost, is that correct?"

"Yes," McDowell nodded, "but he wore black, not brown."

In the time we had lost through the tape change, the ghost had described herself as 16 years of age, wearing a red dress, and the dates 1836 and 1846 both were given. Sybil, of course, had no knowledge of McDowell's experience with the girl in the red velvet dress.

I asked Mr. McDowell to look in the local records for confirmation of some of the names and information that had come through the medium. Offhand, none of it was known to those present, so that confirmation would have to await further research.

We returned to Ballymascanlon Hotel, where the eager German journalist had made an appointment with a local photographer so that he could get my films developed while we were still on location, and if there was anything on the negatives that had not been visible to the naked eye, one could make immediate use of the information. I never anticipated anything of this sort, but one can't know these things in advance either. As it turned out, there *were* two pictures in the batch, taken by Catherine and me with my sealed camera, that showed the same mirror-like effects I had observed on the photographs taken in June Havoc's haunted townhouse in New York and in the haunted trailer of Rita Atlanta, near Boston. Wherever there is present in a room a haunted area, represented by a magnetic field or a coldspot sometimes, such an area occasionally shows up on film with mirror-like effects; that is, reflections of objects in the room occur that could not have occurred under ordinary conditions, there being no mirror or other reflecting surface near.

Peter Rober was clearly elated, showing his pleasure about as much as his North German nature permitted him to. There was still another picture that represented a puzzle to us: in the haunted room upstairs where Helen Meissner had seen the door open by its own volition, Catherine took a picture in what seemed to both of us an empty room. We clearly recall that the doors were both shut. Yet, to our amazement, on the picture the door to the left is quite plainly ajar!

Ernest McDowell suggested we talk to the Meissners firsthand, and the following morning, Mr. and Mrs. Rober and I drove across the border to Northern Ireland, where the Meissners now live in a little town called Warrenpoint.

Mrs. Meissner turned out to be a friendly, talkative lady who readily agreed to tell us what had happened to them during their tenancy at the rectory.

"We lived there twenty-five years, and we left the house in 1960," she began her recollections. "We did not notice anything unusual about the house at first, perhaps because we were so glad to get the house.

"Part of the house was almost Queen Anne period, the rest Georgian. We had two indoor maids and we took our gardener with us, too. Everybody was happy. We did lots of entertaining and life was very pleasant. Then I noticed that local people never came to the rectory *in the evening.* They always made an excuse. Finally, I was informed that there was a ghost in the house. It was supposed to have been the ghost of a sea captain who lived here originally and was lost at sea. The older portion of the house was where he had lived, they said. I never was able to find out anything more than that about this sea captain, however. I was a skeptic myself and went gaily about my business. Then summer came, and I used to be outdoors as late as one could. Several evenings, *something white* passed me, something big, and yet I never heard a sound. I thought this very strange, of course, and wondered if it was a white owl. But there was no sound of wings. Gradually I got to rather expect this phenomenon."

"Any particular time of day?" I interjected.

"At dusk. Outside. And then I saw it from the window. But it had no form, yet I knew it was white. I saw it often, and never a sound."

"After that, did you have any further adventures in the house?" I asked.

"We had a visit from the sister of Ninette de Valois, and she was very interested in the house because it was an ancestor of hers who had owned it. He was a Colonel Stannus. At the same time we had another visitor, a young man from Dublin. The lady and her husband had come rather late in the evening; they were staying at Rostrevor Hotel, and they wanted to see over Carlingford Rectory, and we thought it was rather late in the evening for that, so we asked them to come the next day. At that time the young man from Dublin was here also, but he and the lady had never met.

"When he looked at the lady, he became suddenly white as a sheet. I wondered if he was ill, but he said no, so we moved on to a room that we always regarded as a guest room. The young man from Dublin had often stayed in that room before. But when we entered the room, the lady exclaimed that she had been in that room before! Of course she hadn't.

"The young fellow from Dublin still looked very shaken, so I took him downstairs to one side and said, 'What is wrong with you?'

"Finally he told me.

" 'It's the most extraordinary thing,' he said to me. 'That lady is the ghost.'

" 'What ghost?' I asked.

" 'Often when I slept in that room,' he explained, 'I have been awakened by the feeling of a presence in the room. When I looked up, I saw the face of that lady!'

"What struck me as odd was that he felt something strange immediately upon meeting her and she felt something equally strange about having been to that room before when in fact she hadn't.

"Later, at tea, she asked me if I believed in the transmigration of souls."

The young man, whose name is Ronny Musgrave, evidently was reminded by the lady's appearance of the ghost's, I felt, but that would still not explain *her* reaction to the room, unless she had clairvoyantly foreseen her trip to Carlingford and was now realizing it!

"I've spent so much time in that house," Mrs. Meissner continued, "but I never felt I was alone. My husband's experience was different from mine. He had fallen asleep. He awoke, feeling that there was someone in the room. He thought it was an evil presence and he made the sign of the cross. Then it disappeared. I always thought the presence was female. I've heard footsteps, too. But I never feared this ghost. To me, it was pleasant."

I tried to piece together the past history of the house. Prior to 1932 when the Meissners moved in, there was a rector named Aughmuty there; before that the Reverend Bluett, before him his father-in-law, a Mr. Mailer, and that brings us back to the 19th century, when the Stannus family owned the place. It was just a private house then.

Mrs. Meissner did not recognize any of the names obtained during the trance, incidentally.

While she went to fetch her octogenarian husband to supplement some of the data for us, I had a talk with the daughter, now the widowed Mrs. Thompson, who had come over to the house to see us.

"We had a cocker spaniel," she began, "and the dog was with me in that upstairs room. There was a big mirror there then, and as I looked into it, I saw the door at the far end of the room open by itself, and then close again slowly. The dog got up and snarled and growled, but I saw nothing. That was the only experience that I had, but it was enough for me."

Canon Meissner is a lively and kind man who readily answered my questions as best he knew. None of the names rang a bell with him, as far as churchmen were concerned, and as for private origins, he did not really have the sources in his library. He recommended we take it up with Trinity College in Dublin where there are extensive records. The house had become a rectory about 1870 or 1871, he explained, and was directly purchased from the Stannus family at that time. They had built the newer part onto the already existing old portion.

I started to examine the two heavy books the Canon had brought with him from his study.

No Devine or Devaine showed up in the lists of rectors of Carlingford.

In *The Alumni of Trinity College,* London,

Williams and Norgate, 1924, on page 227, column 1, I found the following entry:

> Devine, Charles, admitted to Trinity, November 4, 1822, age 20 [thus born 1802]; son of John Devine, born County Louth.

That, of course, was the right area, for Carlingford was at that time the principal town in the county.

I further found a listing of "Robert Woodward, graduated Trinity, November 5, 1821, aged 16, son of Henry Woodward. M.A. 1832," on page 94 of the same work.

It seemed extraordinary that we had located two names given in trance by Sybil Leek, and that both names were of the right period claimed and in the right location. But the search was far from finished.

While I was trying to get some corroboration from the local librarian at Dundalk—without success—the German editors packed up and left for Hamburg. I left instructions with Ernest McDowell as to what I needed, and then the three of us, my wife and I and Sybil, went on to the western part of Ireland. There we parted company and Sybil went to her home in the south of England while we returned to New York.

On August 2, 1966, Sybil had a trance-like dream at her house at Ringwood, Hants. In this dream state she saw herself walking back and forth between the rectory and the ruined abbey. There was a girl who had come from some other place and had been waiting a long time for a man to join her. He had been in India. The girl was terribly upset and said that she had married the man but it was not legal and she had to find a Catholic priest to marry them because the whole thing was making her ill. He did not want to be married by a priest because he was a Protestant and his family would cut him off without any money.

He had left her because of her insistence on being married again, but she loved him and wanted to persuade him to agree to being married by a priest. She had been in England, and he told her to come to Ireland to Carlingford, where he could meet her, but he had not turned up. She had to find a priest who would keep the marriage secret, and this was not easy, as everyone said the marriage had to be written down in a book.

The girl claimed that "everything" could be found in the *Yelverton papers* in Dublin. Sybil was sure there was a Court case called the Yelverton case about the 1840–1850 period. But then things in the dream-like state got a bit confused as she found herself drifting in and out of the house, sometimes walking to the Abbey, talking to a priest, then back to the house, which at that time seemed furnished; and the gateway Sybil saw at the back of the house, not where it is now. The girl seemed to be staying with friends; she did not live at Carlingford permanently and indeed went on from there.

That was on August 2nd; on the third, Sybil again "dreamt" exactly the same sequence, which again culminated in the search for the Yelverton case papers. But the dream was more vivid this time; in the morning Sybil found that she had gotten up in the middle of the night, taken off her nightgown and put on a long evening dress, and then gone back to bed in it. She had the distinct feeling of wearing the same kind of clothes this girl wore in the 1840s. The girl said in all her moving around she could not get the right clothes to be married in and would have to buy more. The girl seemed to have an accent and spoke Italian and French in between a lot of crying and sniffling, and she seemed familiar to Sybil.

The latter was only too logical, since Sybil had been her instrument of communication, but we had not until now discussed the details of the case or her trance with Sybil; consequently she could not have known about the religious problem, for instance.

That was a monumental week for this case, for on the following day, and quite independently of Sybil's impressions, Ernest McDowell had come across the needed corroboration in a rare local chronicle. In a work entitled *County Families of the United Kingdom, 1800,* the family named Woodhouse, of Omeath Park, near Carlingford, was listed.

Omeath is the next village after Carlingford and quite close to it.

John Woodhouse, born October 6, 1804, married to Mary Burleigh, June 10, 1834; nine children, the fourth of which was Adeline Elizabeth. Now the Irish would pronounce Adeline rather like Ad'lin, and what I had heard from Sybil's entranced lips sounded indeed like A'lin, or Ad'lin!

The Woodhouse family claimed descent from the Woodhouses of Norfolk, England; thus Sybil's reference to the girl having been to England might fit. Perhaps she had gone to visit relatives.

Further in the same source, there is a listing also for the family Woodward of Drumbarrow. A Robert Woodward, born June 20, 1805, is given, whose father was Henry Woodward. Robert Woodward, according to the source, married one Esther Woodward and had two sons and three daughters. This marriage took place in 1835. This is the same man also listed in the register of Trinity College.

The similarity of the names Woodward and Woodhouse may have been confusing to the ghostly girl. One was presumably her maiden name and the other that of her husband's family.

Unfortunately, we don't have the birth dates for Adeline. But if her father was married only in 1834, she could not very well have married Robert in 1836 or even 1846. If she was sixteen at the time as she claimed in trance, and if she had been born somewhere between 1835 and 1845, we get to the period of around 1850–1860 as the time in which her tragic liaison with Robert might have taken place. But this is speculation.

What we do know concretely is this: nobody, including Sybil Leek, ever heard of a man named Devine, a girl named Adeline Woodhouse, a man named Robert Woodward, before this investigation took place. These names were not in anyone's unconscious mind at the time of our visit to Carlingford Rectory. Yet these people existed in the very area in which we had been and at the approximate time when the ghost had been active there in her lifetime. How can that be explained by any other reasoning than true communication with a restless departed soul?

What were the relationships between the girl in the red velvet dress and her Robert, and how did the father fit into this and which one was the clergyman? Was Devine the clergyman who destroyed their marriage or did he help them? It seems to me that it is his ghost Ernest McDowell observed. Is there a feeling of guilt present that kept him in these surroundings perhaps?

At any rate, the rectory has been quiet ever since

our visit and Ernest McDowell is thinking of moving in soon. That is, if we don't buy the place from him. For the peaceful setting is tempting and the chance of ever encountering the girl in the red velvet dress, slim. Not that any of us would have minded.

Ghost Hunting in County Mayo

ROSS HOUSE stands on a bluff looking directly out into Clew Bay, halfway between Westport and Newport, and in about as nice a position as anyone would wish. From its windows you can see the many islands dotting the bay, one of which is part of the demesne of the house, and the lush green park in back of the house gives a nice contrast to the salty clime of the frontal portion. All in all, it is a house worthy of its owner, Major M. J. Blackwell, retired officer formerly in the British Army and nowadays in business in Chicago, U.S.A., as the second, but by no means minor, half of the celebrated firm of Crosse & Blackwell.

I shan't tell you how to get to Ross House, for it is not easy, what with Western Irish roads, but then there is no need to go there unless you're invited, is there?—and that might well be, for the Major is hospitality personified and his house always rings with the laughter of young relatives and their friends come over for a holiday.

The house itself is exquisitely furnished in both

its stories, the rooms being large and modern, for the house it not too ancient; the broad Georgian staircase is a masterpiece unto itself, and, as I found out later, it also attracted one of the resident ghosts frequently. But about this in good time.

I first heard about Ross House from the Major's young nephew, Edwin Stanley, an American living in New Jersey. Mr. Stanley had read my books and thought it might be worth my while to visit the house. Subsequently Major Blackwell himself invited us to come. We finally made it, driving up from Leenane, where we were staying.

As soon as we had met the brood of youngsters assembled in the house, and the two baby cats, I repaired with the Major to his study upstairs, where we could get down to *ghost* business.

"Let's talk about the house first," I began. "When was it built?"

"It is a Georgian house as you can see, but prior to that, there had been another house here of which we are not quite certain, to the back of the present house. It is on the oldest maps. I inherited it from my mother, and it goes back in her family for quite a long time. My mother's side of the family has proven its descent from 779 A.D., but they even have good claims all the way back to 365 A.D."

"That's about the oldest family tree I've heard of," I said, "even counting my wife's, which goes back to the 800s. You yourself, were you born here?"

"No, I was born in England, but I spent most of my childhood here, always loved the place, the boats, the people. Five years ago I inherited the place from my mother. When I'm not here, I live outside of Chicago."

I asked the Major what his mother's family name

was and it turned out to be O'Malley—the famous O'Malley clan of which Grania O'Malley, the pirate queen of the 16th century, was not its greatest but certainly its best-known member. Then a sudden impulse struck me. During lunch, which we had had in the big downstairs room to the right of the entrance door, Sybil had slipped me a piece of paper, murmuring that it was something that had "come" to her. The name rang a bell and I pulled it out of my pocket now.

Scribbled on it were the words "Timothy . . . Mother . . . O'Malley." There was, of course, a mother O'Malley—the Major's own!

"During the times you've been here, Major," I continued now, "have you ever noticed anything unusual?"

The Major nodded. "About six years ago, the following happened. I was asleep in my room upstairs, when suddenly I woke up; at the end of my bed I saw standing an old maidservant; Annie O'Flynn was her name—she had been a maid of my grandmother's.

"I was completely lucid now, having gone to bed at a normal time the night before. My talking to this ghost woke my wife up, and I pointed her out to my wife, saying—'Look, Annie O'Flynn is here, and she's got a friend with her,' for there was another woman with the maid. When I said this, the ghostly maid smiled at me, apparently happy at being recognized. My wife did not see them, but she can attest to the fact that I was fully awake at the time."

"Amazing," I conceded. "What did you do about it?"

"Well, the next morning I went down to talk to Tommy Moran, an old man who works for us and knows a great deal about the people here, and after I described the other ghost to him he was able to identify her as a local friend of Annie's who had passed on also."

"Was that the first time in your life that you've had a psychic experience?"

"Oh no; for instance when I was in the South of France, where I was brought up, I was going up to see some friends who lived just above Nice, and I was with a friend. We had sat down for a moment on a bridge leading into this chateau when we heard the sound of horses and a coach going at full speed. I said to my friend, let's get out of the way because someone's coach has run away! But the noise just went past us and continued on, no coach, no horses! So we continued to our friend Col. Zane's house. When we told him of our experience he laughed. 'That's nothing, really,' he explained. 'That goes on all the time there. It's a ghost coach.' "

"Any other incidents?" I asked with expectation. Obviously, Major Blackwell was gifted with the sixth sense.

"The only other one was here when I dug up the tomb of Dermot MacGrania." Grania is Irish for grace, incidentally, and it is pronounced more like "gronia."

"I've seen the monolith outside the house, down towards the back end of the estate," I said. "What's the story of that tomb?"

"I started to dig, because I am terribly interested in archaeology. One night I dreamt that I was working on it, as usual, when the stone moved and out from under the stone came this extraordinary figure who was dressed in a kilt and leggings around his feet, and he advanced towards me and I was never so frightened in my life. I couldn't get to sleep at all, and the next morning I went down to the pier, because the two men who had been working on the diggings with me lived across the water and came over by boat.

"Before they landed, they told me immediately, 'We're very, very sorry, but we will not do any more work on the tomb of Dermot MacGrania!'

"Evidently, they too had been frightened off. I have not touched it since then, and that was thirty years ago. I won't permit any digging at the tomb, unless it is for the *good* of it—for I feel that at the time I was not looking into it for that reason, but rather in the hope of finding treasure, and that is why I was stopped."

"This tomb is a pre-Christian relic, is it not?" I asked after a moment of pensive contemplation. Suddenly the 20th century was gone and the very dawn of history was upon us.

"Similar graves exist up in County Sligo. According to the legend told about this particular grave, when Dermot escaped with Grania, they were caught here and killed and buried here by his enemies. That was about 1500 B.C. This is, of course, the very beginning of Irish history."

"Has anyone else had any unusual experience at this tomb?"

"None that I know of. But there have been psychic experiences in the house itself."

I settled back in the comfortable leather chair in the Major's study and listened as Major Blackwell calmly unfolded the record of ghosts at beautiful Ross House.

"Miss Linda Carvel, a cousin of mine, has seen the old maid walking up and down and my wife and I have heard someone walking up and down where the original stairs used to be."

The Major showed me the spot where the wall now covered the stair landing. Only the main staircase exists today.

The former staircase was at the front of the house but structural changes had made it unnecessary.

"My wife has heard it at least four or five times a week. She has also heard the door knocked on."

"Almost like a maidservant," I observed.

"Did anyone *see* the maid?"

"Yes, Linda Carvel actually saw her walking into that front room. This was only two years ago. Everybody had gone to church, and there was nobody in the house at the time except my wife, myself, my daughter and Linda. Linda suddenly came into the room to us, white as a sheet. 'I just saw a woman walk into Granny's room,' she said. 'She was dressed in a white and blue uniform—a starched uniform.' I discussed this with Tommy Moran and he confirmed that that was the uniform the maids wore in my grandmother's time!"

"What do you make of it, Major?"

"I think it is the same one, Annie, who came to see me. She died a normal death, but she was fantastically attached to the family and the house. She spent her whole life here. She married a man named John O'Flynn, a tailor, but she adored it here and even after she left she came back all the time bringing us gifts."

"Have any other phenomena been observed here?"

"In the drawing room, downstairs, Tommy Moran and all his sons have seen two people sitting in front of the fireplace. I know nothing about them firsthand, however. My cousin, Peter O'Malley, also has seen them. He is the one also who had a shocking experience. He saw the most terrible face appear in the window of the drawing room."

"What exactly did he see?" I was all ears now. The whole atmosphere seemed loaded with electricity.

"I wasn't here at the time, but he just says it was a most terrible face. That was ten years ago."

"What about Inishdaff Island, Major?" I asked.

"There is an old monastery there I hope to restore. We've got the records back to 1400 and there it says 'church in ruins.' The peninsula we are on now, where the house stands, also turns into an island at high tide, incidentally, and the path of the pilgrims going over to that ruined church can still be traced. The road would not have been built for any other reason."

"You didn't see anything unusual on the island, though?"

"No, I didn't, but Tommy Moran, and some other relative of mine—actually four people altogether—did. The island has always been considered . . . that there is *something wrong with it.*"

We got to talking about the other members of the family now; Mrs. Blackwell had been unable to join us at lunch since she was staying at Castlebar with their fourteen-year-old daughter, who was in the hospital there because of a broken leg. It appeared, however, that there was more to that accident than a casual mishap.

"The extraordinary thing about it is this. The night before it happened, she dreamt that an ambulance drove up to the *front* of the house. Now the front of the house is blocked off to cars, as you saw. So every car must come through the *back*. She saw the ambulance come to the front entrance, however, pick *someone* up and drive off. Also, the ambulance did not have a red cross or other familiar sign on it, but a circular thing in Irish writing! That was exactly the ambulance that came up the next evening and picked *her* up; it was a Volkswagen ambulance with an Irish inscription on the side in a circle just as she had described it to us! Edie is definitely psychic also."

"So it seems," I said. "Anything else about her I might want to know?"

"One time she dreamt she saw Grandmother—my mother—and described her perfectly in every detail. Being terrified of ghosts, Edie, in her dream, pleaded with my mother's apparition not ever to have to see a ghost again. Granny promised her she wouldn't, but she would always *know*."

There were two more points of psychic interest, I discovered. The unexplained putting on of lights and opening of doors in the nursery, and something else that I only learned towards the end of our most enjoyable stay. But in a way it made a perfect finale.

Right now everybody was handed heavy clothing and overshoes, for we would be sailing—well, motorboating—to the island across the bay and it was wet and chilly, the Major assured us. Cathy looked like a real outdoor girl in the Major's fur jacket, and Sybil was so heavily bundled up she scarcely made the entrance to the cabin of the little boat. The assorted cousins of both sexes also came along in a second boat, and within minutes we were out in the open bay crossing over to the island of Inishdaff, all of which belonged to the Major's estate.

We landed on the island ten minutes later. The

sandy beach was most inviting to a swim and Major Blackwell admitted he was working on just such a project. What with the absence of sharks, I felt this to be about the most ideal place to swim in any ocean.

We next scaled the heights of the hill, taking the center of the island, upon which stood the ruined abbey. It was at once clear to me that we were standing close to the roof of that church and that the lower part had simply filled in with soil over the centuries. In one corner of the "elevated floor" was the simple grave of one of Tommy Moran's sons, a Celtic cross watching over him. Otherwise the island was empty.

While the others stood around the ruined abbey, Major Blackwell, Tommy and I mounted the other side of the wall and then descended onto the wet ground. We then proceeded to the top of the island whence we had a magnificent view of all the other islands around us, all the way out to the farthest, which indeed was Ireland's outpost to the sea, beyond which lay America. It was among these many islands and inlets that the pirates of old hid, safe from prosecution by the law.

We fetched some heavy stones from the enclosure of the church and sat down so that Tommy Moran could talk to me about his experiences.

I first questioned him about the frightening face seen here and in the house.

"Mike Sheils told it to me, sir," Tommy Moran began with a heavy brogue. "He worked the glass house with me for years. He was a man not easily frightened. At the time there were blackthorn trees in the burial ground. He was passing through when he heard some noise. He looked over his shoulder and what he saw was a sheep's head with a human body."

"No," I said.

"Yes, sir," Tommy nodded, "it was a head covered with wool the same as sheep. There were three boys in front of Mike. He knocked them down and ran."

"Did you yourself ever have any such experiences here, Tommy?" I reflected that a disheveled human face might very well look like a sheep's head to a simple, imaginative islander used to lots of sheep.

"During me own time, sir," he began, "they were bringing torf to Ross House by boat, that was Mrs. O'Malley's husband, who was gettin' the torf, and they were rowing, two of them, but they had no sail. They wanted to keep as close to the shore as they could. They were brother and sister, Pat Stanton and his sister Bridget. Suddenly a man came down from the burial ground trying to grasp his oar and take it out of the water. Pat rowed like mad to get away; he recalls the man was stark naked, had no clothes on at all. Finally, they got away."

"There was no one living here at the time?"

"No one, no," Tommy assured me, and the Major nodded assent.

I was fascinated by the old man's tales. Surely, Tommy could not have made them up, for what he had said did make some sense when matched with the horrible face looking into the dining room window. Somewhere along the line a human being living like an animal must have found shelter on the desolate island, and, perhaps brought up by animals, this man was taken for a monster. I did not feel that this was a ghost in the sense I use the term.

Tommy told us other tales, some bordering just barely on the supernormal, and then we rejoined the others and went back to the house. It was time for me to question Sybil Leek about her impressions of the church and burial ground.

"There were impressions, but not a presence as we understand it, Hans," Sybil explained, "but I strongly urge that the place be excavated, for there might be some works of art underneath. There is also a passage, which we discovered this afternoon, on the right hand side. The high altar connecting with the first monastic cell."

We had returned now to the house, and took off the heavy clothing the Major had lent us for the journey. While tea was being prepared, we grouped ourselves around the fireplace, waiting.

It was then that I recalled a chance remark Sybil had made to me earlier about a man she had met when we first came to the house, prior to lunch. Perhaps we could sort this out now, before Tommy Moran left for his chores.

"I left the main party in the house for a while, because I wanted to be on my own," Sybil explained, "so I walked through the path leading to the wrought iron gate which led into a garden. I walked right down as far as I could go, until I came to an open space which was on the other side of the garden to where I had started. I reached the tomb. I stayed by the tomb for a little while, then I went toward the gate, ready to climb over the gate, and I was in deep thought. So I wasn't surprised to see a man there. To me he looked rather small, but of course I was on higher ground than he was. He wore no hat, but he had peculiar hair, gray hair."

"What did he do when he saw you?"

"He smiled at me, and appeared to come towards me. I was continuing to walk towards him. He said, 'So you have come back again?' and I replied, 'But I haven't been here. I don't know this place.' He turned and walked towards the sea and I turned away and went back."

"Did he look like a ghost to you?"

"You know I never know what a ghost looks like. To me, everything seems the same. I have this difficulty of distinguishing between flesh-and-blood and ghosts."

When I informed Major Blackwell of Sybil's encounter, he was taken aback and said: "My God, she's seen the other one—she's seen the Sea Captain!"

It turned out that there was another ghost he had not told us about when we talked about the house. Sybil, he felt, had not made contact with the ghostly maidservant—perhaps she had found a more permanent niche by now—but somehow had picked up the scent of the ghostly seaman.

I questioned Tommy Moran, who at seventy-five knew the place better than any other person, what this sea captain business was all about.

"I don't know his name, sir," Tommy said, "but he was in the house about a hundred years ago. He bought this place and he thought so much about it, he went out to England to bring back his wife and family. He said when he was gone that he would come back, dead or alive!

"He died at sea, and he has since been seen by many, always in daylight, always smoking a cigar; Mike Sheils saw him sittin' in the drawing room once. Several people saw him on the stairway and he always just disappeared. One of my sons saw him and it frightened him. He had no hat, but always this cigar. Very black hair, as tall as you are, sir, according to Mike Sheils."

There you have it, a sea captain *without his cap* but with a cigar! On recollection, Sybil was not sure whether she heard him say, "So you've come back again" or "See, I've come back again."

The Lovers of Carlingford

CARLINGFORD CASTLE and Abbey—or what's left of them, which isn't very much except ruins—stand near the shore of Lough Carlingford in northeastern Ireland, facing England across the sea in one direction, and Northern Ireland in the other. The sea can be quite rough at times in this bay, and there is a certain romantic wildness to the scenery even in the summer. Walking amidst the ruins of what was once an imposing castle and abbey, one gets the feeling of time standing still and also sometimes of an eerie presence. James Reynolds in *More Ghosts in Irish Houses,* reports how an English traveler, who was totally unaware of the haunting reported in these ruins, saw a shadowy figure of a woman and of a man standing in what was once a chapel, only to merge and disappear into the night.

When I visited the ruins of Carlingford with Sybil Leek, she too felt the presence of something unearthly—but to her these ghosts were not frightening or unhappy. Rather she felt a kind of love imprint from the past, something that came and went but somehow was tied to these rocks.

There is a small piece of land between the ruins and the sea, and a road leading down toward it. From the ruined wall of Carlingford all the way down to the shore seems to be the haunted area, or at any rate the area most likely to give a sensitive person the feeling of a presence.

What is left of Carlingford Castle and Abbey is nothing more than a few stone walls without roofs, and a few impressive arches and glassless windows. What was once the chapel, however, is fairly well preserved even though it has neither roof nor floor, nor in fact anything whatsoever to worship by. The niche above the altar is now empty, but it contained a statue of the Virgin at one time.

Who then are the ghostly figures seen by the English tourist? In the first part of the fifteenth century a lady pirate by the name of Henrietta Travescant, after giving up the sea, retired to Carlingford Abbey to serve as its head. Her ship in her active pirate days had been called *The Black Abbess,* so she took the same name when she became the resident abbess of Carlingford.

Perhaps what had prompted her to give up her cherished sea was not only her patriotic desire to give her ship to King Henry V, whom she supported, to serve in his war against France, but also her unhappiness at the loss of her beloved Nevin O'Neill, whom the cruel sea had taken during one of their expeditions.

According to the legend as told by James Reynolds, the years passed by and soon the Black Abbess found herself practically alone in the rambling and partially dilapidated castle and abbey at Carlingford.

One night when praying in front of the madonna, she heard the voice of her dead lover calling to her from out of the mist. Not sure of his identity, she is said to have demanded proof that it was really he who was calling out to her. Soon after, she heard him again calling her from the seashore, ran down toward the sea, and was swallowed up by a huge breaker, never to be found again.

It is her ghost, and that of Nevin O'Neill, who have often been seen walking by the rocky seashore or standing together in the ruined chapel. Quiet summer nights, close to midnight, are the best time to run into this phenomenon—if you are one of those who are capable of registering the very tenuous vibrations of such a haunting.

Carlingford is now only a small town, but at one time in the seventeenth century it was large enough to be the temporary capital of Ireland, and a parliament was once in session there. One reaches Carlingford either by railroad to Dundalk and then about eight miles by car over a winding but otherwise good road, or one can go all the way from Dublin by car. Carlingford is equidistant from Dublin and Belfast. The ruins can be reached on foot only, directly from the village. Like so many other Irish towns, its population has dwindled over the years, and it is now actually more like a village than a small town. But the people of Carlingford are still proud of it and prefer to call it a town.

France

The Musketeer of Avignon

THE HOTEL de l'Europe in Avignon is a distinguished, fashionable hotel famous not only with the French but the better class of British and American tourists. If you are traveling south from Paris to Nice it is a good place to break the journey and miss none of the comforts.

Room No. 2—it may have been renumbered since, for all I know—is a large, comfortable room on the second floor, furnished with exquisite authentic antiques, yet offering the best in contemporary ammenities as well. There is a bathroom off the room, and the only access to the bathroom is from the room itself. This is important, as you will see, for anyone entering the bathroom can only leave it by the door. There is no window and no other way to get out—and the walls are very thick.

In 1945, Capt. George Wood, on the staff of the Duke of Windsor, and his wife, Rose, were occupying the room in question. Mrs. Wood was awakened in the middle of the night by the feeling that there was someone in the room. Fully awake, she noticed a man standing in the middle of the chamber. As she challenged the apparition, the man bolted out of the room—straight through the door! The next morning she queried the hotel staff. The apparition was well known to them. It was called "The General," though no one knew who it actually was or had been.

In 1952, Ruth Thornhill—then Mrs. Ruth Deveries—stayed at the Hotel de l'Europe, in room No. 2. This was their second visit, but to their surprise, the room had been redecorated in the meantime. In particular, a large antique wardrobe had been placed in it, which Mrs. Deveries estimated to belong to the period of Francis I, around 1530.

Although she had slept in this very room before without the problems encountered by the earlier occupant—but not without a restless feeling—this time Ruth was rudely awakened in the middle of the night.

The noise that awoke her was due to the doors of the wardrobe bursting open with great force. Out of it came a man dressed in the military garb of the sixteenth century!

He approached her bed and for an agonizing moment she could actually feel his icy fingers on her hand. Then the specter turned around abruptly and went into the bathroom. Minutes later, when nothing further had occurred, Ruth got up and looked in the bathroom. It was empty. No one could have left by natural means.

The Hotel de l'Europe is still open for business, and presumably room No. 2 can be booked for the night—that is, if you care to.

The Ghost at La Tour Malakoff, Paris

MAISON-LAFITTE is a rustic, elegant suburb of metropolitan Paris, reached easily by car within half an hour. Near the race course there is a cluster of townhouses within a park setting, aristocratic reminders of a disappearing elegance. More and more highrise, high-price apartment houses have replaced the old residences.

On the corner of rue Racine and avenue Montaigne there stands a three-story residence within about an acre of landscaped grounds. When I visited the house it was exactly as it had been since it was built during the Second Empire, in the 1860s. A glass-enclosed conservatory faced toward the garden and a tower reached up beyond the roof in the romantic Victorian manner of the period. The only new addition was a low-ceilinged projection room on the other end of the garden: the last tenant had been motion picture personality Robert Lamoureux.

Inside the house, the appearance of an elegant townhouse in the country was further maintained by the presence of high ceilings, white walls, gold appliances and wrought-iron staircases in the front and rear.

No. 3 avenue Montaigne was built by Emperor Napoleon III for his own account. Ostensibly a hunting lodge (Maison-Lafitte was then still rural), in reality it housed a favorite mistress, whose portrait the Emperor had had painted and placed on the outside wall.

With the advent of the Republic, the house became state property and was maintained as a "Residence of State" until World War II. Important visitors —but not those important enough to be housed in the Elysée Palace—were lodged there. During World War II German soldiers occupied the house and, in the process, looted it of anything that was not nailed down. When Allied troops took over the property, they completed the job. Subsequently it was purchased by M. DuPrès, a gentleman interested in real estate. When Mme. DuPrès saw the house, she had him take it off the market and moved in with their family.

In the fall of 1949, Mr. and Mrs. D. rented it for their own use. Mr. D. was a high-ranking diplomat at the American Embassy in Paris. Mrs. D., Pennsylvania-born, was of English, Welsh, and Irish descent and was born with a caul, a fact some people regard as a sign of psychic talents. She and Mr. D. have four children and now live near Washington, D.C., where Mr. D. practices law.

When the D.'s rented the house, they also took over the services of Paulette, the "bonne-à-tout-faire" who had been with the DuPrès family for many years. The house had meanwhile been tastefully refurnished and the appointments included a fine grand piano in the "salon," the large downstairs reception room where the lady in Napoleon's life presumably met her illustrious lover whenever he visited her.

Mrs. D. liked the house from the start; but she could not help wondering about the oval portrait of the lovely lady attached to the wall of the tower.

Shortly after moving to the house, Mr. D. had to travel for three weeks on government business. Mrs. D. was left with her children, Paulette the maid, and a nursemaid—neither of whom spoke a word of English. Mrs. D.'s French was then almost nonexistent, so she looked forward to a somewhat unusual relationship with her servants.

Several nights after her husband's departure, Mrs. D. was awakened at 3:00 A.M. by the sound of music. It was a rambling but lovely piano piece being played somewhere nearby. Her first reaction was how inconsiderate the neighbors were to make music at such an hour, until she realized that she had no neighbors near enough to hear anything. It then struck her that the music came from *inside* her house, or, to be specific, from the salon downstairs. She rushed to the bathroom and sat down on an ice-cold bathtub to make sure she was awake. An hour later the playing stopped. During that hour she was much too scared to go down and see who was playing her piano. The music had not been particularly macabre, but rather more on the pleasant side and somewhat rambling.

Who was she to discuss her experience with? The Embassy staff would hardly react favorably to such matters and her French did not permit her to question the servants.

The next night, the ghostly piano music came on

again, promptly at 3 A.M., and stopped just as promptly at 4 A.M. Night after night, she was being treated to a concert by unseen hands. Mrs. D. still would not venture downstairs at the time of the spooky goings-on, but prior to retiring she tried to set traps for her unknown visitor, such as closing the piano lid or leaving sheet music open at certain pages. But the ghost did not respond: everything was exactly as she had left it, and the music was as clear as ever.

She greeted her husband with a sigh of relief on his return. When she told him of her ordeal, he was amazingly understanding. Had the ghost been playing that night, Mr. D. would have sat up to listen, but unfortunately, his return abruptly ended the nocturnal concerts.

Gradually the matter of the ghostly pianist faded into memory, especially as the D.'s did a lot of entertaining in the house. Among their guests were Neill O., her husband's assistant, and his wife. One Sunday morning they descended the stairs to breakfast in a somewhat shaken condition. When questioned by Mrs. D., the couple complained about the inconsiderate "neighbor" who had kept them awake playing the piano at 3 A.M. Their room had been exactly above the salon. Mrs. O. added that she had clearly heard a hunting horn outside the house and that it had awakened her.

Other overnight guests of the D.'s complained similarly about nocturnal concerts downstairs. What could the hosts do but say they hoped their guests would sleep better the next night?

Eventually Mrs. D., with the help of Neill O., interrogated the maid about the house in which she had served for so long.

"What about that portrait of a lady outside?" Mrs. D. wanted to know. Apparently Napoleon had wearied of his mistress after a while and left her to live by herself in the house. During those lonely years as a former Imperial mistress she had little company to comfort her: only a grand piano for her amusement, and soon it became her one and only passion. When Mrs. D. asked the maid about a ghost in the house, the girl blanched. Living on the third floor, Paulette had often heard the ghostly piano concert downstairs but had been too scared to investigate. During the DuPrès residency, Paulette had been alone with the children on one occasion when the nurse had gone to sleep.

One of the children started to cry and Paulette rushed to the room. She found the little girl standing in her bed wide awake, pointing to a corner of the room and saying, "Look at the pretty lady!" Paulette, however, could not see anyone or anything.

After the D.'s left Paris, the house passed into the hands of Robert Lamoureux, who added the projection room on the grounds but left everything else as it was.

He, too, gave up the house and eventually moved elsewhere. The house then became part of a real estate parcel acquired by speculators for the purpose of tearing down the old houses and erecting a new apartment house on the spot. In August 1968, I was granted permission by the La Tour Malakoff Society to visit the house, with the tense suggestion that I do so as soon as possible if I wanted to find the house still standing.

Finally, in 1969, I did so, and fortunately the wreckers had not yet come. The house already showed its state of abandonment. The once carefully kept garden was overgrown with weeds, the windows were dirty and the absence of all furniture gave it an eerie, unreal feeling.

I walked up and down the staircase, taking pictures and "listening with an inner ear" for whatever vibrations might come my way. I did not hear any music, but then the grand piano was no longer there. An Italian watchman, who had spent hundreds of nights on the property guarding it from intruders, looked at me and wondered what I wanted there. I asked if he had had any unusual experiences in the house. He shook his head and explained he wouldn't have—he never slept there and wouldn't dream of doing so. Why not? He just smiled somewhat foolishly and changed the subject.

When my photographs were developed by the professional service I use, one of them showed a strange light streak I could not account for. It was a picture of the iron staircase in the house. The shapeless light streak appears between the second and first floors. Was it perhaps Napoleon's lady friend rushing downstairs to welcome her lover?

One can't be sure about those things.

The Eight Young Ladies of the Château de la Caze

THE CHÂTEAU de la Caze is a solid, well preserved Renaissance castle perched on a hill in the center of the picturesque Gorges du Tarn, in southeastern France. It is not easy to reach and the winding road requires skillful driving. But the country around Caze is of such unusual beauty that it pays for the traveler to take the extra time and descend into the ravine of the Tarn river.

Caze was long eclipsed by the importance of the nearby monastery of St. Enimie. The Abbot's brother had a marriagable daughter named Soubeyrane who was engaged to another local dignitary named de Montclar. As part of the wedding contract, William Alamand de Montclar and his bride Soubeyrane built the fortified castle in 1489. Unfortunately, the marriage remained without issue and the castle passed into the hands of another family, the Mostuéjouls. The head of that family was Captain Bertrand de Mostuéjouls, king's lieutenant in the district of Gevaudan and a famous warrior who had successfully done battle with the Huguenots. His daughter inherited the castle and through her marriage to a certain M. de Malian, produced eight lovely daughters whose portraits still adorn the walls of the castle. Because of their presence, Caze soon became the rallying point for the young men of the district who came to pay court to the demoiselles.

Allegedly, these young women could not find proper husbands. Their frustrated ghosts are said to haunt the corridors of the south tower where their well-guarded quarters had been.

Travelers have reported being disturbed at night —if that's the word—by the transparent apparition of one or more young women entering their bedrooms as if in search of something or someone. It is, of course, possible that these witnesses were merely picking up impressions from the past psychometrically. Either way, the Château de la Caze is now an elegant inn which can be visited without difficulty. The nearest train station is at La Malene, on the Paris-Biziers line, or by car from Milan.

Germany

Haunted Wolfsegg Fortress, Bavaria

THE FORTIFIED castle at Wolfsegg, Bavaria, is not state property and can be visited only through the kindness and permission of its owner. It is one of the few privately owned fortresses in the world, I believe, and thereby hangs a tale.

The late Georg Rauchenberger, by profession a painter and the official guardian of monuments for the province of The Upper Palatinate, which is part of the state of Bavaria, purchased this ancient fortress with his own savings. Since he was the man who passed on monies to be spent by the state for the restoration of ancient monuments in the province, he had of course a particularly touchy situation on his hands, for he could not possibly allow any funds to be diverted to his own castle. Consequently, every penny spent upon the restoration of this medieval fortress came from his own pocket. Over the years he gradually restored this relic of the past into a livable, if primitive, medieval fortress. He put in some of the missing wooden floors, and turned the clock back to the eleventh century in every respect.

Two persons, so far, can sleep comfortably in the large fortress, but as it is still in the process of being restored, it will be a long time before it can compare with some of the "tourist attractions" under state control. Nevertheless, small groups of interested visitors have been admitted most days of the week for a guided tour through the Hall of Knights and other parts of the fortress. Ordinarily visitors are not told of the hauntings at Wolfsegg, but I am sure that anyone referring to these lines will find at least a friendly reception.

Because of the nearness of the River Danube, the fortress at Wolfsegg was always of some importance. It rises majestically out of the valley to the equivalent of four or five modern stories. Quite obviously constructed for defense, its thick bulky walls are forbidding, the small windows—high up to discourage aggressors—and the hill upon which the fortress perches making attack very difficult.

As a matter of fact, Wolfsegg never fell to an enemy, and even the formidable Swedes, who besieged it for a long time during the Thirty Years' War, had to give up. Built in 1028, Wolfsegg belonged to several noble Bavarian families and was always directly or indirectly involved in the intricate dynastic struggles between the various lines of the Wittelsbachs, who ruled Bavaria until 1918. Many of the masters of Wolfsegg made a living by being "Raubritter"—that is to say, robber barons. All in all, the area had an unsavory reputation even as early as the twelfth and thirteenth centuries. The walls are thick and the living quarters located well above ground.

The Knights Hall on the third floor is reached by a broad staircase, and one flight down there is also a lookout tower which has been restored as it was in the sixteenth century. In the inner court there is a wooden gallery running along part of the wall (at one time this gallery covered the entire length of the wall). The lower stories have not yet been fully restored or even explored.

Georg Rauchenberger himself heard uncanny noises, footsteps, and experienced cold drafts at various times in various parts of the fortress. The late Mrs. Therese Pielmeier, wife of the custodian, actually saw a whitish form in the yard, full of luminescence, and she also heard various unexplained noises. On one occasion, Mr. Rauchenberger saw a young lady coming in with a small group of visitors, and when he turned to speak to her she disappeared.

I held a séance at Wolfsegg with a Viennese lady who served as my medium at the time. Through the trance mediumship of Mrs. Edith Riedl, I was able to trace the terrible story of a triple murder involving a beautiful woman, once the wife of a Wolfsegg baron, who had become the innocent victim of a political plot. The legend of the beautiful ghost at Wolfsegg had, of course, existed prior to our arrival on the scene. Apparently, greedy relatives of a fourteenth-century owner of Wolfsegg had decided to take over the property, then of considerable value, by trapping the young wife of the owner with another man. The husband, told of the rendezvous, arrived in time to see the two lovers together, killed both of them, and was in turn murdered in "just revenge" by his cunning relatives.

The portrait of the unlucky lady of Wolfsegg hangs in one of the corridors, the work of the father of the current owner, who painted her from impressions received while visiting the castle.

Although I was able to make contact with the

atmosphere surrounding the "white woman" of Wolfsegg, and to shed light upon a hitherto unknown Renaissance tragedy, it is entirely possible that the restless baroness still roams the corridors to find recognition and to prove her innocence to the world.

One reaches Wolfsegg on secondary roads in about a half hour's drive from Regensburg, and it is situated near a small and rather primitive village, northwest of the city on the north side of the Danube River. There is only one inn in this village, and staying overnight, as I once did, is not recommended.

This is a remote and strange area of Germany, despite the comparative nearness of the city of Regensburg. By the way Regensburg is sometimes also called Ratisbon, and is the center of one of the few remaining strongly Celtic areas in Germany.

The Haunted Ruin at Schwärzenberg, Bavaria

SCHWÄRZENBERG IS an early medieval fortress, now largely in ruins, topping one of the hills between Regensburg and the Czechoslovakian border. It is due northeast of Regensburg, and it takes about an hour and a half to two hours on good country roads to reach it. Surrounded by parklike natural state forests, the area is extremely deserted and very beautiful. One can drive only to the foot of the hill upon which the fortress sits. One must walk the rest of the way, but the ascent is not difficult. The square towers of Schwärzenberg are still standing, and part of the halls are intact although the floors have all disappeared. Since the fortress has not been taken care of by the monument service, it is overgrown with various examples of the lush Bavarian flora, and rain and snow have partially filled the fortress with earth.

Those unable to drive up to the ruin can also reach it by railroad on a secondary line between Schwandorf and Fürth. The station to get off at is called Neubäu. From there one must either hire a car or walk for about two hours. No permission is needed to visit Schwärzenberg Fortress. There really isn't anyone there to give it. But it is best visited during the daytime. The forest paths leading up the hill are not easy to find in the dark of night, and there are absolutely no lights in the area.

Built around 1300, Schwärzenberg was destroyed twice. The first time it was sacked during the Hussite Wars, when the Bohemian raiders came south to fight the Catholic armies of the emperor. This was in 1415 at the height of the first religious wars in Central Europe. In 1634, at the same time that the Swedes besieged Wolfsegg without success, they came to Schwärzenberg with considerable success. As a result of the Swedish destruction, Schwärzenberg is now only a ruin.

Legend has it that it is inhabited by a kind mountain spirit called Rotmantel or Redcoat.

Many years ago, Georg Rauchenberger spent a night at Schwärzenberg in the company of several friends. The purpose of the visit was to find out whether there was a ghost inhabiting the ancient ruin. On the first try nothing happened, but when they returned a second time, there was indeed something more than the noise of the surrounding forest or the animals running for shelter. In the middle of the night, they were all awakened by the sound of footsteps. It sounded to them as if a group of men was returning to the fortress, perhaps after a successful raid into the countryside. Schwärzenberg, like so many castles in the forests of Bavaria, was headquarters for robber-barons whose sole occupation was the pillaging of the countryside. While the group of observers lay still on the ground, the footsteps of long-dead, medieval soldiers could be clearly heard reverberating in the ruined halls of Schwärzenberg.

I brought Mrs. Edith Riedl to Schwärzenberg after our visit to Wolfsegg, and she was able to trace much of the violent history of this outpost.

Visibly shaken, she spoke of gangs of marauders coming from the fortress, spilling out into the countryside and returning later with much loot. She turned in horror from an area in the lower portion of the ruin, where the dungeons must have been located at one time. She still felt the impression of past cruelty and sufferings.

Even the conquering Swedes managed to imprint something of themselves upon the ruins. Mrs. Riedl vividly described the "foreigners" from the north who had come to destroy the fortress.

Schwärzenberg is not on any tourist map, but it is well worth a visit from the psychic point of view alone.

Austria

Ghosts Around Vienna

WHAT GHOSTS are, you know by now, and those of my readers who are unfamiliar with the term *gemütlichkeit* ought to be told that it is a German word meaning "pleasant, go-easy way of life." When we flew into Hamburg, we did not expect *gemütlichkeit,* which is mostly found in southern countries like Switzerland and Austria anyway. But we found a genuine interest in psychic matters among radio and television people, although the vast masses of Germans are quite unaware of the seriousness with which sixth-sense experiences are studied in the Anglo-Saxon world. A small, keenly intelligent minority is, of course, trying to establish research on a respectable basis. Hans Bender and his parapsychological laboratory at Freiburg are unique, though. In Hamburg, we met with Erich Maria Koerner, author and translator of books on extrasensory perception, and Milo Renelt, a medium, called "the seer of Hamburg." But, simply because people are reluctant to talk, we could not find any leads to haunted houses, of which there must be many.

When we arrived in Vienna, Austria, things were a little better. For one thing, my dear friend Turhan Bey had kept me abreast of existing research, and the very day of our arrival in the Danube city, we went to see Countess Zoe Wassilko-Serecki, the president of the Austrian society for psychical research. She brought us up to date on the situation in Austria, where the press was openly hostile and derisive of any serious efforts to report parapsychological studies. An American of Austrian descent myself, I found the use of the local tongue most helpful when I called on the television and radio people the next day. I quickly found out that radio would have nothing to do with me, since a local magician had convinced the responsible producers that all psychic experiences were hokum and could be reproduced by him at will. Somewhat more of an open mind awaited me at the newly created television headquarters of Austrian TV, which is about ten years behind ours, but full of good will and operating under great handicaps of low budgets and pressures. Finally, a reporter named Kaiser agreed to accompany Catherine and me on a ghost hunt and to do a straight reporting job, without bias or distortion. I must say he kept his word.

We drove to the Imperial Castle, which is a sprawling array of buildings in the very heart of Vienna. There we went on foot into the portion known as Amalienburg, the oldest part of the castle. All I had to go on was a slim report that a ghost had been observed in that area.

Right off the bat, Kaiser turned to the police officer at the gate and asked him if he knew of any ghosts.

"Ghosts?" the officer asked, somewhat perplexed, and scratched his head. "None that I know of." He suggested we pay the *Burghauptmann,* or governor, a visit.

The governor was a fortyish gentleman with the unusual name of Neunteufel, which means Nine Devils. Far from being hellish, however, he invited us into his office and listened respectfully, as Kaiser explained me to him. Considering that we were in arch-Catholic Vienna, in the inner offices of a high government official, I admired his courage. But then Kaiser had admitted to me, privately, that he had experienced an incident of telepathy he could not dismiss. His open-mindedness was not a drafty head but sincere.

"Well," the governor finally said, "I am so sorry, but I've only been in this post for five years. I know nothing whatever about ghosts. But there is an old employee here who might be able to help you."

My heart had begun to falter and I saw myself being ridiculed on television. "Please, boys," I said inaudibly, addressing my Friends Upstairs, "help us a little."

Mr. Neunteufel dialed and asked to speak to a Mr. Sunday. There was a pause. "Oh, I see," he then said. "You mean Mr. Sunday isn't in on Friday?" Black Friday, I thought! But then the governor's face brightened. Mr. Sunday would be over in a moment.

The man turned out to be a quiet, soft-spoken clerk in his later years. He had worked here practically all his adult life. "Yes," he nodded. "There is indeed a ghost here; but not in the Amalienburg. Come, I'll show you where."

You could have heard a pin drop, or, for that matter, a ghost walk, when he had spoken. Kaiser gave me a look of mixed admiration and puzzlement. He and his cameraman were already on their feet.

With the governor at our side, we followed Sunday up and down a number of stairs, along corridors, through musty halls, and again up a staircase into a back portion of the castle.

"I've never been here myself," the governor apologized to me, as we walked. "In fact, I didn't even know this part existed," he added.

What the hell! I thought. It's a big house.

Now we stood in front of a *Marterl,* a peculiarly Austrian type of Blessed Virgin altar built into the wall and protected by a metal screen. To the left were the stairs we had come up on, and to our right was another, smaller stairway, closed off by a wooden door.

"Where are we?" Kaiser asked.

"This is the private apartment of Baroness Vecera," Sunday said.

Baroness Vecera was the sweetheart of Crown Prince Rudolph, central characters of the famed Meyerling tragedy, resulting in a major national scandal that rocked the Austria of the 1880s.

"The Crown Prince arranged for this flat," Sunday explained, "so he could see his lady friend quietly and privately. These stairs are not marked on the plans of the building."

"No wonder!" The governor sighed with relief.

Part of the castle had evidently been rented out to private citizens in recent years, since the Republic had toppled the monarchy, and the officials of the castle had paid scant attention to that wing since then.

"Has anyone seen a ghost here?" I inquired.

Sunday nodded. "A *Jaeger* reported seeing a white woman here some years ago, under the Empire." A *Jaeger* is a soldier belonging to a Tyrolean or other Alpine regiment. "Then there is the guardist Beran," Sunday continued, "who saw this white woman right here, by the altar of the Virgin Mary. As a matter of fact, many servants have seen her, too."

"When did all this start—I mean, how far back has she been seen?" I asked.

"Not too far back," Sunday answered, "about eighty years or so."

Since the death of Rudolph and Vecera, then, I thought. Of course! This was their home, the only refuge where they could meet in secrecy. There are among historians growing voices that say the suicide of Meyerling wasn't a suicide at all, but an execution.

Would the restless ghost of Baroness Vecera demand satisfaction or was the spectre her remorseful form, praying by the shrine, seeking forgiveness for the tragedy she had caused?

Sunday now took us farther down the narrowing corridor into what must have been the oldest part of the castle. The thick walls and tiny slit windows suggested a fortress rather than a showplace of the Habsburgs.

"Not long ago," he said, "a patient of Dr. Schaefer, who had his offices here, saw a Capuchin monk walk down the corridor."

"What would a monk be doing here?" I demanded.

"In the early days, the Emperors kept a small number of monks here for their personal needs. There was a Capuchin monastery built into the castle at this very spot."

We waited for a while, but no Capuchin showed up. They were probably all too busy down in the Imperial Crypt, where the Capuchin Fathers do a thriving tourist business letting visitors look at the gaudy Imperial coffins for fifty cents a head.

I looked at Kaiser, and there was a thoughtful expression on his face.

We returned to the TV studio and filmed some footage, showing me with photographs of haunted houses. Then a reporter took down my dialogue, and the following day, as is their custom, the daily newsreel commentator read the story of our ghost hunt to some seven million Austrians who had never before been told of psychic research.

The chain of events is sometimes composed of many links. A friend of a friend in New York introduced me to Herta Fisher, a medium and student of the occult, who, in turn, suggested that I contact Edith Riedl when in Vienna.

Mrs. Riedl offered to take us to the two haunted castles I wanted to visit in southern Austria. In fact, even before I arrived in Vienna, she was able to help me. The *Volksblatt,* a local newspaper, had published a highly distorted report of my activities two weeks before our arrival. Mrs. Riedl sent me the clipping for such action as I might see fit to take.

I picked up the phone and dialed the *Volksblatt.*

"The 'responsible editor,' please," I said, in German. Austrian newspapers employ "responsible editors," usually minor clerks, who must take the blame whenever the newspaper publishes anything libelous.

"Hello," said a pleasantly soft voice on the other end of the line.

"Hello, yourself," I replied. "Did you not publish a piece about Hans Holzer, the Ghost Hunter, recently?"

"Ja, ja," the voice said. "We did."

"Well," I said in dulcet tones, "I am he, and I'm suing you for five million schillings."

There was a gasp at the other end. "Wait!" the voice pleaded. "Let us talk this over."

The following afternoon, Turhan Bey drove us to the editorial offices of the newspaper, awaiting our return in a nearby café. I had a three-o'clock appointment with the publisher. At three fifteen I reminded the receptionist that time was of the essence. When nothing further had happened five minutes later, I sent in my card with a note: "Sorry can't wait—am on my way to my lawyer, from whom you will hear further."

Faster than you can say "S. O. B.," the publisher came running. I repaired to his offices, where I was joined by his editor and a man named Hannes Walter, a reporter.

It was agreed that I could indeed sue for libel. But they were willing to print another piece, far more thorough and bereft of any libelous matter. Would I agree?

I always believe in giving felons a second chance. When I read the piece a few weeks later, I realized I should have sued instead. Mainly the brain child of Herr Walter, it was still full of innuendoes, although it did report my activities with some degree of accuracy. Austrian TV is only ten years old and its press goes back several hundred years—yet the only fair treatment I received in public was on the home screens. As is the case in many countries, newspapermen frequently underestimate the intelligence of their readers. That is why so many TV sets are sold.

Mrs. Riedl turned out to be a cultured lady in her late fifties or early sixties, capable of speaking several languages, and full of intellectual curiosity. Of noble

Hungarian ancestry, she is married to one of the owners of the Manners chocolate factory, and lives in a sprawling villa in the suburb of Dornbach.

At first, she was to drive us to the Burgenland Province in her car, but, when Turhan Bey offered to come along, we switched to his larger car. The four of us made a marvelous team as we discovered mutual bonds in many areas. I wanted to know more about Edith Riedl's mediumship, and asked her to tell me all about herself.

We were rolling towards the south, that part of Austria annexed in 1919 which had been a Hungarian province for many centuries, although the people of the area always spoke both German and Hungarian. Soon we left the sprawling metropolis of Vienna behind us and streaked down the southern highway towards the mountains around Wiener Neustadt, an industrial city of some importance. Here we veered off onto a less-traveled road and began our descent into the Burgenland, or Land of Castles.

"Tell me, Mrs. Riedl," I asked, "when did you first notice anything unusual about yourself—I mean, being psychic?"

Speaking in good English interlarded with an occasional German or French word, the lively little lady talked freely about herself. "I was only three years old when I had my first experience," she replied. "I was in my room when I saw, outside my window, smoke billowing, as if from a fire. This, of course, was only an impression—there was no smoke.

" 'We'll get a war!' I cried, and ran to my mother. Imagine a small child talking about war. I certainly did not know the meaning of the word I was using!"

"Amazing," Turhan Bey said, and I agreed. I had

never before heard of psychic experiences at such an early age.

"Thirty years later, the house was hit by a bomb, and smoke rose indeed at the spot where I had seen it as a child, and the house burned down."

"When was the next time you experienced anything unusual along psychic lines?" I asked. The countryside was getting more and more rustic and we encountered fewer cars now.

"I was seventeen years old. A cousin of mine served with the Hungarian Hussar Regiments, and we were engaged to be married. The First World War was already on, but he did not serve at the front. He was stationed deep inside the country, near Heidenschaft.

" 'I don't mind fighting at the front,' he often told me. 'I'm not afraid of the enemy. The only thing I'm afraid of, somehow, is fog.' "

"Fog?" I said. "Strange for a Hussar officer in Hungary to worry about fog. You don't have much fog down here, do you?"

"No, I couldn't understand why fog could be something for him to fear. Well, Christmas came, and I sent him a card, showing an angel. Without thinking much about it, I wrote the word 'Peace' into the halo of the angel, and sent the card off to my fiancé.

"Later, I regretted this—after all, one should wish a soldier victory, not peace—I wanted the card back, because the whole idea bothered me. I got the card back all right—with a notation by a strange hand across it, reading, 'Died in service, December 22nd.'

"I couldn't understand how he could have died in the war at Heidenschaft, where there was no enemy within many hundred miles. I felt terrible. I wanted to die, too. I went to my room and put out the lights; I wanted to go to bed early. I was not yet asleep—in fact, still wide awake—when I saw a kind of light near me, and within this luminous disc I recognized a rock, a tree, and at the bottom of the tree, a crumbled mass of something I did not have the courage to look at closely. I knew at this moment that I could either join him in death, or live on. Being very young, my life force triumphed. As I decided to stick to the world of the living, the vision slowly lost color and faded away. But I still wondered how he could have died where he was stationed. The vision immediately returned, but my power of observation was weakening; perhaps the excitement was too much for me. At any rate, I could not make it out clearly.

"The next morning, I reported the incident to my parents. Mother and father looked at each other. 'It is better to tell her,' mother said, but my father shook his head. A year passed by, but I had never forgotten my fiancé.

"One day I helped my father sort some papers in his study. As I helped him go through his desk, my eyes fell on a letter with a black border. I had the feeling it had to do with Francis, my fiancé. I asked my father if I could take it, and my father, preoccupied with his own affairs, nodded in affirmation.

"I immediately went to my own room and opened the black-bordered letter. It was from one of Francis' friends, and he told the family how my fiancé had died. He was flying a small plane on a reconnaissance mission towards the Italian front, but he was stopped short by sudden fog. In the dense fog, he underestimated his altitude and hit a rock. The plane broke into pieces and his body was later found at the foot of a tree. Just as I had seen in my vision!"

"I believe you mentioned to me some startling experiences with premonitions—your ability to warn of impending disaster," I said.

"It happens quite often," Mrs. Riedl replied. "During the last war, for instance, on one occasion when my children were away at Laa on Theyer, in school, I went to visit them by school bus along with many children and a few mothers. I was seated behind the driver, when there was one of those sudden thunderstorms we have in the area. Suddenly, I heard myself shout to the driver, 'Stop, stop at once!'

"He stopped and turned around. 'Are you out of your mind? What is it?' he demanded. Before he had finished talking, a huge tree fell onto the road hitting the spot where the bus would have been if I hadn't stopped it.

"On another occasion, after the last war, my daughter and I were invited to go to Mistelbach, out in the country, to a wedding. At that time it was not possible to use your own car, trains weren't running yet, and transportation was quite primitive.

"There were two groups of people: one was our wedding party, the other was a funeral party also going in that direction. Transportation was by bus. Our numbers were called, and we were about to board the bus, when I cried out to my daughter, 'Come back, this isn't our bus.'

"Our entire group turned back and I was asked why I had recalled them, when our numbers had obviously been called.

"I could not tell them. I never know why I do these things. All I know is I must do it.

"Meanwhile the other party, those going to that funeral, boarded the bus, taking our place. I said, 'The bus is supposed to return to take us next.' "

"Did it?" I asked.

"The bus was supposed to come back in half an hour. Three hours went by and no bus. Then the news came—there had been an accident. We were saved by my warning, but the funeral party were badly hurt."

"How often have you had these warning flashes?"

"Maybe twenty times during the last five years."

"You also have the ability to sense where objects might be safe, as well as people, isn't that right?"

"Yes," Mrs. Riedl nodded. "As you know my husband has a valuable collection of rare books. When war broke out, he decided to send the most valuable ones to a safe place in the country. But as soon as the books had been unloaded there, I had to order the driver to take them back again. I felt the place was far from safe. We went to a parish house and tried to hide them there, but again something warned me against the location. Finally, we did unload the books at another parish house. The priest had already received some books belonging to a Vienna book seller and invited me to add ours to this pile. But I politely refused. Instead, I went around until I found what my Inner Voice told me was the only safe place in the house: the washroom!"

"How did the priest take that?"

"Well, he didn't like it. He remonstrated with me, but to no avail. As it turned out, the house was consumed by fire, except the washroom, and our books were safe at the end of the war!"

"Have you accepted this gift of yours as something that is part of you?"

"Certainly. Just think how much good it has brought me already."

By now we had reached the border country

where today's Hungary meets Austria, and we had to be careful not to pierce the Iron Curtain accidentally by taking the wrong road. The land was green and fertile and the road ran between pleasant-looking hills sometimes crowned by ancient castles or fortresses, a striking demonstration of how the country got its name—Land of Castles.

Our destination was Forchtenstein, a yellow-colored compound of imposing buildings sitting atop a massive hill that rises straight out of the surrounding landscape. As we wound our way up the hill we could see its towers beckoning to us.

Shortly after, we drove up at the imposing castle and Turhan parked the car. This is one of the biggest of Esterhazy castles, of which there are many, since that family was wealthy and powerful in Hungary and southeastern Austria for many centuries, and though the Communists have taken the Esterhazy lands in Hungary, the family still controls huge estates in Austria, and is likely to continue to do so. Today, Forchtenstein is run as a museum. Its fortifications, long, vaulted galleries and rooms, its magnificent collection of paintings and enough medieval and seventeenth-century arms to equip a small army make it a major tourist attraction in this part of Central Europe. Although it was started in the fourteenth century, it really reached importance only in the time of the Turkish wars, when the Crescent and Star were very near indeed.

During that time also the Court of Justice for the entire land was held here and executions took place in the courtyard.

We passed over the front ditch, over a wooden bridge, into the outer courtyard.

"There are noises and all sorts of goings on in this castle," Mrs. Riedl explained.

"There is a well, four hundred and twenty feet deep, dug out by Turkish prisoners of war. When the well was completed, the prisoners were thrown into it. I am sure some of them are still around."

"How do you know?"

"Many people have heard sighing in the vicinity of the well."

Turhan Bey, who is half Turkish, half Austrian, smiled. "I am here as ambassador of peace," he said.

"Also chain rattling," Mrs. Riedl continued.

"Did you ever feel anything unusual here?"

"I was here once before," Mrs. Riedl replied, "and whenever I could be by myself, away from the others in the group being shown around, I felt a presence. Someone wanted to tell me something, perhaps to plead with me for help. But the guide drove us on, and I could not find out who it was."

If there is one thing I dislike intensely, it is guided tours of anything. I went to the local guide and asked him for a private tour. He insisted I buy a dozen tickets, which is the smallest number of people he could take around. We started out at once, four humans, and eight ghosts. At least I paid for eight ghosts.

We walked into the inner courtyard now, where a stuffed crocodile hung high under the entrance arch, which reminded us of the days when the Esterhazys were huntsmen all over the world.

"This is supposed to scare away evil spirits," Mrs. Riedl remarked.

"They must have had a bad conscience, I guess," I

said grimly. The Hungarians certainly equaled the Turks in brutality in those days.

We walked past the monument to Paul Esterhazy, ornamented with bas-reliefs showing Turkish prisoners of war in chains, and into the castle itself. Our guide led us up the stairs onto the roof which is now overgrown with shrubbery and grass.

Suddenly, Mrs. Riedl grabbed my arm. "Over there, I feel I am drawn to that spot. Somebody suffered terribly here."

We retraced our steps and followed to where she pointed. The ground was broken here, and showed a small opening, leading down into the castle.

"What is underneath?" I asked our guide.

"The dungeon," he replied. He didn't believe in ghosts. Only in tourists.

Quickly we went down into the tower. At the gate leading into the deep dungeon itself, we halted our steps. Mrs. Riedl was trembling with deep emotion now.

"Somebody grabbed my skirts up there," she said, and pointed to the roof we had just left, "as if trying to call attention to itself."

I looked down into the dimly lit dungeon. A clammy feeling befell all of us. It was here that the lord of the castle threw his enemies to die of starvation. One time he was absent from the castle, leaving its administration to his wife, Rosalie. She mistreated some of his guests and on his return he had her thrown into this dungeon to die herself.

Her ghost is said to haunt the castle, although her husband, taken with either remorse or fear of the ghost, built a chapel dedicated to Rosalie, on a nearby hill.

"What do you feel here?" I asked Mrs. Riedl.

"A woman plunged down here from a very high place. I feel her very strongly."

"What does she want?"

Mrs. Riedl kept still for a moment, then answered in a trembling voice, "I think she wants us to pray for her."

With the guide pointing the way, we walked up another flight of stairs into the private chapel of the Esterhazys. To a man with twelve tickets there were no closed doors.

Mrs. Riedl quickly grabbed the railing of the gallery and started to pray fervently. Underneath, in the chapel itself, the lights of many candles flickered.

After a moment or two, Edith Riedl straightened up. "I think she feels relieved now," she said.

We continued our inspection of the building. "This is the execution chamber," the guide said casually, and pointed out the execution chair and sword. Then the guide, whose name is Leitner, took us to the prisoners' well, showing us its enormous depth by dropping a lighted flare into it. It took the flare several seconds to hit bottom. "Five thousand Turks built it in thirteen years' time," he said.

Mrs. Riedl stepped closer to the opening of the well, then shrank back. "Terrible," she mumbled. "I can't go near it."

I wondered how many of the murdered Turks were still earthbound in this deep shaft.

Outside, there was sunshine and one of those very pleasant late-summer afternoons for which southern Austria is famous.

We passed the chapel dedicated to Rosalie, but in

our hearts we knew that it had not done much good. Quite possibly our visit had done more for the tormented spirit of the ancient *Burgfrau* than the self-glorifying building atop the hill.

We consulted the maps, for our next destination, Bernstein, lay some thirty miles or more to the west. We drove through the backwoods of the land, quiet little villages with nary a TV aerial in sight, and railroad tracks that hadn't seen a train in years. It was getting cooler and darker and still no sign of Bernstein!

I began to wonder if we had not taken a wrong turn somewhere when all of a sudden we saw the castle emerge from behind a turn in the road.

Not as imposing as Forchtenstein, Bernstein impresses one nevertheless by its elegance and Renaissance-like appearance within a small but cultured park. There is a mine of semiprecious stones called *smaragd* nearby, and the downstairs houses a shop where these stones are on display. This is a kind of wild emerald, not as valuable as a real one, of course, but very pretty with its dark green color and tones.

Bernstein castle goes back to the thirteenth century and has changed hands continuously between Austrian and Hungarian nobles. Since 1892 it has belonged to the Counts Almassy, Hungarian "magnates" or aristocrats.

We arrived at a most inappropriate time. The Count had a number of paying guests which helped defray the expenses of maintaining the large house, and it was close to dinnertime. Nevertheless, we were able to charm him into taking us to the haunted corridor.

On November 11, 1937, Count Almassy, a tall, erect man now in his late sixties, was sitting in his library when one of his guests asked for a certain book. The library can be reached only by walking down a rather narrow, long corridor connecting it with the front portion of the building.

"I left the library, walked down the passage with a torch—I don't like to turn on the main lights at night—well, when I came to this passage, I saw by the light of my torch [flashlight] a female figure kneeling in front of a wooden Madonna that stands at that spot. It was placed there in nineteen fourteen by my mother when both my brothers and I were away in the war. Of course I had often heard talk of a 'White Lady of Bernstein,' so I realized at once that I was seeing a ghost. My first impression was that she looked like a figure cast in plaster of Paris with hard lines. She wore a Hungarian noblewoman's dress of the fifteenth century, with a woman's headgear and a big emerald-green stone on her forehead which threw a dim, green light around her. She had her hands folded under her left cheek."

"What did you do when you saw her?" I asked.

"I had time to switch on the light in the passage," the Count replied, "so that I had her between two lights, that of my torch and the electric light overhead. There was no possible mistake, I saw her clearly. Then just as suddenly, she vanished."

"What is the tradition about this ghost, Count Almassy?" I asked.

"Well, she is supposed to be an Italian woman, Catherine Freschobaldi—of a Florentine family which still exists, in fact—mentioned in Dante's *Inferno.* She married a Hungarian nobleman, Count Ujlocky, of a very old Hungarian family. Her husband was the last King of Bosnia. The family died out. He was very jealous, without any reason, and so he killed her, according to one version, by stabbing her; according to another, by walling her in. That is the story."

"Has anyone else seen the White Lady of Bernstein?"

"Many people. When I was a boy, I remember every year someone or other saw her. When I was in the army, between nineteen ten and nineteen thirteen, she was seen many, many times. In nineteen twenty-one she was seen again when there were Hungarian occupation troops garrisoned at Bernstein during the short-lived Austro-Hungarian campaign of that year—and the ghostly lady chased them away! Then, of course, in nineteen thirty-seven, as I told you, and that was the last time I saw her."

"I believe also that a friend of yours saw her in Africa in the Cameroons? How does this fit in?"

Count Almassy laughed. "Well, that's another story, that one. An Army friend of mine—I really did not know him too well, I met him in nineteen sixteen, and he left Austria in nineteen thirty-seven and bought a farm in the Cameroons. He became a wealthy man. In nineteen forty-six he experienced a strange incident.

"An apparition very much like the White Lady of Bernstein (although he knew nothing whatever about our ghost) appeared to him and spoke to him in Italian.

"In nineteen fifty-four he came to see me to check on the story this ghost had told him. The ghost claimed to be the famous White Lady and he decided to come to Austria to see if there was such a ghost."

"Remarkable," I said. "I can only assume that the apparition in the Cameroons was a thought projection, unless, of course, your ghost is no longer bound to this castle."

The Count thought for a moment. "I do hope so," he finally said. "This is a drafty old castle and Africa is so much warmer."

The Secret of Mayerling

IN A world rife with dramatic narratives and passionate love stories, with centuries of history to pick and choose from, motion picture producers of many lands have time and again come back to Mayerling and the tragic death of Crown Prince Rudolph of Austria as a subject matter that apparently never grows stale.

This is probably so because the romantic Mayerling story satisfies all the requirements of the traditional tearjerker: a handsome, misunderstood prince who cannot get along too well with his stern father, the Emperor; a loving but not too demonstrative wife whom the prince neglects; a brazen young girl whose only crime is that she loves the prince—these are the characters in the story as seen through Hollywood eyes.

To make sure nobody objects to anything as being immoral, the two lovers are shown as being truly in love with each other—but as the prince is already married, this love cannot be and he must therefore die. The Crown Princess gets her husband back, albeit dead. In the motion picture version the political differences between father and son are completely neglected, and the less than sterling qualities of the young Baroness Vetsera are never allowed to intrude on the perfect, idyllic romance.

The prince goes to the Prater Park in Vienna, sees and falls in love with the young girl, secret meetings are arranged, and love is in bloom. But then the piper must be paid. Papa Franz Josef is upset, reasons of state must be considered, and commoners (to a crown prince a mere baroness is like a commoner!) do not marry the heir to the imperial throne. They could run away and chuck it all—but they don't. In this, perhaps, the movie versions come closer to the truth than they realized: Rudolph would never have run off, and Vetsera was too much in love with him to do anything against his wishes.

Nothing is made of the Emperor's political jealousy or the total lack of love between the crown prince and the wife that was forced upon him by his father. In the pictures, she is the wronged woman, a pillar of moral concern to the millions of married moviegoers who have paid to see this opus.

There is apparently a never-ending attraction in the yarn about an unhappy, melancholy prince in love with a young girl who wants to die for and with him. Perhaps the thrill of so close a juxtaposition of life-creating love and life-taking death holds the secret to this powerful message, or perhaps it is the age-old glamor of princely intrigue and dashing romance that keeps moviegoers enthralled from generation to generation.

But does this tell the *true* story of the tragedy that came to a head at the imperial hunting lodge at

Mayerling, or were the real secrets of Mayerling quite different?

To seek an understanding of the unfortunately rather grim facts from which the screenwriters have spun their romantic versions, we must, first of all, look at the secret undercurrents of political life in the Austrian Empire of the 1880s.

For decades, the military powers of the great empire had been declining, while Germany's star had kept rising. A reactionary political system holding sway over Austria seemed out of step with the rest of Europe. A reluctance on the part of a starchy court and its government to grant any degree of self-determination to the many foreign elements in the empire's population was clearly leading toward trouble.

Especially there was trouble brewing with the proud Hungarians. Never reconciled to the incorporation of their kingdom into the Austrian Empire, the Magyars had openly rebelled in 1848 and done it with such force that the Austrians had to call for Russian troops to help them.

In 1849 the revolt was quashed, and Hungary became more enslaved than ever. But the struggle that had been lost on the battlefield continued in Parliament and the corridors of the Imperial Palace. Hungary pressed for its national identity until, in 1867, the government gave in: the so-called *Ausgleich,* or reconciliation, acknowledged the existence of a Hungarian nation, and the Empire was changed into a dual monarchy, with separate Austrian and Hungarian parliaments, ministers, and of course languages, all under the rule of the Habsburg Emperor.

Austro-Hungary was now a weaker but less turbulent giant, united only around the person of its ruler, the aging Emperor Franz Josef. Still, the

Hungarian magnates pursued a separatist policy, gradually driving wedges between the two halves of the Danube monarchy, while the Germanic Austrian ruling class tried everything within its power to contain the Hungarians and to keep a firm upper hand.

By the 1880s there was no question of another armed insurrection. The Hungarians knew it would be unsuccessful, and they weren't going to take a chance unless they were sure of positive results. But they thought they could get greater attention for Hungarian affairs, greater influence by Hungarians in the councils of state and in trade matters. The Magyars were on the march again, but without a leader.

Then they found a sympathetic ear in the most unlikely quarter, however: Rudolph, the crown prince, who had grown up in the shadow of his illustrious father, but who was also very critical of his father's political accomplishments, because he did not share his father's conservative views.

Rudolph was born in 1858, and in 1888 he was exactly thirty years old. Although he was the heir apparent and would some day take over the reins of the government, he was permitted little more than ceremonial duties. He had himself partly to blame for this situation, for he was outspoken, and had made his sympathies with the underdogs of the Empire well known. He did not hold his tongue even among friends, and soon word of his political views reached the Court. Even if his father had wanted to overlook these views, the Prime Minister, Count Eduard von Taaffe, could not. To him, an archconservative, Rudolph was clearly not "on the team," and therefore had to be watched.

Hoping to keep Rudolph from the center of

political activity, Count von Taaffe managed to get the crown prince and the crown princess sent to Hungary, but it turned out to be a mistake after all. While residing in Budapest, Rudolph endeared himself to the Hungarian partisans, and if he had nurtured any doubts as to the justice of their cause, he had none when he returned to Vienna.

Also, during his sojourn in Hungary, Rudolph had learned to be cautious, and it was a sober, determined man who re-entered the princely apartments of the Imperial Castle. Located on the second floor in the central portion of the palace and not very close to the Emperor's rooms, these apartments could easily be watched from both inside the walls and from the outside, if one so desired, and Count von Taaffe desired just that.

Perhaps the most fascinating of recent Mayerling books is a bitter denunciation of the Habsburg world and its tyranny underneath a façade of Viennese smiles. This book was written in English by Hungarian Count Carl Lonyay, whose uncle married the widowed ex-Crown Princess Stephanie. Lonyay inherited the private papers of that lady after her death, and with it a lot of hitherto secret information. He did a painstaking job of using only documented material in this book, quoting sources that still exist and can be checked, and omitting anything doubtful or no longer available, because of Franz Josef's orders immediately after the tragedy that some very important documents pertaining to Rudolph's last days be destroyed.

"Rudolph was a virtual prisoner. He was kept under strict surveillance. No one could visit him unobserved. His correspondence was censored." Thus

Lonyay describes the situation after Rudolph and Stephanie returned to the old Imperial Castle.

Under the circumstances, the Crown Prince turned more and more to the pursuit of women as a way to while away his ample free time. He even kept a diary in which each new conquest was given a rating as to standing and desirability. Although Rudolph's passing conquests were many, his one true friend in those days was Mizzi Kaspar, an actress, whom he saw even after he had met the Baroness Vetsera.

Mizzi was more of a confidante and mother confessor to the emotionally disturbed prince, however, than she was a mistress. Moodiness runs in the Habsburg family, and mental disease had caused the death of his mother's cousin, Ludwig II of Bavaria. Thus, Rudolph's inheritance was not healthy in any sense, and his knowledge of these facts may have contributed to his fears and brooding nature, for it is true that fear of unpleasant matters only hastens their arrival and makes them worse when they do occur, while rejection of such thoughts and a positive attitude tend to smooth their impact.

There is a persistent hint that Rudolph's illness was not only mental, but that he had somehow also contracted venereal disease along the highways and byways of love. In the latter years of his life he often liked the company of common people in the taverns of the suburbs, and found solace among cab drivers and folksingers.

As Rudolph's frustrations grew and he found himself more and more shunted away from the mainstream of political activity, he often hinted that he wished to commit suicide. Strangely, he did not expect death to end all his problems: He was not a materialist, but he had mystical beliefs in a hereafter and a deep curiosity about what he would find once he crossed the threshold.

Perhaps this direction of his thoughts got its start after an incident during his residence in Prague some years before. At that time, the daughter of a Jewish cantor saw him pass by and immediately fell in love with the prince. Her parents sent her away from Prague, but she managed to get back and spent the night sitting underneath his windows. The next morning she had contracted pneumonia, and in short order she died. Word got to the Crown Prince and he was so touched by this that he ordered flowers put on her grave every day. Although he had conquered many women and immediately forgotten them, the attachment of the one girl he had never even met somehow turned into a romantic love for her on his part. Until he crossed paths with Mary Vetsera, this was the only true love of his life, unfulfilled, just as his ambitions were, and very much in character with his nihilistic attitudes.

Now, in the last year of life, he kept asking people to commit suicide with him so that he need not enter the new world alone. "Are you afraid of death?" he would ask anyone who might listen, even his coachmen. A classical Austrian answer, given him a day before his own death, came from the lips of his hired cab driver, Bratfisch:

"When I was in the Army, no, I wasn't afraid of death. *I wasn't permitted to.* But now? Yes."

It didn't help to put Rudolph's mind at rest. But people who announce beforehand their intentions to do away with themselves, seldom carry out their threat.

"Rudolph announced his decision to commit

suicide, verbally and in writing, to a number of persons. Of these, not even his father, his wife, his cousin, or the two officers on his staff ever made a serious attempt to prevent him from carrying out his plan, although it was clear for all to see that Rudolph's state of mind gave rise to grave concern," Lonyay reports.

But despite this longing for death, Rudolph continued a pretty lively existence. It was on November 5, 1888, that he saw Mary Vetsera for the first time in the Freudenau, a part of the large Prater Park that was famed for its racing. The girl was not yet eighteen, but she had led anything but a sheltered life. The daughter of the widowed Baroness Helen Vetsera had already had a love affair with a British officer in Cairo at age sixteen, and was prematurely developed beyond her years. Her mother's family, the Baltazzis, were of "Levantine" origin, which in those days meant anything beyond the Hungarian frontiers to the east. Lonyay calls them Greeks, but Lernet-Holenia describes them as Jewish or part-Jewish. Their main claim to fame was an interest in, and a knowledge of, horse breeding, and since Vienna was a horsey city, this talent opened many doors to them that would otherwise have remained closed. Helen's husband, Victor von Vetsera, had been an interpreter at the Austrian Embassy in Constantinople, and this later enabled her to move to Vienna with her daughter Mary.

What struck Rudolph immediately when he saw the girl was her similarity to the cantor's daughter who had died for him in Prague. Although they had never spoken, he had once glimpsed her and did remember her face. Mary had lots to offer on her own:

She was not beautiful in the strictest sense, but she appeared to be what today we call "very sexy."

After the initial casual meeting in the Freudenau, Mary herself wrote the prince a letter expressing a desire to meet again. Rudolph was, of course, interested, and asked his cousin, Countess von Larisch, to arrange matters for him discreetly. Marie Larisch gladly obliged her cousin, and the two met subsequently either in Prater Park or at various social functions. So far there had been no intimate relations between them. The relationship was a purely romantic one as Rudolph found himself drawn to the young girl in a way none of his other conquests had ever attracted him. It wasn't until the thirteenth of January, 1889, that the two became lovers in Countess Larisch's apartment at the Grand Hotel.

Eventually, Mary's mother found out about the meetings, and she did not approve of them. Her daughter was not about to become the crown prince's mistress if *she* could help it, and Rudolph became aware of the need to be very circumspect in their rendezvous. Shortly after, he requested Countess Larisch to bring Mary to him at the Imperial Castle. This was a daring idea and Marie Larisch didn't like it at all. Nevertheless, she obeyed her cousin. Consequently, she and Mary arranged for the visit at the lion's den.

Dressed in "a tight-fitting olive green dress," according to Countess Larisch's own memoirs, Mary was led to a small iron gate which already stood open, in the castle wall. They were received by Rudolph's valet, Loschek, who led the two women up a dark, steep stairway, then opened a door and stopped. They found themselves on the flat roof of the castle! Now he motioned them on, and through a window they descended into the corridor below. At the end of this passage, they came to an arsenal room filled with trophies and hunting equipment. From there, they continued their journey through the back corridors of the castle into Rudolph's apartments.

Rudolph came to greet them, and abruptly took Mary Vetsera with him into the next room, leaving his cousin to contemplate the vestibule. Shortly after, Rudolph returned and, according to Countess Larisch's memoir, told her that he would keep Mary with him for a couple of days. That way Mary's mother might realize he was not to be trifled with. Countess Larisch was to report that Mary had disappeared from her cab during a shopping expedition, while she had been inside a store.

Marie Larisch balked at the plan, but Rudolph insisted, even threatening her with a gun. Then he pressed five hundred florins into her hand to bribe the coachman, and ushered her out of his suite.

Evidently Mary Vetsera was in seventh heaven, for the next two weeks were spent mainly at Rudolph's side. She had returned home, of course, but managed to convince her mother that she was serious in her love for the Crown Prince. Baroness Helen had no illusion about the outcome. At best, she knew, Rudolph would marry her daughter off to some wealthy man after he tired of her. Nevertheless, she acquiesced, and so Mary kept coming to the castle via the secret stairs and passages.

The Imperial Castle is a huge complex of buildings, spanning several centuries of construction. It is not difficult to find a way into it without being seen by either guards or others living at the castle, and the back door was reasonably safe. Although rumors had

Rudolph meet his lady love within the confines of the castle, nobody ever caught them, and chances are that their relationship might have continued for some time in this manner had not the tragedy of Mayerling cut their lives short.

As we approach the momentous days of this great historical puzzle, we should keep firmly in mind that much of the known stories about it are conjecture, and that some of the most significant details are unknown because of the immediate destruction of Rudolph's documents—those he left behind without proper safeguard, that is.

The accounts given by Lonyay and the historian and poet Alexander Lernet-Holenia are not identical, but on the whole Lonyay has more historical detail and should be believed. According to this account, on January 27, 1889, at a reception celebrating the birthday of German Emperor William II, Franz Josef took his estranged son's hand and shook it—a gesture for public consumption, of course, to please his German hosts, with whom he had just concluded a far-reaching military alliance. This gesture was necessary, perhaps, to assure the German allies of Austria's unity. Rudolph took the proffered hand and bowed. This was the last time the Emperor and his only son met.

At noon, the following day, Rudolph ordered a light carriage, called a gig, to take him to his hunting lodge at Mayerling, about an hour's drive from Vienna. He had arranged with his trusted driver Bratfisch to pick up Mary Vetsera at her home in the third district, and to bring her to Mayerling by an alternate, longer route. Mary, wearing only a cloak over her negligee, slipped out from under her mother's nose and was driven by Bratfisch to the village of

Breitensee, halfway between Vienna and Mayerling. There she joined her lover, who dismissed his gig and continued the journey with Mary in Bratfisch's cab.

At this point, reports Lernet-Holenia, the carriage was halted by a group consisting of Mary's uncle Henry Baltazzi, a doctor, and two seconds, who had come to challenge the Crown Prince to a duel. In the ensuing scuffle, Henry was wounded by his own gun. This encounter is not of great importance except that it furnishes a motive for the Baltazzis to take revenge on Rudolph—Henry had wanted Mary for himself, even though she was his niece.

As soon as the pair reached the safety of the Mayerling castle walls, Lernet-Holenia reports, the Countess Larisch arrived in great haste and demanded he send the girl back to Vienna to avoid scandal. The mother had been to the chief of police and reported her daughter as missing. Lonyay evidently did not believe this visit occurred, for he does not mention it in *his* account of the events at Mayerling on that fateful day. Neither does he mention the fact that Rudolph gave the countess, his favorite cousin, a strongbox to safekeep for him.

"The Emperor may order my rooms searched at any moment," the countess quotes him in her memoirs. The strongbox was only to be handed over to a person offering the secret code letters R.I.U.O.

After the tragedy, this strongbox was picked up by Archduke John Salvator, close friend to Rudolph, and it is interesting to note that Henry W. Lanier, in a 1937 book titled *He Did Not Die at Mayerling,* claims that Rudolph and John Salvator escaped together to America after another body had been substituted for Rudolph's. Both archdukes, he says, had been involved in an abortive plot to overthrow Franz Josef, but the plot came to the Emperor's attention.

However interesting this theory, the author offers no tangible evidence which makes us go back to Lernet-Holenia's account of Countess Larisch's last words with Rudolph.

She left Mayerling, even though very upset by the prince's insistence that he and Mary were going to commit suicide. Yet, there was no privacy for that, if we believe Lernet-Holenia's version, which states that immediately after the countess's carriage had disappeared around the bend of the road, Rudolph received a deputation of Hungarians led by none other than Count Stephan Karolyi, the Prime Minister. Karolyi's presence at Mayerling is highly unlikely, for it surely would have come to the attention of the secret police almost immediately, thereby compromising Rudolph still further. Lonyay, on the other hand, speaks of several telegrams Rudolph received from the Hungarian leader, and this is more logical.

What made a contact between the Hungarians and Rudolph on this climactic day so imperative really started during a hunting party at Rudolph's Hungarian lodge, Görgény. Under the influence of liquor or drugs or both, Rudolph had promised his Hungarian friends to support actively the separation of the two halves of the monarchy and to see to it that an independent Hungarian army was established in lieu of the militia, at that time the only acknowledgment that Hungary was a separate state.

Austria at this juncture of events needed the support of the Hungarian parliament to increase its armed forces to the strength required by its commitments to the German allies. But Karolyi opposed the government defense bill for increased recruiting, and instead announced on January 25 that he had been assured by Rudolph that a separate Hungarian army would be created. This of course turned the Crown Prince into a traitor in the eyes of Count von Taaffe, the Austrian Prime Minister and father of the defense bill, and Rudolph must have been aware of it. At any rate, whether the Hungarian deputation came in person or whether Karolyi sent the telegrams, the intent was the same. Rudolph was now being asked to either put up or shut up. In the face of this dilemma, he backed down. The telegrams no longer exist, but this is not surprising, for a file known as "No. 25—Journey of Count Pista Karolyi to the Crown Prince Archduke Rudolph re defense bill in the Hungarian parliament" was removed from the state archives in May 1889, and has since disappeared. Thus we cannot be sure if Karolyi did go to Mayerling on this day in January or not.

But all existing sources seem to agree that two men saw Rudolph on January 29: his brother-in-law, Philip von Coburg, and his hunting companion, Count Joseph Hoyos. Rudolph begged off from the shoot, and the two others went alone; later Philip went back to Vienna to attend an imperial family dinner, while Rudolph sent his regrets, claiming to have a severe cold.

The next morning, January 30, Philip von Coburg was to return to Mayerling and together with Hoyos, who had stayed the night in the servants' wing of the lodge, continue their hunting. Much of what follows is the account of Count Hoyos, supported by Rudolph's valet, Loschek.

Hoyos and Coburg were to have breakfast with

Rudolph at the lodge at 8:00 A.M. But a few minutes before eight, Hoyos was summoned by Loschek, the valet, to Rudolph's quarters. Now the lodge was not a big house, as castles go. From the entrance vestibule, one entered a reception room and a billiards room. Above the reception area were Rudolph's private quarters. A narrow, winding staircase led from the ground floor directly into his rooms.

On the way across the yard, Loschek hastily informed Hoyos why he had called him over. At six-thirty, the Crown Prince had entered the anteroom where Loschek slept, and ordered him to awaken him again at seven-thirty. At that time he also wanted breakfast and to have Bratfisch, the cab driver, ready for him. The prince was fully dressed, Loschek explained, and, whistling to himself, had then returned to his rooms.

When Loschek knocked to awaken the prince an hour later, there was no response. After he saw that he was unable to rouse the prince—or the Baroness Vetsera, who, he explained, was *with* the prince—he became convinced that something was wrong, and wanted Count Hoyos present in case the door had to be broken down. Hardly had Hoyos arrived at the prince's door, which was locked, as were all other doors to the apartment, when Philip von Coburg drove up. Together they forced the door open by breaking the lock with a hatchet. Loschek was then sent ahead to look for any signs of life. Both occupants were dead, however. On the beds lay the bodies of the two lovers, Rudolph with part of his head shot off seemingly by a close blast, and Mary Vetsera also dead from a bullet wound.

Hoyos wired the imperial physician, Dr. Widerhofer, to come at once, but without telling him why, and then drove back to Vienna in Bratfisch's cab.

At the Imperial Castle it took some doing to get around the protocol of priority to inform the imperial couple of the tragedy. Franz Josef buried his grief, such as it was, under the necessity of protecting the Habsburg *image,* and the first announcements spoke of the prince having died of a heart attack. After a few days, however, this version had to be abandoned and the suicide admitted. Still, the news of Mary Vetsera's presence at the lodge was completely suppressed.

Rudolph had been found with his hand still holding a revolver, but since fingerprints had not yet become part of a criminal investigation procedure, we don't know whose revolver it was and whether he had actually used it. But there wasn't going to be any kind of inquest in this case, anyway. Mary's body was immediately removed from the room and hidden in a woodshed, where it lay unattended for two days. Finally, on the thirty-first the Emperor ordered Rudolph's personal physician, Dr. Auchenthaler, to go to Mayerling and certify that Mary Vetsera had committed suicide. At the same time, Mary's two uncles, Alexander Baltazzi and Count Stockau, were instructed to attend to the body. Without any argument, the two men identified the body and then co-signed the phoney suicide document which had been hastily drawn up. Then they wrapped Mary's coat around the naked body, and sat her upright in a carriage with her hat over her face to hide the bullet wound. In the cold of the night, at midnight to be exact, the carriage with the grotesque passenger raced over icy roads toward the monastery of Heiligenkreuz, where the Emperor had decided Mary should be buried. When the body threatened to topple over, the men put a cane down her back to keep it upright. Not a word was spoken during the grim journey. At the Cistercian monastery, there was some difficulty at first with the abbot, who refused to bury an apparent suicide, but the Emperor's power was so great that he finally agreed.

And so it was that Mary Vetsera was buried in the dead of night in a soil so frozen that the coffin could be properly lowered into it only with difficulty.

Today, the grave is a respectable one, with her name and full dates given, but for years after the tragedy it was an unmarked grave, to keep the curious from finding it.

Rudolph, on the other hand, was given a state funeral, despite objections from the Holy See. His head bandaged to cover the extensive damage done by the bullet, he was then placed into the Capuchins' crypt alongside all the other Habsburgs.

However, even before the two bodies had been removed from Mayerling, Franz Josef had already seized all of Rudolph's letters that could be found, including farewell letters addressed by the couple to various people. Although most of them were never seen again, one to Rudolph's chamberlain, Count Bombelles, included a firm request by the Crown Prince to be buried with Mary Vetsera. Strangely enough, the count was never able to carry out Rudolph's instructions even had he dared to, for he himself died only a few months later. At the very moment his death became known, the Emperor ordered all his papers seized and his desk sealed.

In a letter to a former lover, the Duke of Braganza, Mary is said to have stated, "We are extremely anxious to find out what the next world looks like," and in another one, this time to her mother, she confirms her desire to die and asks her mother's forgiveness. Since the letter to the Duke of Braganza also bore Rudolph's signature, it would appear that Rudolph and Mary had *planned* suicide together. But, according to Lonyay, a fragment of Rudolph's letter to his mother somehow became known, and in this farewell note, Rudolph confessed that he had murdered Mary Vetsera and therefore had no right to live. Thus, apparently, Rudolph shot the girl first but then had lacked the courage to kill himself until the next morning. Many years later, when the Emperor could no longer stop the truth from coming out, reports were made by two physicians, Kerzl and Auchenthaler, in further support of the view that Mary had died some ten hours before Rudolph.

In the letter to her mother, Mary had requested that she be buried with Rudolph, but to this day, *that desire has not been honored: Her* remains are still at the Heiligenkreuz cemetery, and *his* are in the crypt in Vienna.

After the deaths, Mary Vetsera's mother was brusquely told to leave Austria; the daughter's belongings were seized by police and, on higher orders, were burned.

Ever since, speculation as to the reasons for the double "suicide" had raced around the world. In Austria, such guessing was officially discouraged, but it could hardly be stopped. Lonyay dismisses various reasons often advanced for the suicide: that Franz Josef had refused his son a divorce so he could marry Mary Vetsera; that a lovers' pact between Rudolph and Vetsera had taken place; or that his political *faux pas* had left Rudolph no alternative but a bullet. Quite rightly, Lonyay points out that suicide plans had been on Rudolph's mind long before things had come to a head. He also discounts Rudolph's great love for the girl, hinting that the Crown Prince simply did not wish to die *alone,* and had made use of her devotion to him to take her with him. Thus it would appear that Mary Vetsera, far from being the guilty party, was actually the victim—both of Rudolph's bullets, and of his motives. No one doubts Mary's intention to commit suicide if Rudolph did and if he asked her to join him.

But—is the *intention* to commit suicide the same as actually doing it?

Too many unresolved puzzles and loose ends remained to satisfy even the subdued historians of those days, to say nothing of the unemotional, independent researcher of today, who is bent only on discovering what really happened.

The official report concerning the two deaths was finally signed on February 4, 1889, and handed to the Prime Minister for depositing in the Court archives. Instead, Count von Taaffe took it with him to his private home in Bohemia for "safekeeping." It has since disappeared.

Of course, there was still Loschek, the valet. He could not help wondering why the Prime Minister was in such good spirits after the Crown Prince's death, and especially when the report was filed, thus officially ending the whole affair. While the ordinary Viennese mourned for their prince, von Taaffe seemed overjoyed at the elimination of what to him and his party had been a serious threat. And in the meantime Franz Josef now maintained that he and Rudolph had always been on the best of terms and that the suicide was a mystery to one and all.

Helen Vetsera wrote a pamphlet telling the

family's side of the story: but it was seized by the police, and so the years passed and gradually the Mayerling events became legendary.

The Austro-Hungarian monarchy fell apart in 1918, just as Rudolph had foreseen, and the Habsburgs ceased to be sacrosanct, but still the secret of Mayerling was never really resolved nor had the restless spirit of the girl, who suffered most in the events, been quieted.

True, the Emperor had changed the hunting lodge into a severe monastery immediately after the tragedy: Where the bedroom once stood there is now an altar, and nuns sworn to silence walk the halls where once conviviality and laughter prevailed. In Vienna, too, in the corridor of the Imperial Castle where the stairs once led to Rudolph's apartment, a *marterl,* a typically Austrian niche containing a picture of the Virgin Mary, has been placed.

But did these formal expressions of piety do anything to calm the spirit of Mary Vetsera? Hardly. Nor was everything as quiet as the official Court powers would have liked it to be.

The English Prime Minister, Lord Salisbury, had some misgivings about the official version of the tragedy. In a letter that Edward, the Prince of Wales, wrote to his mother, Queen Victoria, we find:

"Salisbury is sure that poor Rudolph and that unfortunate young lady were murdered."

But perhaps the most interesting details were supplied by the autopsy report, available many years later:

> "The gun wound of the crown prince did not go from right to left as has been officially declared and would have been natural for *suicide,* but from left, behind

> the ear toward the top of the head, where the bullet came out again. Also, other wounds were found on the body. The revolver which was found next to the bed had *not* belonged to the crown prince; all six shots had been fired.
>
> "The shotgun wound of the young lady was not found in the temple as has been claimed, but on top of the head. She, too, is said to have shown other wounds."

Had Count von Taaffe seized upon the right moment to make a planned suicide appear just that, while actually murdering the hesitant principals?

We have no record of secret agents coming to Mayerling that day, but then we can't be sure that they didn't come, either. So confusing is this comparatively recent story that we can't be too sure of *anything,* really. Certainly there was a motive to have Rudolph eliminated. Von Taaffe knew all about his dealings with Karolyi, and could not be sure that Rudolph might not accept a proffered Hungarian crown. To demand that Rudolph be restrained or jailed would not have sat well with the image-conscious Emperor. Yet the elimination of Rudolph, either as an actual traitor or as a potential future threat to von Taaffe's concepts, was certainly an urgent matter at that moment.

Just as von Taaffe was aware of the Hungarian moves and had read the telegrams from Karolyi, so he knew of Rudolph's suicide talk. Had the Karolyi move prompted him to act immediately, and, seeing that the Crown Prince had gone to Mayerling with Mary Vetsera, given him an idea to capitalize on what *might* happen at Mayerling . . . but to make sure it did? Rudolph's lack of courage was well known. Von

Taaffe could not be sure the Crown Prince would really kill himself. If Rudolph returned from Mayerling alive, it would be too late. The Hungarian defense bill had to be acted upon at once. Rebellion was in the air.

Perhaps von Taaffe did not have to send any agents to Mayerling. Perhaps he already *had* an agent there. Was someone around the Crown Prince in von Taaffe's employ?

These and other tantalizing questions went through my mind when I visited the old part of the Imperial Castle with my (then) wife Catherine. I was following a slender thread: a ghostly white lady had been observed in the Amalienburg wing. Our arrival was almost comical: Nobody knew anything about ghosts and cared less. Finally, more to satisfy the curiosity of this American writer, the *burghauptmann* or governor of the castle summoned one of the oldest employees, who had a reputation for historical knowledge. The governor's name was Neunteufel, or "nine devils," and he really did have a devil of a time finding this man whose Christian name was Sonntag, or "Sunday."

"Is Herr Sonntag in?" he demanded on the intercom.

Evidently the answer was disappointing, for he said, "Oh, Herr Sunday is not in on Friday?"

Fortunately, however, the man was in and showed us to the area where the phenomenon had been observed.

Immediately after the Mayerling tragedy, it seemed, a guard named Beran was on duty near the staircase leading up toward the late Crown Prince's suite. It was this passage that had been so dear to

Mary Vetsera, for she had had to come up this way to join her lover in his rooms. Suddenly, the guard saw a white figure advancing toward him from the stairs. It was plainly a woman, but he could not make out her features. As she got to the *marterl,* she vanished. Beran was not the only one who had such an unnerving experience. A Jaeger, a member of an Alpine regiment serving in the castle, also saw the figure one afternoon. And soon the servants started talking about it. Several of them had encountered the "white woman," as they called her, in the corridor used by Mary Vetsera.

I looked at the *marterl,* which is protected by an iron grillwork. Next to it is a large wooden chest pushed flush against the wall. And behind the chest I discovered a wooden door.

"Where does this door lead to?" I asked.

"No place," Sonntag shrugged, "but it *used* to be a secret passage between the outside and Rudolph's suite."

Aha! I thought. So that's why there is a ghost here. But I could not do anything further at that moment to find out *who* the ghost was.

On September 20, 1966, I returned to Vienna. This time I brought with me a Viennese lady who was a medium. Of course she knew where we were—after all, everybody in Vienna knows the Imperial Castle. But she had no idea why I took her into the oldest, least attractive part of the sprawling building, and up the stairs, finally coming to an abrupt halt at the mouth of the corridor leading toward the haunted passage.

It was time to find out what, if anything, my friend Mrs. Edith Riedl could pick up in the atmosphere. We were quite alone, as the rooms here have long been made into small flats and let out to various people, mainly those who have had some government service and deserve a nice, low-rent apartment.

With us were two American gentlemen who had come as observers, for there had been some discussions of a motion picture dealing with my work. This was their chance to see it in its raw state!

"Vetsera stairs. . . ." Mrs. Riedl suddenly mumbled. She speaks pretty good English, although here and there she mixes a German or French word in with it. Of noble Hungarian birth, she is married to a leading Austrian manufacturer and lives in a mansion, or part of one, in the suburb of Doebling.

"She stopped very often at this place," she continued now, "waiting, till she got the call. . . ."

"Where did the call come from?" I asked.

"From below."

Mrs. Riedl had no knowledge of the fact that Mary Vetsera came this way and *descended* into Rudolph's rooms by this staircase.

"The Madonna wasn't here then . . . but she prayed here."

She walked on, slowly, as if trying to follow an invisible trail. Now she stopped and pointed at the closed-off passage.

"Stairway . . . that's how she went down to Rudolph . . . over the roof . . . they met up here where the Madonna now is . . . and sometimes he met her part of the way up the stairs."

No stairs were visible to any of us at this point, but Mrs. Riedl insisted that they were in back of the door.

"She had a private room here, somewhere in the castle," she insisted. Officially, I discovered, no such room belonging to Mary Vetsera is recorded.

"There were two rooms she used, one downstairs and another one farther up," Mrs. Riedl added, getting more and more agitated. "She changed places with her maid, you see. That was in case they would be observed. In the end, they were no longer safe here, that's when they decided to go to Mayerling. That was the end."

I tried to pinpoint the hub of the secret meetings within the castle.

"Rudolph's Jaeger . . . ," Mrs. Riedl replied, "Bratfisch . . . he brought the messages and handed them to the maid . . . and the maid was standing here and let her know . . . they could not go into his rooms because his wife was there, so they must have had some place of their own. . . ."

We left the spot, and I followed Mrs. Riedl as she walked farther into the maze of passages that honeycomb this oldest part of the castle. Finally, she came to a halt in a passage roughly opposite where we had been before, but on the other side of the flat roof.

"Do you feel anything here?" I asked.

"Yes, I do," she replied, "this door . . . number 77 . . . 79 . . . poor child. . . ."

The corridor consisted of a number of flats, each with a number on the door, and each rented to someone whose permission we would have had to secure, should we have wished to enter. Mrs. Riedl's excitement became steadily greater. It was as if the departed girl's spirit was slowly but surely taking over her personality and making her relive her ancient agony all over again.

"First she was at 77, later she changed . . . to 79 . . . these two apartments *must* be connected. . . ."

Now Mrs. Riedl turned to the left and touched a window giving onto the inner courtyard. Outside the window was the flat roof Countess Larisch had mentioned in her memoirs!

"She came up the corridor and out this window," the medium now explained, "something of her always comes back here, because in those days she was happiest here."

"How did she die?" I shot at her.

"She wouldn't die. She was killed."

"By whom?"

"Not Rudolph."

"Who killed him?"

"The political plot. He wanted to be Hungarian King. Against his father. His father knew it quite well. He took her with him to Mayerling because he was afraid to go alone; he thought with her along he might not be killed."

"Who actually killed them?"

"Two officers."

"Did he know them?"

"She knew them, but he didn't. She was a witness. That's why she had to die."

"Did Franz Josef have anything to do with it?"

"He knew, but he did not send them. . . . *Das kann ich nicht sagen!*" she suddenly said in German, "I can't say this!"

What couldn't she say?

"I cannot hold the Emperor responsible . . . please don't ask me. . . ."

Mrs. Riedl seemed very agitated, so I changed the subject. Was the spirit of Mary Vetsera present, and if so, could we speak to her through the medium?

"She wants us to pray downstairs at that spot . . ." she replied, in tears now. "Someone should go to her grave. . . ."

I assured her that we had just come from there.

"She hoped Rudolph would divorce his wife and make her Queen, poor child," Mrs. Riedl said. "She comes up those stairs again and again, trying to live her life over but making it a better life. . . ."

We stopped in front of number 79 now. The name on the door read "Marschitz."

"She used to go in here," Mrs. Riedl mumbled, "it was a hidden door. Her maid was at 75, opposite. This was her apartment."

At the window, we stopped once more.

"So much has changed here," the medium said.

She had never been here before, and yet she *knew*.

Later I discovered that the area had indeed been changed, passage across the flat roof made impossible.

"There is something *in between,*" she insisted.

A wall perhaps? No, not a wall. She almost *ran* back to the Madonna. There the influence, she said, was still strongest.

"Her only sin was vanity, not being in love," Mrs. Riedl continued. "She wishes she could undo something . . . she wanted to take advantage of her love, and that was wrong."

Suddenly, she noticed the door, as if she had not seen it before.

"Ah, the door," she said with renewed excitement. "That is the door I felt from the other side of the floor. There should be some connection . . . a secret passage so she could not be seen . . . waiting here for the go-ahead signal . . . no need to use the big door . . . she is drawn back here now because of the Virgin Mary. . . . Mary was her name also . . . she can pray here. . . ."

I asked Mrs. Riedl to try to contact the errant spirit.

"She is aware of us," my medium replied after a pause in which she had closed her eyes and breathed deeply. "She smiles at us and I can see her eyes and face. I see this door *open* now and she stands in the door. Let us pray for her release."

On Mrs. Riedl's urging, we formed a circle and clasped hands around the spot. At this moment I thought I saw a slim white figure directly in front of us. The power of suggestion? "She is crying," Mrs. Riedl said.

We then broke circle and left. My American friends were visibly shaken by what they had witnessed, although to me it was almost routine.

The following day, we returned to the castle. This time we had permission from the governor to open the secret door and look for the passage Mrs. Riedl had said was there. At first, the door would not yield, although two of the castle's burly workmen went at it with heavy tools. Finally, it opened. It was evident that it had not been moved for many years, for heavy dust covered every inch of it. Quickly, we grouped ourselves around the dark, gaping hole that now confronted us. Musty, moist air greeted our nostrils. One of the workmen held up a flashlight, and in its light we could see the inside of the passage. It was about a yard wide, wide enough for one person to pass through, and paralleled the outer wall. A stairway had once led from our door down to the next lower floor—directly into Crown Prince Rudolph's apartment. But it had been removed, leaving only traces behind. Likewise, a similar stairway had led over from the opposite side where it must have once linked up with the corridor we had earlier been in—the window Mrs. Riedl had insisted was significant in all this.

The castle's governor shook his head. The secret passage was a novelty to him. But then the castle had all sorts of secrets, not the least of which were corridors and rooms that did not show on his "official" maps. Some parts of the Imperial Castle date back to the thirteenth century; others, like this one, certainly as far back as Emperor Frederick III, around 1470. The walls are enormously thick and can easily hide hollow areas.

I had taken a number of photographs of the area, in Mrs. Riedl's presence. One of them showed the significant "reflections" in psychically active areas. The day of our first visit here, we had also driven out to Mayerling with the help of Dr. Beatrix Kempf of the Austrian Government Press Service, who did everything to facilitate our journey. Ghosts or no ghosts, tourists and movie producers are good business for Austria.

At Mayerling, we had stood on the spot where the two bodies had been found on that cold January morning in 1889. I took several pictures of the exact area, now taken up by the altar and a cross hanging above it. To my surprise, one of the color pictures shows instead a whitish mass covering most of the altar rail, and an indistinct but obviously male figure standing in the right corner. When I took this exposure, nobody was standing in that spot. Could it be? My camera is double exposure proof and I have occasionally succeeded in taking psychic pictures.

If there is a presence at Mayerling, it must be Rudolph, for Mary Vetsera surely has no emotional ties to the cold hunting lodge, where only misery was her lot. If anywhere, she would be in the secret passageway in the Vienna castle, waiting for the signal to come down to join her Rudolph, the only place where her young heart ever really was.

I should point out that the sources used by me in my Mayerling research were only read long *after* our investigation, and that these are all rare books which have long been out of print.

We do know, however, that Mary Vetsera was not a suicide. A planned suicide never leads to the ghostly phenomena observed in this case. Only a panic death, or murder, leaving unresolved questions, can account for her presence in the castle. To the unfortunate victim, eighty years are as nothing, of course. All others who were once part of this tragedy are dead, too, so we may never know if Count von Taaffe ordered Rudolph killed, or the royal family, or if he himself committed the act.

The strange disappearance of the most vital documents and the way things were hushed up leads me personally to believe that the medium had the right solution: The Hungarian plot was the cause of Rudolph's downfall. There was neither suicide nor a suicide pact at the time the pair was in Mayerling. There was an earlier *intention,* yes, but those letters were used as a smoke screen to cover the real facts. And without accusing some presently honorable names, how can I point the finger at Rudolph's murderers?

Let the matter rest there.

But apparently, it wouldn't. Several years after I first published this version of the Mayerling tragedy, hitherto secret documents were discovered in the archives which fully bore out what psychics had only pointed at: the sinister implications of a deliberate frameup to kill Rudolph and also eliminate his cousin and co-conspirator, John Salvator. Whether the old Emperor knew of the killings beforehand or not is a moot question: he surely knew *afterwards,* and did nothing to expose the true facts. And there, dear reader, truly the matter must rest.

The Black Knight of Pflindsberg

NOT FAR from Altaussee, a picturesque village southeast of Salzburg, stand the remnants of a fortress atop a high ridge which is not easy to scale even today. The spot was already important to the Romans, who maintained a guard post there for the north-south trade route pass over which so much of the local salt reached Italy. Access today is from the rear across a deep, man-made moat, although some hardy souls may want to climb up from the front.

The oldest records show the mountain to have been leased by a certain Aribo to the warlike Archbishop of Salzburg in A.D. 909. But it was not until 1252 that an actual fortress was erected there. The occasion was the need to forestall Hungarian incursions into the Salzburg area. Later, the fortress served as headquarters for the superintendent of the Archbishop's salt mines in the area. Still later the tower was used as a jail and criminals were executed in the adjacent meadow. By 1587, the small fortress was in a state of sad disrepair, but Archduke Charles restored it and his mining superintendents lived there in relative comfort. Nevertheless, the primitive building gradually became uninhabitable and by 1755 the fortress was abandoned, even though the Domain of Pflindsberg existed in the records until 1848. Today, only a few walls are standing but the fervent efforts of Police Inspector Louis Mayrhuber, chairman of the local museum, may yet result in restoring the ruins to their pristine glory in the years to come.

According to tradition, back in the Middle Ages the last Knight of Pflindsberg had a beautiful daughter who had caught the roving eye of a neighbor, the Baron von Wildenstein, Lord of nearby Ischl. She did not care for him, so the gentleman appeared at Pflindsberg with some soldiers and forced the gates. The daughter was thrown into the dungeon, while the father was permitted the freedom of his own house. When the girl failed to change her mind, he threw her father into the dungeon with her. After a while, their relatives began to worry about them. Thus, when they received word of Pflindsberg's troubles, the Lords of Wolkenstein and Strechau approached the fortress from two sides in order to free their relatives.

Meanwhile, the younger brother of the usurper had also arrived at Pflindsberg, where he had not visited in some time. Just as he arrived he found his elder brother in the act of beating a helpless girl. The younger man remonstrated with him over it and the usurper threw him into the dungeon as well. When the two armies of the Knight's relatives arrived at the fortress, the Baron von Wildenstein realized he could not withstand such a force and fled the castle on his black horse. He made good his escape to his own castle at Ischl, but the pursuers, including his own brother, stormed it.

Wielding his sword in anger, the younger brother then executed the usurper on the spot. From that moment on, a Knight on a black horse has been reported around Pflindsberg. This legend must have had some basis in fact, for the fortress found no buyer when it and its valuable properties were eventually put up for sale to the highest bidder. It was as if a curse adhered to the masonry. Eventually Pflindsberg was abandoned to the elements. According to another local tradition, the horseman hit the rocks so hard that the horseshoes were torn from the legs of his horse. Only after the four horseshoes shall be recovered and returned to fortress Wildenstein will the Baron find peace.

I am indebted for this account to Louis Mayrhuber, Police Inspector and local historian. It so happened that a medieval horseshoe was found in the summer of 1971 by Mayrhuber and his friend Peter Bruschke.

Now only three more need to be discovered. Meanwhile, the Black Knight is presumably still riding the airwaves around Pflindsberg when the memory of his righteous pursuers becomes too strong to bear.

Switzerland

A Haunted Former Hospital in Zurich

THE HOUSE in question is now a private residence, owned by Colonel and Mrs. Nager. The Colonel is a professional officer and takes a cautious attitude towards psychic phenomena. Mrs. Catherine Nager is not only a talented medium herself, but also serves as secretary to the Swiss Society for Parapsychology headed by the Zurich psychiatrist Dr. Hans Negele-Osjord.

Rather aristocratic in design and appearance, the house stands on upper Hoenger Street at a spot where it overlooks much of downtown Zurich. It is a square, heavy-set stone house with three stories, and an attic above the top story. In this attic there is a window that does not want to stay closed—no matter how often one tries to close it. When this happened all the time, the Nagers kept accusing each other of leaving the window open, only to discover that neither of them had done it.

The house is set back from the road, in a heavily protected garden; it is painted a dark gray and there is a wrought-iron lantern over the entrance.

When I first visited the house in the company of the owner, the attic immediately depressed me. The famous window was open again and I had no difficulty closing it. But it could not have opened by its volition.

Down one flight there is a small room which for many years has served as a maid's room. It was here that the most notable phenomena have been observed. A maid named Liesl saw a man wearing a kind of chauffeur's cap standing between the bed and the wall with a candle in his hand. She panicked and ran from the room screaming in terror. Mrs. Nager checked the room immediately and found it empty. No one could have escaped down the stairs in the brief interval. Another servant girl took Liesl's place. A year and half after the initial incident, the new girl saw the same apparition.

Next to the maid's room is another room famous for uncanny atmospheric feelings. Guests who have stayed there have frequently complained about a restlessness in the room, and nobody ever slept well.

On the third floor there is still another maid's room where a girl named Elsbeth saw the ghostly apparition of a man wearing a peculiar beret. When Mrs. Nager's son was only eight, he saw a man emerge from between the window curtains of his room. He, too, emphasized the peculiar cap the man wore—something not seen today.

Other servants have described the ghost as being a man of about thirty-five, wearing the same peculiarly Swiss cap; they have seen him all over the house.

The explanation is this: during the seventeenth century the house had been a military hospital. Many wounded soldiers who came there died. The cap worn by the apparition was the soldier's cap worn in the period. Most likely the man is lost between two states of being and would like to get out—if only someone would show him the way.

Estonia

The Concerned Castle Ghost

THE BUXHOEVEDEN family is one of the oldest noble families of Europe, related to a number of royal houses and—since the eighteenth century when one of the counts married the daughter of Catherine the Great of Russia—also to the Russian Imperial family. The family seat was Lode Castle on the island of Eesel, off the coast of Estonia. The castle, which is still standing, is a very ancient building with a round tower somewhat apart from the main building. Its Soviet occupants have since turned it into a museum.

The Buxhoevedens acquired it when Frederick William Buxhoeveden married Natalie of Russia; it was a gift from mother-in-law Catherine.

Thus it was handed down from first-born son to first-born son, until it came to be in the hands of an earlier Count Anatol Buxhoeveden. The time was the beginning of this century, and all was right with the world.

Estonia was a Russian province, so it was not out of the ordinary that Russian regiments should hold war games in the area, and on one occasion when the maneuvers were in full swing, the regimental commander requested that his officers be put up at the castle. The soldiers were located in the nearby town, but five of the staff officers came to stay at Lode Castle. Grandfather Buxhoeveden was the perfect host, but was unhappy that he could not accommodate all five in the main house. The fifth man would have to be satisfied with quarters in the tower. Since the tower had by then acquired a reputation of being haunted, he asked for a volunteer to stay in that particular room.

There was a great deal of teasing about the haunted room before the youngest of the officers volunteered and left for his quarters.

The room seemed cozy enough and the young officer congratulated himself for having chosen so quiet and pleasant a place to spend the night after a hard day's maneuvers.

And being tired, he decided to get into bed right away. But he was too tired to fall asleep quickly, so he took a book from one of the shelves lining the walls, lit the candle on his night table, and began to read for a while.

As he did so, he suddenly became aware of a greenish light toward the opposite end of the circular room. As he looked at the light with astonishment, it changed before his eyes into the shape of a woman. She seemed solid enough and, to his horror, came over to his bed, took him by the hand and demanded that he follow her. Somehow he could not resist her commands, even though not a single word was spoken. He followed her down the stairs into the library in the castle itself. There she made signs indicating that he was to remove the carpet. Without questioning her, he flipped back the rug. She then pointed at a trap door that was underneath the carpet. He opened the door and followed the figure down a flight of stairs until they came to a big iron door that barred their progress. Now the figure pointed to the right corner of the floor and he dug into it. There he found a key, perhaps ten inches long, and with it he opened the iron gate. He now found himself in a long corridor that led him to a circular room. From there another corridor led on and again he followed eagerly, wondering what this was all about.

This latter corridor suddenly opened into another circular room which seemed familiar—he was back in his own room. The apparition was gone.

What did it all mean? He sat up trying to figure it out, and when he finally dozed off it was already dawn. Consequently he overslept and came down to breakfast last. His state of excitement immediately drew the attention of the Count and his fellow officers. "You won't believe this," he began and told them what had happened to him.

He was right. Nobody believed him.

But his insistence that he was telling the truth was so convincing that the Count finally agreed, more to humor him than because he believed him, to follow the young officer to the library to look for the alleged trap door.

"But," he added, "I must tell you that on top of that carpet are some heavy bookshelves filled with books which have not been moved or touched in over a hundred years. It is quite impossible for any one man to flip back that carpet."

They went to the library, and just as the Count had said, the carpet could not be moved. But Grandfather Buxhoeveden decided to follow through anyway and called in some of his men. Together, ten men were able to move the shelves and turn the carpet back. Underneath the carpet was a dust layer an inch thick, but it did not stop the intrepid young officer from looking for the ring of the trap door. After a long search for it, he finally located it. A hush fell over the group when he pulled the trap door open. There was the secret passage and the iron gate. And there, next to it, was a rusty iron key. The key fit the lock. The gate, which had not moved for centuries perhaps, slowly and painfully swung open and the little group continued their exploration of the musty passages. With the officer leading, the men went through the corridors and came out in the tower room, just as the officer had done during the night.

But what did it mean? Everyone knew there were secret passages—lots of old castles had them as a hedge in time of war.

The matter gradually faded from memory, and life at Lode went on. The iron key, however, was preserved and remained in the Buxhoeveden family until some years ago, when it was stolen from Count Alexander's Paris apartment.

Ten years went by, until, after a small fire in the castle, Count Buxhoeveden decided to combine the necessary repairs with the useful installation of central heating, something old castles always need. The contractor doing the job brought in twenty men who worked hard to restore and improve the appointments at Lode. Then one day, the entire crew vanished to a man—like ghosts. Count Buxhoeveden reported this to the police, who were already being besieged by the wives and families of the men who had disappeared without leaving a trace.

Newspapers of the period had a field day with the case of the vanishing workmen, but the publicity did not help to bring them back, and the puzzle remained.

Then came the revolution and the Buxhoevedens lost their ancestral home. Count Alexander and Count Anatol, my former brother-in-law, went to live in Switzerland. The year was 1923. One day the two men were walking down a street in Lausanne when a stranger approached them, calling Count Alexander by name.

"I am the brother of the Major Domo of your castle," the man explained. "I was a plumber on that job of restoring it after the fire."

So much time had passed and so many political events had changed the map of Europe that the man was ready at last to lift the veil of secrecy from the case of the vanishing workmen.

This is the story he told: when the men were digging trenches for the central heating system, they accidentally came across an iron kettle of the kind used in the Middle Ages to pour boiling oil or water down on the enemies besieging a castle. Yet this pot was not full of water, but rather of gold. They had stumbled onto the long-missing Buxhoeveden treasure, a hoard reputed to have existed for centuries but which was never found. Now, at this stroke of good fortune, the workmen became larcenous. To a man, they opted for distributing the find among themselves, even though it meant leaving everything behind—their families, their homes, their work—and striking out fresh somewhere else. But the treasure was large enough to make this a pleasure rather than a problem, and they never missed their wives, it would seem, finding ample replacements in the gentler climes of western Europe, where most of them went to live under assumed names.

At last the apparition that had appeared to the young officer made sense: it had been an ancestor who wanted to let her descendants know where the family gold had been secreted. What a frustration for a ghost to see her efforts come to naught, and worse yet, to see the fortune squandered by thieves while the legal heirs had to go into exile. Who knows how things might have turned out for the Buxhoevedens if *they* had gotten to the treasure in time.